Intelligence, Security and Policing Post-9/11

Intelligence, Security and Policing Post-9/11

The UK's Response to the 'War on Terror'

Edited By

Jon Moran
University of Wolverhampton, UK

and

Mark Phythian
University of Leicester, UK

First published 2008 by
PALGRAVE MACMILLAN

Palgrave Macmillan in the UK is an imprint of Macmillan Publishers Limited,
registered in England, company number 785998, of Houndmills, Basingstoke,
Hampshire RG21 6XS.

Palgrave Macmillan in the US is a division of St Martin's Press LLC,
175 Fifth Avenue, New York, NY 10010.

Palgrave Macmillan is the global academic imprint of the above companies
and has companies and representatives throughout the world.

Palgrave® and Macmillan® are registered trademarks in the United States,
the United Kingdom, Europe and other countries.

ISBN-13: 978–0–230–55191–6 hardback
ISBN-10: 0–230–55191–2 hardback

This book is printed on paper suitable for recycling and made from fully
managed and sustained forest sources. Logging, pulping and manufacturing
processes are expected to conform to the environmental regulations of the
country of origin.

A catalogue record for this book is available from the British Library.

Library of Congress Cataloging-in-Publication Data

Moran, Jon.
    Intelligence, security and policing post-9/11 : the UK's response
to the war on terror / Jon Moran, Mark Phythian.
        p. cm.
    Includes bibliographical references and index.
    ISBN 978–0–230–55191–6 (alk. paper)
        1. Terrorism – Great Britain – Prevention. 2. Terrorism – Prevention.
    3. Intelligence service – Great Britain. 4. Intelligence service.
    I. Phythian, Mark. II. Moran, Jon. III. Title.
HV6433.G7M67 2008
363.325'1630941—dc22   2008029971

10 9 8 7 6 5 4 3 2 1
17 16 15 14 13 12 11 10 09 08

Printed and bound in Great Britain by
CPI Antony Rowe, Chippenham and Eastbourne

To Harriet

To Jamie and Hayley

Contents

List of Abbreviations   ix

List of Contributors   xi

Introduction   1
Jon Moran and Mark Phythian

Part I   Security, Intelligence and Counterterrorism

1   Politics, Security, Intelligence and Liberty after 9/11   11
    Jon Moran

2   In the Shadow of 9/11: Security, Intelligence and
    Terrorism in the United Kingdom   32
    Mark Phythian

3   The Pursuit of Terrorism with Intelligence   54
    Clive Walker

4   Counterterrorist Finance Policies in the
    United Kingdom: The 'Silver Bullet' for Terrorism?   79
    Peter A. Sproat

Part II   Civil Liberties and Counterterrorism

5   A Chilling Consensus: Political Protest in the
    United Kingdom and the 'War on Terror'   99
    Christopher J. Newman

6   National Security, Religious Liberty and
    Counterterrorism   115
    Ian Leigh

7   The Torture Debate: A Perspective from the
    United Kingdom   135
    Philip N.S. Rumney

Part III   Comparative Perspectives

8   Law, Intelligence and Politics in Australia's
'War on Terror'   159
Christopher Michaelsen

9   Counterterrorism in the Netherlands after 9/11:
The 'Dutch Approach'   183
Beatrice A. de Graaf and Bob G.J. de Graaff

10   The Spanish Experience of Countering Terrorism:
From ETA to al-Qaeda   203
Rogelio Alonso

Conclusion: Future Directions in the 'War on Terror'   222
Jon Moran and Mark Phythian

Bibliography   230

Index   255

Abbreviations

AIVD	*Algemene Inlichtingen- en Veiligheidsdienst*
AML	anti-money laundering
ARA	Assets Recovery Agency
ASEAN	Association of South East Asian Nations
ASIO Act	Australian Security Intelligence Organisation Legislation Amendment (Terrorism) Act
ASIS	Australian Secret Intelligence Service
ASTA	Interdepartmental Steering Committee Terrorist Actions
ATCSA	Anti-Terrorism, Crime and Security Act 2001
BIF	Benevolence International Foundation
BVD	Dutch National Security Service (Dutch: *Binnenlandse Veiligheidsdienst*)
BZC	Special Cases Agency
CAB	Criminal Assets Bureau
CCTV	Closed-circuit television
CESID	*Centro Superior de Información de la Defensa*
CIA	*Central Intelligence Agency*
CNCA	*Centro Nacional de Coordinación Antiterrorista*
CNI	*Centro Nacional de Inteligencia*
COTER	Committee on Terrorism
CRI	Central Criminal Investigation Intelligence
CT	counterterrorism
CTF	counterterrorist finance
CTG	Counter Terrorist Group
CEMU	*Comité Ejecutivo para el Mando Unificado*
DIB	*Directie Inlichtingen Buitenland*
DPP	Director of Public Prosecutions
DSD	Defence Signals Directorate
DST	Directorate for Territorial Surveillance (French: *Direction de la Surveillance du Territoire*)
ECHR	European Convention on Human Rights
ECtHR	European Court on Human Rights
FIU	Financial Investigation Unit
GAL	*Grupos Antiterroristas de Liberación*
GCHQ	Government Communications Headquarters

GRAPO	*Grupo de Resistencia Antifascista Primero de Octubre*
GSPC	*Groupe Salafiste pour la Prédication et le Combat*
ICBMs	intercontinental ballistic missiles
ICC	Interception of Communications Commissioner
ICCPR	International Covenant on Civil Political Rights
ICM	Institute for Conflict Management
IPCC	Independent Police Complaints Commission
ISC	Intelligence and Security Committee
ISI	Inter-Services Intelligence
JIC	Joint Intelligence Committee
JTAC	Joint Terrorism Analysis Centre
KLPD	National Police Agency
KSM	Khaled Sheik Mohammed
LBT	National Support Team Counterterrorism
LIFG	Libyan Islamic Fighting Group
LPF	*Lijst Pim Fortuyn*
NCIS	National Criminal Intelligence Service
NCTb	Dutch National Coordinator for Counterterrorism (Dutch: *Nationaal Coördinator Terrorismebestrijding*)
NTFIU	National Terrorist Finance Investigation Unit
PACE	Police and Criminal Evidence Act
PIRA	Provisional Irish Republican Army
PoCA	Proceeds of Crime Act
PSOE	Partido Socialista Obrero Español-
RaRa	*Revolutionaire Anti-Racistische Actie*
SARs	Suspicious Activity Reports
SIAC	Special Immigration Appeals Commission
SOCA	Serious and Organised Crime Agency
SOCPA	Serious Organized Crime and Police Act

Contributors

Rogelio Alonso is Professor of Political Science at the University of King Juan Carlos and Coordinator of the Terrorism Analysis and Documentation Unit, Madrid. He is the author of *The IRA and Armed Struggle* (Routledge, 2006) and numerous articles on terrorism in Spain in *Terrorism and Political Violence* and elsewhere.

Beatrice A. de Graaf, PhD, is Assistant Professor/research coordinator at the Centre for Terrorism and Counterterrorism at The Hague campus of Leiden University. Her research focuses on intelligence, terrorism and counterterrorism in Western Europe and the United States, mainly during the late Cold War period.

Bob G.J. de Graaff, PhD, worked on the Srebrenica-research project at the Netherlands Institute for War Documentation from 1999 to 2002. He holds an Extraordinary Chair for Political and Cultural Reconstruction at Utrecht University, and in February 2007, de Graaff was appointed Professor of Terrorism and Counterterrorism at Leiden University.

Ian Leigh, is Professor of Law at the University of Durham and author of *In from the Cold: National Security and Parliamentary Democracy* (Oxford University Press, 1994), with Laurence Lustrate, and editor of *Who's Watching the Spies: Establishing Intelligence Service Accountability* (Potomac Books, 2005) with Hans Born and Loch Johnson, and *Religious Freedom in the Liberal State* (Oxford University Press, 2005), with Rex Adaro.

Christopher Michaelsen is Human Rights Officer (Anti-Terrorism) at the Office for Democratic Institutions and Human Rights (ODIHR) of the Organization for Security and Cooperation in Europe (OSCE). He graduated in law from the University of Hamburg and holds a Master of Laws degree (LLM) from the University of Queensland.

Jon Moran is Reader in Criminal Justice at the University of Wolverhampton. He has published on policing, security, corruption and democratization in *Intelligence and National Security, Crime, Law and Social Change* and others. He is the author of *Policing the Peace in Northern Ireland* (Manchester University Press, 2008).

Christopher J. Newman is Lecturer in Law at the University of Sunderland. Previously employed as a detective in the Metropolitan

Police Service, he also worked within the field of criminal defence in a legal aid firm of solicitors. He has recently published on the issue of free speech and public order in the *Journal of Criminal Law.*

Mark Phythian is Professor of Politics in the Department of Politics and International Relations at the University of Leicester, UK. His research interests are in the areas of intelligence, national security and foreign policy. He is the author or editor/co-editor of nine books including: *Arming Iraq* (1996); *The Politics of British Arms Sales Since 1964* (2000); *Intelligence in an Insecure World* (with Peter Gill, 2006); *The Labour Party, War and International Relations 1945–2006* (2007); and *Intelligence and National Security Policymaking on Iraq: British and American Perspectives* (edited with Jim Pfiffner, 2008), as well as various articles and book chapters.

Philip N.S. Rumney is Reader in the Law School at the University of the West of England. His research interests are in the areas of criminal law, criminal justice and civil liberties. He has written several articles that examine the effectiveness of coercive interrogation and is currently working on the use of the necessity defence in the context of coercive interrogation.

Peter A. Sproat is Senior Lecturer in Fraud Management at the Centre for Fraud Management Studies, University of Teesside. His research interests include terrorism, counterterrorism law, and counterterrorism finance. He has published in *Terrorism and Political Violence, Crime, Law and Social Change and the Journal of Money Laundering Control.*

Clive Walker is Professor of Criminal Justice Studies at the School of Law, University of Leeds. He is the author of numerous articles and books, including *The Anti-Terrorism Legislation* (Oxford University Press, 2002). In 2003, he was a special adviser to the UK Parliamentary select committee, which was considering what became the Civil Contingencies Act 2004, and authored *The Civil Contingencies Act 2004: Risk, Resilience and the Law in the United Kingdom* (Oxford University Press, 2006).

Introduction

Jon Moran and Mark Phythian

This book has been designed to provide analyses of key aspects of the British experience of the 'war on terror', as declared by the US Bush Administration shortly after the 11 September 2001 (9/11) terrorist attacks on the United States. In the wake of 9/11 the United Kingdom stood, to use American terminology, 'front and centre' with the United States in its war to remove the Taliban from power in Afghanistan, a war for which there was broad international support, and in its war to remove Saddam Hussein from power in Iraq, a war for which there was not. Domestically the United Kingdom ramped up its counter-terror legislation and focussed resources on the police and security services. Nevertheless, by 2005 the United Kingdom had experienced suicide bombings in London, which killed fifty-two, while the number of Islamist plots that were being detected and frustrated had mushroomed.

All books aim to be distinctive and this is no exception. Although the 'war on terror' has generated a voluminous literature, there is still much to be dissected. Therefore, a few words are in order to explain what this book *is* and what it *is not*. It does not deal with the US experience given that so much has already been written on the role of the United States in framing and leading the 'war on terror', ranging from the domestic and international politics of the 'war on terror', to its effects on international law, security and intelligence, military affairs, civil liberties and the media. One purpose of this book is to move beyond the US-centric focus of much 'war on terror' writing. Second, this book does not focus exclusively on the vexed issue of civil liberties (which have been examined in detail in a voluminous literature) but integrates them with other issues, particularly at the micro level. Third, the book is multi-disciplinary. The chapters that follow stem from the fields of politics, criminology, law and sociology but each one speaks to the other, stressing the need to integrate the disciplines when analysing terrorism. One cannot examine intelligence or public order without at the same time examining politics, law and order, liberty and culture.

With this in mind we should set out some positive pointers as to what the book *does* set out to achieve. First, the book provides an examination of the policies, discourse, laws and counter-terrorism *practice* of the United Kingdom's 'war on terror' a term that is itself – and rightly – now out of official favour as a serious description of events in the United Kingdom since 9/11 and 7/7 (7 July 2005). We emphasize practice as one of the aims of the book, that is, to place a tight, even forensic, focus on the *nature and effectiveness* of counter-terrorist strategies. It is this part of the analysis that we wish to integrate with civil liberties, for what has often escaped examination is a detailed examination of the actual record in practice of many of the 'magic bullets' for countering terrorism. As part of this examination the first part of this book focusses on intelligence. A great amount has been written in this area, and it is assuming almost mythic importance, both as a counter-terrorist tool and as a threat to civil liberties. The chapters here examine intelligence critically in terms of its relation to politics, law and accountability and finance and whether it provides an effective platform for counter-terrorism policies.

Moran's introductory chapter begins by laying out some of the major debates that have characterized the UK experience, setting out a number of themes that are developed in subsequent chapters. One of these concerns the nature of state power in the United Kingdom. Moran argues that the idea of a weakened state 'hollowed out' by globalization and a vibrant civil society now seems far less convincing in the face of post-9/11 terrorism legislation and special measures. He also discusses the politics of the 'war on terror', including the remarkable media strategy of the Labour government, the development of special measures to counter terrorism and the effectiveness of these measures. A number of Moran's themes relate to intelligence and are taken up in subsequent chapters. The events of 9/11 were to transform the fortunes of the security and intelligence agencies in the United Kingdom. Having struggled throughout the post-Cold War 1990s to identify a legitimating threat that would protect them from assuming their share of the 'peace dividend', the 'war on terror' bestowed on these agencies a centrality that they had never previously enjoyed. Earlier calls that MI5, for example, be disbanded and its functions reallocated elsewhere now appear to belong to a bygone era. Nevertheless, issues relating to the operation of the security and intelligence agencies have remained controversial in the post-9/11 world, in part because of the manner in which the Blair government (mis)used intelligence in articulating its case for war in Iraq during 2002–2003, and the extent to which the intelligence underpinning the case was considerably wide of the mark in its assessment of Iraq's weapons programmes, and in part because the spectre of intelligence failure has followed MI5 since the London suicide bombings of 7/7.

However, as Mark Phythian argues, we need to be clear about both what we expect from intelligence and what we mean by 'failure' in this context. Phythian examines the constraints on intelligence and provides a critique of the way in which intelligence has been used by successive governments in the 'war on terror'. There is only so much that intelligence can be expected to deliver given the physical, financial and legislative limits within which the security and intelligence agencies operate. Moreover, it is important that they continue to operate within such clearly defined limits if we are to avoid compromising the very liberties the agencies exist to safeguard. In this context, Phythian argues, intelligence failure is likely to remain an ever-present possibility, and harbouring very high expectations as to what the agencies can deliver is almost bound to lead to periodic disappointment.

Clive Walker analyses the legal aspects of using intelligence, and argues that the dichotomy between evidence and intelligence has become increasingly blurred. Although it was never completely distinct, intelligence has increasingly intruded into the legal world, particularly with regard to terrorism. Walker explores perhaps the most controversial aspect of this intrusion, the use of intelligence as the basis for placing suspected terrorists who cannot be deported or convicted under control orders. As he argues, while 'there appear to be no fundamental objections to the melding of intelligence into the evidence-based legal process' it must be properly defined and subject to rigorous structures of accountability. For Walker this means the involvement of judges, and he rejects the idea that this will 'stain' the judiciary by its involvement in special closed courts relying on intelligence. Instead the judiciary must be involved at all stages, for there is a clear danger in allowing politicians alone to claim special expertise in national security measures.

Peter Sproat deals with the key issue of counter-terrorist finance, based around squeezing terrorist funds out of the financial system, identifying financial transactions by terrorists as a basis for an operation to disrupt or charge them, or simply seizing assets identified as being used by terrorists or their supporters. These initiatives rely on intelligence from private sector institutions (banks, building societies, insurance companies) for their lifeblood. Flagging up terrorist transactions and seizing assets seems an obvious winner, but in practice a number of problems emerge. As Sproat demonstrates, squeezing money out of the system and identifying suspicious transactions are both difficult in the current technology-based financial system, which either fails to pick up suspicious transactions or provides *too much* (often poor) intelligence about suspicious transactions.

These chapters also introduce important debates concerning the appropriate 'balance' between civil liberties and state power, which the chapters that follow address directly. While this issue has generated a massive amount of debate, the discourse has in general been characterized by well-rehearsed arguments. On the one hand, government supporters or sympathizers argue that changes to police powers and executive authority are necessary and proportionate (while providing only shaky evidence). On the other, defenders of civil liberties argue (at times, somewhat apocalyptically) that the changes propel us towards an authoritarian national security state. Another purpose of this volume is to go beyond this debate to analyse in detail the changes that have occurred and analyse their rationale, operation and accountability. It is often held that the techniques which adhere to human rights principles are the most effective. This may or may not be true – it is a rhetorical technique. If a technique radically contravenes human rights it should not be used whether it works or not, but an important point is to examine the claims of effectiveness around it. In this context, Philip Rumney provides a comprehensive overview of the highly charged debate concerning coercive interrogation. He bases his analysis on a critique of both those who advocate the use of this technique and those who state it should never be countenanced. Rumney argues that the case on both sides is characterized by declamatory and unsupported statements rather than the forensic analysis that it demands, concluding that in some very specific cases coercive interrogation may provide benefits, but that those who advocate it leave too many questions unanswered. Some might consider Rumney's chapter controversial, but its purpose is to throw down a challenge to those who oppose coercive interrogation in any context, one which needs to be taken up as the debate is advanced further if the arguments in opposition are to demonstrably carry the day, as we believe they should.

Beyond this there are a whole range of techniques that rub against or even begin to dissolve civil liberties without 'cracking' them and represent areas in which the capillaries of state power are to be observed intermeshing with civil society's boundaries. Christopher Newman deals with public order and the 'war on terror', and demonstrates how counter-terrorist powers have seeped out into the policing of mainstream protest. Contrary to many observers, Newman argues that the courts have not been greatly activist in challenging police powers in this area, even though their decisions may give the appearance of this. He also argues that the effects can be seen not only in practical terms but also in the more general manner in which freedom of expression has been 'chilled'. Newman is followed by Ian Leigh, who discusses the implications of the government's responses within the 'war on terror' for freedom of expression. He argues that the government's strategy has been contradictory. At the same time as the government has followed a path of building bridges to the Muslim community, it has also introduced a raft of legislation with regard to extremist speech that risks alienating Muslims as it chills free speech. Far from winning hearts and minds, this may in turn provide a critical space for extremists to engage in radicalization by arguing that the state is oppressing the Muslim community.

Here, the book continually poses the question: are special measures justified? As should be clear, we do not advocate any means-end analysis. Indeed, a focus on a lack of effectiveness strengthens any critique of special measures. However, examining effectiveness at all can be a controversial issue, and was manifested to the editors by a comment that this volume was actually advocating *an increase* in state power in the United Kingdom. As the chapters that follow clearly show, this was a significant misreading but one which can be understood in the context of the strongly held (nay, polarized) positions from which academics, journalists and politicians view the 'war on terror'.

Finally, this book makes a contribution to comparative analysis that moves beyond the US-centric focus of much 'war on terror' writing. We have chosen comparative studies of countries which have adopted a criminalisation rather than a 'war' approach to countering political violence. As with the first two sections in regard to the United Kingdom, the three comparative chapters are particularly adept at relating the 'war on terror' to political, legal and social developments while keeping an eye on the actual effectiveness of the measures. These three chapters show that even within the criminalization strategy, important distinctions remain across nations. Australia was deeply affected by the deaths of 88 of its nationals among the 202 killed in the October 2002 Bali bombings and was subsequently a contributor of troops to the Bush Administration's war in Iraq. As Michaelsen shows, a dynamic evident in the United Kingdom is also in operation here where more and more counterterror legislation is being passed regardless of whether attacks happen or not. Indeed, in a stark example of the politics of terror he demonstrates that ramped up counterterror legislation has often not resulted from planned or completed terrorist attacks but after failures by the government and security services. This legislation has, moreover, been implemented in the absence of a nationally active judiciary based around a domestic bill of rights and in the absence of a regional supranational human rights convention (the ICCPR does not have the force of the ECHR). The chapter provides a clear analysis of the dynamic that can develop between governments seeking to be tough on terror, the media and the electorate, a dynamic that can reach accelerated speed in the absence of informed and inclusive discussion about the actual nature of the threat.

The Netherlands is an extremely interesting example and one that requires more focus, especially in the English language. Beatrice de Graaf and Bob de Graaff show how in the Netherlands the visceral examples of extremism in the form of the political murders of Pim Fortuyn and Theo van Gogh forced the Dutch polity to re-examine its liberal approach to issues of integration and expression, a culture even the Dutch intelligence services had followed. After 9/11 had been followed by these individual acts of political violence, policies towards groups and acts identified as extremist shifted and came to have more in common with those being pursued in the United Kingdom, and were arguably more stringent in some respects. The Dutch polity continues to re-evaluate its distinctive liberal approach to security and intelligence as well as to social issues.

The final comparative chapter sees Rogelio Alonso stressing how in Spain the government was faced with a double terrorist threat in the form of jihadist terrorism and the continuing threat from armed Basque separatist group ETA in the Basque regions, but the Spanish experience also illuminates a road not followed by the United Kingdom. In Spain the state responded to the twin threats posed by ETA and al-Qaeda without passing rafts of legislation. Indeed, a key to countering the threat posed by ETA lay at the political level, and was to be found in both the impact of Basque devolution and (controversial) restrictions on ETA's political wing, *Batasuna*. At the same time, the Spanish state also concentrated on reorganising security and policing and improving intelligence. With regard to al-Qaeda the need for the security services to adopt a multi-faceted strategy is still evident, but limited by the lack of success in penetrating extremist networks. With regard to al-Qaeda in Europe, the government has realized that reducing radicalism requires building links (and developing an intelligence base) within

Spain's long-standing Muslim communities. Nevertheless, focussing too exclusively on al-Qaeda, Alonso argues may risk underestimating the continuing threat posed by ETA.

Hence, this book addresses key UK responses to the evolving 'war on terror' and provides a valuable comparative focus, highlighting lessons, opportunities, and risks. It is vital that there is an informed debate about these issues, one that feeds into policy-making, given that the 'war on terror' is increasingly seen as a phenomenon generational in duration, during which time the range of potential governmental responses could have serious implications for civil liberties and human rights. This book is intended to make a contribution to such debates and encourage others to follow.

Part I

Security, Intelligence and Counterterrorism

1
Politics, Security, Intelligence and Liberty after 9/11

Jon Moran

Introduction

At the start of David Rees' sharp satirical comic-strip critique of the post 9/11 world, *Get Your War On*, one character declaims:

> Oh my God, this War on Terrorism is gonna rule! I can't wait until the war is over and there's no more terrorism!

The other responds:

> I know! Remember when the U.S. had a drug problem and then we declared a War on Drugs, and now you can't buy drugs anymore? It'll be just like that! (Rees, 2003, p. 2)

Like the best satire, the strip zeroed in on uncomfortable truths. The quote aptly summed up the idea that the 'war on terror' might never end, and also questioned whether success was possible. Rees deals with the United States, and could not have foreseen the way in which the United Kingdom would become embroiled in the 'war on terror' not only on the international front of Afghanistan and Iraq, but also on the domestic front. On 7 July 2005 British Muslim citizens exploded a series of devices on London public transport above and below ground that killed 52 people and injured over 700 others.[1]

Each individual nation state that has been sucked – or has walked purposefully – into the maelstrom of the 'war on terror' has experienced it via its specific political and legal structures and civil society. However, each experience raises general issues of importance, and this chapter highlights a number of these and relates some of these to the chapters which follow, particularly those concerned with intelligence. The United Kingdom's experience in the 'war on terror' presents both analytical and practical challenges in a number of areas. The first is the way in which post 9/11 events lead us to rethink notions of state power. The second is the need to analyse the course of government policy in concrete political terms rather than in the shadow of the Manichean concept of the 'war on terror'. Each nation state affected by the post 9/11 environment, whether authoritarian or democratic, from Australia to Pakistan to Uzbekistan, has seen an intense period of political manoeuvring in the face of varying levels of threat.

Third, to this idea of the politics of the 'war on terror' can be added, the need to study the mechanics of the 'war on terror' in the United Kingdom. What reorganization has taken place in the security, intelligence and police bureaucracies? What new laws have been passed with regard to countering terrorism? Here the United Kingdom's approach can be set against the varied experiences of nation states in Europe alone.

A fourth question follows from this. Simply, have these policies been effective? Have the 'magic bullets' that have been proposed for tackling terrorism – intelligence, pre-charge detention, financial surveillance – hit home? This type of analysis is sorely required as there has been a great deal of analysis in academic and civil society of the 'war on terror' and its effects on civil liberties but little in terms of a forensic examination of the effectiveness or otherwise of counterterror policies.

Finally, and certainly not least, there is a need to examine practically what systems of accountability are in place with regard to these specialist measures, and the effect that the measures have had on civil liberties and human rights in light of the increase in state power.

State power and the 'war on terror'

The 'war on terror' has raised important questions about the scope and penetration of state power, challenging particularly ideas that it was in terminal decline in the face of its internal contradictions, globalization, the strength or versatility of civil society and the failure of statist economics (Moran, 2005, pp. 335–59). Indeed:

> Whatever is written about hollowed out states and soft power, governments retain the capacity to take decisions in areas such as defence and international relations which ignore the niceties of parliamentary accountability and the political constraints of party

policy if it feels that such decisions serve the strategic interests of the UK state in international matters. (Doig and Phythian, 2005, p. 370)

Certainly, the field of international relations has witnessed the development of an activist interventionist foreign policy on the part of the US, UK and Australian governments. At the same time, in the fallout from the 'war on terror' Iran emerged as a regional power, while Russia and the People's Republic of China flexed their soft power muscles on the international stage. The idea of the withering national interest proposed by advocates of globalization now looks decidedly fragile. However, it is not just in the area of international relations that 'the state is back.'

The UK state currently imprisons over 80,000 of its citizens, has introduced a national DNA database, is expanding the collection of DNA, is establishing other large databases on its citizenry, has expanded CCTV (Closed Circuit Television) coverage beyond any comparable nation state, is introducing ID cards, has introduced preventive detention theoretically applicable to UK citizens as well as foreign nationals and has given powers to a wide range of central and local public authorities to gain access to the details of the landline and mobile communication calls of citizens. Political scientists, sociologists and (particularly) criminologists have been clearly wrongfooted regarding developments in state power in the post 9/11 world. If criminologists argued for the need to think 'beyond the state', one overview of the field prior to 9/11 showed the dangers of taking this too far and exposed a criminology ill-equipped to focus on the state as the core principle of political organization and security once the 'war on terror' had commenced (Garland and Sparks, 2000). The response to post 9/11 developments has been most effective in the field of international relations and political science (although it should be noted that in these fields globalization was disproportionately influential for a long period) (Ross, 2004; Tilly, 2004; Naylor, 2006; Beland, 2005).

The response might be made that the disastrous invasion of Iraq and the practical exercise of domestic laws and powers in the United Kingdom and the United States show that state power is not always effective. As a counter argument this is insufficient, since this has always been the case with state power. In England and Wales capital punishment was the supreme criminal sanction until 1965. However hanging was hedged in practice with all sorts of restrictions, and the system did not prevent murder rates fluctuating. Nevertheless to argue that this expresses the limits of state power would be disingenuous, particularly to those 7000 people out of 35,000 sentenced to death who went to the scaffold between 1770 and 1830 (Gattrell, 1996, p. 7). A disjuncture between state power and state capacity (the exercise of that power in practice) has always existed (Cuéllar, 2004), and theorists who posit a crisis of the state and assert its current limitations as proof neglect this (Garland, 2000, ch. 5). Whether effective or not, British citizens are now likely to encounter state power in their day-to-day activities (for this concept, see Mouer and Sugimto, 1986; Tremewan, 1994) much more than was the case in the 1990s: for example, via the mandatory information provision required under the Proceeds of Crime Act 2002 when taking out a mortgage or engaging in other financial transactions; via the CCTV systems which may be linked to the police as part of Automatic Number Plate Recognition; if their DNA is taken after mere arrest; if they are involved with the Child Support Agency; if their child is declared as 'at risk' for some reason; if they are designated as being involved in antisocial behaviour; in terms of the powers the central and local authorities have over new taxing and environmental provisions, and so forth (Furedi, 2002; Penna, 2005; for the United States see Simon, 2007). Further, UK citizens might be awash in carnival and 'play' and the joys of late modern consumption, but while they are, data are being collected on them by private sector companies that the state may later access.

Further, the power of the private sector vis à vis the state, which has been a central focus in the arguments of globalization theorists and other analysts, is certainly evident but the 'Balkanization' seen by some,[2] exaggerates the extent of the retreat of the state. The state and the private sector have always existed in symbiosis; the purpose of any analysis is to trace the changing relationships between them. Even in the golden age of Keynesianism, mainstream and radical critiques talked of business elites driving state policy and the increasing power of the private sector (Wright Mills, 1956; Useem, 1986). Conversely, in the contemporary period, certainly states have become more business friendly, but they have also expanded state regulation, and in the area of crime and security, currently in the United Kingdom (and the United States) the state has obliged the private sector to open itself to scrutiny and access by police and security agencies seeking information on matters from airline bookings to financial transactions, and has obliged the private sector to pay the substantial and ongoing costs of instituting antimoney laundering systems (Harvey, 2005; Sproat, 2007). If more exemplars were needed there is much talk of the role and growth of the private security industry in Iraq (Johnson, Woolf and Whitaker, 2007), but their role has demonstrated their limits in producing public order and supplanting state authority in the streets of Baghdad, and they have clearly been operating in an environment structured by the state and the US military who took the decision to invade Iraq in the first place.[3]

Politics and the 'war on terror'

Following the shattering 9/11 attacks on the United States that killed nearly 3000 people, the politics of the 'war on terror' have influenced each nation state in specific ways. For those whose citizens have been attacked the experience has been a jolt to the political system and the stress on national security and the need to prevent further attacks is evident. This has not prevented them (and other nations who have not been attacked) from being accused of 'playing politics' with the 'war on terror'.

Some political elites used the 'war on terror' to bolster the position of the existing regime (e.g. for Pakistan, Algeria, Uzbekistan, see BBC, 2005f, 2005g, 2006h, 2007f). Other governments (e.g. in Spain) either found themselves toppled in the wake of terrorist attacks or saw the existing administration come under severe political pressure (e.g. the United States). Other governments (e.g. the United States) saw the existing administration under severe political pressure. The United Kingdom has been no exception. The Labour governments under Tony Blair were regularly accused of 'playing politics' with the 'war on terror', despite their consistent arguments that they wished to maintain a bipartisan consensus, and their political strategy has involved an aggressive media management of all the issues related to countering terrorism (Oborne, 2006).

The idea of the political nature of the 'war on terror' can be highlighted by the fact that in the United Kingdom by 2007 even the government seemed to view the term as no longer acceptable (Burke, 2006; BBC, 2007j). However, whatever term is used, the idea of a long-term conflict continues. Almost the first act by Sir Alan West, appointed by new Prime Minister Gordon Brown as Security Minister in 2007, was to state that the struggle against terrorism would continue for perhaps 15 years (BBC, 2007m).

The intensity of the United Kingdom's place in the post 9/11 environment has arisen from the government's decision to stand side by side with the administration of George Bush in the US military interventions in Afghanistan and Iraq, which fitted in with an already developing interventionist UK foreign policy, as seen in Kosovo and Sierra Leone at the end of the 1990s (Kampfner, 2004). Of clear political importance is the idea that the war in Iraq had a direct effect of bringing terrorism home to the United Kingdom. There is evidence of the radicalization of young British Muslims taking place before the invasion of Iraq in March 2003 (BBC2; Honigsbaum and Dodd, 2005; Husain, 2007).[4] However following the invasion, UK interests, and finally the United Kingdom itself, became a target for terrorism. In November 2003 the British Consulate and the HSBC bank in Istanbul were bombed, killing three British citizens among the twenty-eight dead. Then in July 2005 the bombings in London took place, the visceral manifestation of a growing radicalism in networks across the United Kingdom. It is clear, despite government denials, that the invasion of Iraq not only led to the United Kingdom becoming a hotbed of international terrorism, it also transformed the United Kingdom from being merely a haven for radical Islamists – 'Londonistan' as French and US analysts termed it – to a target for home-grown Islamist terrorists (albeit often with links abroad via personal family/networks or the Internet) (Kampfner, 2002; Younge, 2005).

As Jason Burke railed,

> I was angry at the British government's stubborn and utterly unjustified pretence that there was no link between the [7/7] attack and their policy in Iraq. Britain had indeed been a target for terrorism before the war in Iraq, as the government claimed, but the UK had become a far more likely target as a result of its close support for the United States and the policy of the Bush administration. (Burke, 2007, pp. 265–6)

Therefore, although the government has attempted to manage the 'war on terror' the management has been affected by the particular imagery and discourse used. The struggle is presented in absolutist terms: terrorists 'hate our way of life', they are influenced by a 'death cult' into which young impressionable men are 'groomed' and so forth. This completely neglects how the dynamics of recruitment changed. As Burke has noted,

> At the beginning of the 1990s, most of the Islamic activists living in London, or 'Londonistan' as it was called by critics of the British government's liberal asylum policy, were highly politicised, educated and relatively moderate. By the end of the decade militants in the west included far more men like Richard Reid, a British petty

criminal who tried to blow himself up on a transatlantic jet ... These were poor, unemployed, angry people. The number of former convicts or asylum seekers among recently recruited Islamic militants is striking. (Burke, 2004, pp. 283–4)

Since Burke wrote, it is apparent that recruits to jihadism have come from even more varied backgrounds.

Hence, it is possible to identify a considerable degree of cognitive dissonance in government policy, which has had the effect of conditioning and undermining some of its counter-terror strategy.

The government, the media and the 'war on terror'

Much has been written on the government's use of the media in the 'war on terror'. Arguing, as some have, that the government is using panic to maintain political authority is too simplistic.[5] The government genuinely believes that the terrorist threat is multifaceted and serious – because it is. However, the government seems to have succeeded in panicking *itself more than the general population*, who, as polls show, remain less concerned about the terrorist threat than sexual crime or environmental issues or house price falls.[6] Indeed, the government's public relations (PR) strategy under the Blair government seemed to become more apocalyptic as the UK population became *less* panicked. Further, in the age of twenty-four hour news media and a more aggressive manner of covering stories, the government became addicted to 'spinning' the 'war on terror' in much the same way as it did National Health Service reform, education reform or crime or any other issue (Rawnsley, 2001; Oborne, 2006).

As a result, but particularly after the invasion of Iraq, the government's rhetoric adopted a supercharged and absolutist tone, presenting the United Kingdom as part of an apocalyptic global struggle. As Tony Blair argued in July 2005,

> What we are confronting here is an evil ideology. It is not a clash of civilisations. All civilised people, Muslim or other, feel revulsion at it. But it is a global struggle, and it is a battle of ideas, hearts and minds. (Blair, 2005a)

In his short term as Home Secretary John Reid was particularly splenetic, warning of 'the scale of the threat which we face. In responding to it, the struggle has to be at every level, in every way and by every single person in this country.'

> It's evil terrorists on one side against all civilised people on the other. There can be no compromise, no appeasement with terrorism. Faced with the terrorist threat, as John F. Kennedy said, we must be prepared to 'bear any burden, pay any price, face any foe and support any friend'. (Reid, 2006a)

The intense news management strategy, characterized by such overcooked language, did little to advance government aims in other areas, notably building trust in Muslim communities. Since the government's participation in the invasion of Iraq in 2003 was not accepted as a factor in leading some Muslim youth to jihadist violence, the radicalization of individuals was not presented as a complex political and psychological process, but as an equivalent of paedophile grooming. John Reid urged:

> They believe, and they would have you believe that the West is evil, in all its works and that all modern values are corrupting to Muslims and to Islam, when in fact it is they who are wicked and ruthless and they who are attempting to corrupt young minds, mainly young Muslim minds [...] there is no nice way of saying this, but there are fanatics who are looking to groom and brainwash children in these communities, including your children, and they are grooming them for one thing: to kill themselves in order to murder many others as they do. So all I say is look for those telltale signs now, be herdsmen to your family. (Reid, 2006b)

This contrasted sharply with the government's approach to building peace in Northern Ireland where, over a long period of time, republican and loyalist paramilitary groups were co-opted through a complex (and often chaotic) process of security action, concessions and political manoeuvring (Moloney, 2002; Taylor, 2002). Although a comparison of republican and jihadist terrorism is fraught with difficulties, it is nevertheless true to say that any effective response to terrorism requires a sophisticated political and PR strategy rather than simplistic megaphone chanting. The premiership of Gordon Brown (from June 2007) did see a change in PR following the attempted suicide attack at Glasgow airport, but the damage had been done. As Leigh shows in Chapter 6, there has been a clear tension in the government's political strategy between highlighting the uniquely threatening 'war on terror', its rafts of anti-terror legislation and its need to build links with Muslim communities.

Indeed, this PR strategy may in fact have limited the ability of the police and security services to recruit informants in potential terrorist networks in the Muslim community or receive reports from citizens concerned at suspicious behaviour (Clarke, 2007, p. 6). It is plausible that the lack of intelligence partly results from the simplistic media strategy outlined above, coupled with the consistent leaking from government and police during anti-terror operations and capped by a media focus that increasingly ignores any written or unwritten contempt of court reporting restrictions (BBC, 2007g; Judd, 2007; O'Neill, 2007).

Discussing practical matters such as intelligence brings us to the third variable mentioned at the start of this chapter, what have been the mechanisms used by the government to counter terrorism in the United Kingdom and what concerns do these raise?

The mechanics of the 'war on terror'

The UK government has not engaged in the kind of major reorganiza-tion that has taken place in the United States, where a Department of Homeland Security was established in response to the alleged intelli-gence failure of the major agencies before the attacks of 9/11 (Gill, 2004; 2006). Although the Joint Terrorism Analysis Centre (JTAC) was created in 2003, this was a body aimed at improving coordination in the area of threat assessment rather than assuming authority over existing agencies. It took until 2007 for a major change to take place when the Home Office (which in the two centuries of its existence had come to oversee a massive range of issues from immigration to national security) was split into two Ministries, a Ministry of Justice, dealing with normal criminal justice matters and another ministry, still termed the Home Office, with responsibility for security policy. Once again, however, this is more of a coordinating change than a case of the Home Office becoming a centralized, supreme body for counter-terror work. MI5, MI6 and GCHQ (Government Communications Headquarters) remain autonomous. Indeed, previous to this, the government had rejected the idea of a counterterrorism 'Czar'. Further developments, such as the establishment of regional Counter Terrorism Units which link the local police and the security services across Britain are again aimed at coordinating rather than supplanting the existing system (Moran, 2007a, pp. 29–30). The National Security Strategy, produced in early 2008, brought no major changes; however a common theme running through all these changes has been the idea that if intelligence is used more rapidly and more effectively, terrorist attacks can be disrupted and, if appropriate, convictions gained.

It is in the area of law that successive Labour governments have been most active in changing the techniques of counter terrorism. Labour has had a zeal for passing legislation. Since the party was returned to power in 1997 it has created over 3000 new offences via a constant stream of legislation. Terrorism has been a part of this with the passing of the Terrorism Act 2000, the Anti-Terrorism, Crime and Security Act 2001, the Prevention of Terrorism Act 2005, the Terrorism Act 2006, and relevant legislation such as the Proceeds of Crime Act 2002 and the Serious Organised Crime and Police Act 2005. As the chapters by Walker, Leigh, Newman and Sproat show these laws cover a range of areas from introducing new offences of terrorism, to extending periods of pre-charge detention for those accused of terrorism offences, to changing the rules on stop and search, to changing public order powers, to facilitating information storage and access, and increasing financial surveillance.

By 2003 the government's strategy had solidified into CONTEST, involving Prevent (preventing the radicalization of individuals and engaging in the battle of ideas by challenging the ideologies that extremists believe can justify violence), Pursue (intelligence, legal change, disruption and international cooperation), Protect (securing borders, and public infrastructure) and Prepare (risk and contingency measures in case of attack) (Home Office, n.d.). No strategy is perfect and, as argued above, it appeared that the government's media policy actually conflicted with its Prevent strand, as did its participation in the Iraq war. Further, the core of the government's Pursue strand (law and intelligence) not only raised issues of effectiveness but also of its effect on civil liberties.

Judging the effectiveness of the strategy and technique of the UK 'war on terror'

The next question raised by this change is straightforward: what have been the results? The first point to make is that the 'war on terror' cannot be judged by convictions alone, since strategies are involved that might not lead to convictions. Here we are in the territory of what constitutes evidence that can be used to charge an individual with a criminal offence and what constitutes intelligence, which might be used to counter terrorist activity through measures short of prosecution. For example, police and security service activity might aim for the disruption of terrorist activities, including the prevention of terrorist activity through arrests or other measures aimed at hampering terrorist operations (e.g. neutralizing explosives). Many of these successes might come from the recruitment of informants within terrorist networks. Informants can also destabilize networks from within, by promoting dissent and suspicion. Success might also come from picking up and preventing suspected terrorist activity through technical surveillance or information from the financial system via bank and other institutional reporting of suspicious activity. Similarly, suspected terrorists might not be brought to trial, and instead be deported.

The experience of Northern Ireland provides a guide. Although approximately 30,000 convictions were secured during the period of conflict in Northern Ireland (1968–98), and this was the bedrock of an effective counter-terror strategy, many analysts argue that the qualified success against republican and loyalist paramilitaries lay in the fact that by the 1980s they were thoroughly penetrated by high-level British military intelligence or police informants (Holland and Phoenix, 1997; Moloney, 2002; Taylor, 2002). These informants assisted in the disruption of terrorist activities as well as undermining internal confidence within the republican and loyalist groups. In addition, counter terrorism involved measures to undermine terrorist financial structures through changing regulations, requiring the production of accounts by pubs, clubs and other small businesses linked to paramilitaries (Norman, 1998).

In terms of convictions during the 'war on terror', by early 2007, 41 individuals had been convicted of terrorism offences with a further 183 convicted of a variety of crimes, including murder, explosives and firearms offences, conspiracy, fraud and others, and 100 were awaiting trial.[7] A number of the more serious offenders had been given sentences of up to 40 years in prison.[8] Further, apart from the 7/7 attacks Britain has faced no successful terrorist attack, although fifteen attacks have been attempted since 2001 (BBC, 2007l).

However, a critical analysis of this overall picture raises some questions about the practical efficacy of many of the major anti-terrorist tools that have been portrayed as being vital to the successful prosecution of the 'war on terror'.

Intelligence and other 'magic bullets'

Intelligence is repeatedly identified as the key to combating terrorism. This is self-evident as a general statement. Once we move to specifics, important questions arise: what is 'good' intelligence? How should it be used? Under what conditions is its use effective? How important is it to maintain the distinction between intelligence (i.e. information gained from a variety of sources with varying levels of reliability) and evidence (information that is robust enough to be used in a courtroom having been subjected to challenge by the defence and assessment by a jury and, if successful, leading to a conviction on the basis of being beyond reasonable doubt)? (Gill, 2000). As Clive Walker has argued in a series of sophisticated papers, intelligence can feed into policing and security processes in a variety of ways, and its increasing use is controversial, not just in terms of its legitimacy but also in terms of effectiveness. However, there is no fundamental objection to the use of intelligence, providing it is subject to a continuing process of professionalization and independent oversight (Walker, 2002, 2004, 2005).

Intelligence is such a flexible datum, as demonstrated by the fact that its use stretches from low-level policing of burglaries to high-level political decisions to wage war. As Phythian argues, it is this political nature of intelligence that also calls into question its efficacy. One only needs to mention the British government's 2003 dossier on the threat from Iraq (which incorporated plagiarized detail from an American PhD thesis on Iraq) to see both how politicized and how poor it can be as a result. Searching for perfect intelligence on which to make decisions is always going to be a difficult process, considering the practical limits of resources and the highly charged arena in which intelligence agencies operate. In the period up to the Iraq war, the United Kingdom followed the United States in respect of the politicization of intelligence assessments (Doig and Phythian, 2005). Intelligence cannot be the key to combating terrorism if it does not both take account of the changing nature of the threat and screen out the often powerful white noise of political context. The nature of al-Qaeda is a case in point. As Jason Burke argued, 'Though united by an ideology and a vision of the world, Islamic militancy is now, operationally, as fragmented as it has ever been' (Burke, 2004, p. 272). Intelligence failure is, therefore, not only quite common in the highly politicized context in which it is produced and interpreted, it is also an ever-present possibility.

The search for magic bullets in the 'war on terror' has seen the government adopt or rework a number of policies that rely on intelligence, including counter terrorist finance. The United States developed the idea that instituting mandatory reporting of 'suspicious' transactions in the financial system might squeeze out illicit money or that, in addition, if suspicious money or other assets were discovered at some later date after investigation or through trial, legislation should give the state the power to freeze the assets, or even confiscate them. These strategies began with regard to drug trafficking but spread elsewhere (Levi, 1997; Alldridge, 2003).

In the United Kingdom such ideas were tested in the 1980s in Northern Ireland with regard to the finances behind paramilitary groups. In Northern Ireland the idea of simply beginning an investigation into the financial operations of businesses linked to paramilitaries could be enough to disrupt their operations. The Criminal Assets Bureau (CAB) in the Republic of Ireland also provided a model. Set up in the 1990s in the aftermath of the assassination of journalist Veronica Guerin, the CAB investigates financial affairs and institutes penalties on the basis that the individual has unlawfully gained his/her assets. This is the context for the UK government's counter terrorist finance policies, which aim to squeeze terrorist funds out of the financial system, identify financial transactions by terrorists as a basis for an operation to disrupt (or charge) them, or seize assets identified as being used by terrorists or their supporters. These initiatives appear promising but in practice a number of problems are evident. Terrorist attacks can be undertaken for relatively (or even absolutely) small amounts of money, and the transactions that might provide the finance are no different from those of millions of other citizens, particularly in the credit-based economy of the United Kingdom. Indeed loans of thousands of pounds that would not trigger any suspicion are provided by high street banks to anyone with a half decent credit rating. As Sproat shows, these overarching policies have not provided the 'silver bullets' for combating terrorism; it is the more mundane extra powers given to police on the ground in terms of access to the financial details of suspected terrorists which have demonstrated their usefulness.

This realization follows the now-much-publicized failure of the Assets Recovery Agency (ARA) to dry up the financial lifeblood of criminal organizations. Established in 2003 as the solution to serious crime by depriving criminals of their assets, the ARA was hit with problems from its inception, including the long duration of cases, internal disorganization and its failure to receive high-profile cases from various police forces. By 2007 it had been announced that the ARA would be merged into the Serious and Organised Crime Agency (SOCA).

Finally, extending the time in which suspects can be held by the police before charge is another technique held to be a major leap forward in combating terrorism, and highlights the classic opposing points of view in the 'war on terror'. The government argued that it was necessary and proportionate. Many Members of Parliament and members of the House of Lords (including Law Lords) argued it was not. The breadth of argument covered the issue of whether the United Kingdom in fact faced a public emergency or a threat to the life of the nation sufficient to justify exceptional measures. The higher echelons of the Metropolitan Police argued forcefully for 90 days and in a public letter Metropolitan Police Assistant Commissioner Andy Hayman set out the police case, backed up by the Commissioner Sir Ian Blair. Much of the argument for the 90 days limit stressed the newness of al-Qaeda, its use of technology and the need for longer times for forensic examination of computers. Much of this case was itself subject to scrutiny, and thus the police had clearly drawn themselves into a political debate. Later, the police in the form of Deputy Assistant Commissioner Peter Clarke argued that this was not a political intervention, (Clarke, 2007, pp. 9–10) but coupled with the statements of Sir Ian Blair in the course of the 'war on terror' it looked dangerously like it (Moore, 2006). Indeed, as the Home Affairs Committee of the House of Commons pointed out, the melding of politics (government) and police did not benefit either party:

> [W]e found the case for extending the maximum detention period to 28 days was convincing, but did not find the arguments for the 90 day period compelling. On such a major issue, with very significant human rights implications, we would have expected the case made by the police to have been better developed. The police should have been able to present an evidence based analysis of the type we have endeavoured to undertake. It is clear that this was not done, despite their reliance on their 'professional judgement'. We think it is reasonable for the Prime Minister and Home Secretary to rely on advice from the police on such issues, but we would also expect them to have challenged critically the advice in order to assure themselves of the case that was being made. We heard no evidence that this had happened: this is unsatisfactory. (Home Affairs Select Committee, 2006, p. 48 para 1)

The government was defeated in the House of Commons, although the House agreed to extend the pre-charge period to 28 days via the Terrorism Act 2006. Following the London and Glasgow attempted bombings in 2007 an extension to 42 days was back on the agenda. The government argued that with the prospect of multiple suspects with multiple identities, international links, multiple mobile phones and the need to collect a wide range of forensic data, the pre-charge detention period would have to be increased. Opponents argued that in previous cases although the police had detained suspects right up to 28 days, there was no case for extending the period, as there was no case yet in which the police had needed it (Joint Committee on Human Rights, 2007, section 2) and a range of critics failed to be convinced of the case for any extension, including former Attorney General Lord Goldsmith

(Branigan, 2007a). An increase to 42 days was scrambled through the House of Commons in mid-2008 not because the government had won the argument but because it became bound up with PM Gordon Brown's political survival.

The essentials to an effective 'war on terror' domestically have come from traditional methods of investigation. Here the new financial powers to examine accounts as part of standard police investigations have proved effective (see Sproat, this volume). Technical surveillance, enhanced through taps on mobile phones, has provided important information as have, to a lesser extent, informants within radical networks – an area that requires more focus by MI5 – and information from British citizens.

Indeed, looking abroad, the Spanish experience in combating both ETA and al-Qaeda demonstrates that the Spanish state was able to cope without relying on extraordinary measures. Rather, political strategy, police and intelligence professionalization and reorganization and inter-agency cooperation remain keys. Indeed it seems to be the Anglo-Saxon democracies (the United Kingdom, United States and Australia – see Michaelsen's Chapter 8) that have reached for extraordinary measures rather than the statist democracies of Europe.[9] Although the British government, as Rumney notes, unlike the USA rejected the magic bullet of 'coercive interrogation' – inhuman or degrading treatment, or torture for those without a gift for euphemism (see Poole, 2007, ch. 7) – it has allegedly received valuable intelligence from sources abroad who have used these unlawful techniques, including Pakistan's ISI (Plett, 2007).

Accountability and the 'war on terror'

Flowing through the discussion of policy, intelligence, law and practice in the 'war on terror' is the issue of accountability. The scope of the structures of accountability that govern these new or charged up counter-terror mechanisms clearly fit in with the overall debate about state power eroding civil liberties in the 'war on terror'. However as argued above, the standard dichotomy that sees all special measures as eroding civil liberties lacks the sophistication to see the changes in context. As Walker argues,

> The 21st century concept of normality in criminal justice embodies the contingency and reality of 'special' powers dealing with 'special' situations or risks, whether terrorism, serious frauds, sex offenders or the anti-social. This trend towards fragmentation and specialisation

may be warranted, provided sensible safeguards and scrutiny are built upon. (Walker, 2004, p. 325).

What might these safeguards be? Accountability takes many forms: courts and courts of appeal, internal organizational oversight, external bureaucratic oversight, the media and civil society groups.

The courts have been vigorous in critiquing the mechanisms of the 'war on terror'. In pre-trial hearings and in the trials themselves evidence has been challenged and not guilty verdicts reached. The court judgements that have been given the most attention have been those of the higher courts. Some of the judgements of the House of Lords have contained remarkable language, and it is the House of Lords' judgement in December 2004 that put paid to the government's policy of detaining in prison those suspected international terrorists who could not be charged with an offence or deported. Following this judgement the government had to change the policy, placing suspected international terrorists under house arrest via control orders. Then the Court of Appeal quashed a number of control orders in 2006 on procedural grounds. As Walker argues in this volume, 'judges will no longer be passive bystanders in the processes by which intelligence is assessed and applied to individuals.' Elsewhere the Court of Appeal in early 2008 quashed the convictions under s57 of the Terrorism Act 2000 of five Bradford students who had downloaded extremist material. The judgement argued that this was not evidence of their intent to commit terrorist acts (BBC, 2008). However, arguments that the Human Rights Act has facilitated an active judiciary must be tempered (Walker, 2005; Rasiah, 2006). Although the Lords initially raised queries over the idea that there is a national security threat to the extent the government claims,[10] generally they have deferred to the executive in terms of national security, for example, as Newman shows in this volume, interpreting public order legislation as being consistent with the European Court of Human Rights (ECtHR).

Although New Labour Ministers have railed that they are shackled by the ECtHR, it has not prevented the passing and operation of fundamental changes to policing and security (not all of them restricted to the 'war on terror'). These include the expansion of CCTV, the taking of DNA merely as a result of being arrested, extended pre-charge detention (discussed above), indefinite house arrest under control orders, even while others have been declared incompatible, including indefinite detention for foreign suspected terrorist nationals in prison (see above) and accepting evidence from torture. The situation is complex.

Parliament has been active in a patchy manner. The House of Commons has rebelled once, over 90-day detention. Individual parliamentary committees have often been more critical. The Joint (Lords and Commons) Parliamentary Committee on Human Rights has been forceful in its public reports, which have challenged much of the government's architecture of the 'war on terror' for necessity, effectiveness and accountability. The Home Affairs Select Committee has been critical of a number of government anti-terror measures. However, the government's independent scrutineer of anti-terrorist legislation, Liberal peer Lord Carlile, has generally agreed with the government, albeit with some mild qualifications.

In terms of specific national security agencies, oversight is generally bureaucratic and less vigorous than in the United States, for example. External accountability mechanisms in the form of the Intelligence Services Commissioner and the Interception of Communications Commissioner (ICC) are evident, although these are bureaucratic (the ICC also covers the police) and inapplicable if individuals simply do not know they are being surveilled. The Parliamentary Intelligence and Security Committee has been criticized for its lack of scope, power and activity (Phythian, 2005).

The police, despite facing much criticism, are generally more constrained than other agencies via the Police and Criminal Evidence Act (PACE) 1984 and its voluminous Codes of Practice covering the actual operation of PACE in practice. Although police and security service surveillance was virtually unregulated until the late 1980s, legislation such as the Regulation of Investigatory Powers Act 2000 has necessitated the police developing clear internal guidelines on the use of covert technical and human surveillance that may provide the basis for challenge in court. Further, the police are subject to an oversight watchdog the Independent Police Complaints Commission (IPCC), which has not been 'captured'. Indeed it has been accused of being both too aggressive and a whitewash organization.[11] Clearly critics would want to see more independent agencies such as the IPCC replace these bureaucratic oversight mechanisms.

This legislative and bureaucratic oversight is, of course, insufficient unless buttressed by a vigorous civil society. The 'war on terror' has been pursued in the full phosphorescent glare of 24-hour media coverage, conjoined with pressure groups such as Liberty and activist groups of protestors and individuals from comedian Mark Thomas to artists such as Banksy and Mark Wallinger (for the latest critique see Atkins, Bee and Button, 2007). When all is said and done, the 'war on terror' is probably the most scrutinized in history. One only has to compare the current situation with Northern Ireland in the 1980s. However the initiative rests with the state, and the concern is the idea of a never-ending war that may mitigate against proportionality, and the actual robustness of accountability in practice.

Civil liberties and state power

The balance between state power and civil liberties has generated a massive amount of quality debate, although it is too often characterized by well-rehearsed arguments, with government supporters or sympathizers arguing that changes to police powers and executive authority are necessary and proportionate but providing shaky evidence while defenders of civil liberties exaggerate and simplify by arguing that the changes propel us towards an authoritarian state (Waddington, 2005; Haubrich, 2006; Waddington, 2006; Moran, 2007b). Two points seem clear: state power has increased and the United Kingdom does face a terrorist threat, leading us to ask: what is the nature of the threat and are the special measures against it proportionate? In light of this it is interesting to move away from this sphere and urge that those who are concerned with state power and civil liberties in the United Kingdom maintain a focus on the other challenges to individual autonomy in late modern societies, and ones that do not have the justifiable rationale of threats to national and public security behind them. One interesting recent development has been the way in which the idea that civil liberties are under threat has come from the margins to the centre. For the right-wing press civil liberties were historically an issue that concerned naïve metropolitan liberals. However, under the Blair governments (1997–2007) conservative and right-wing commentators have begun to campaign on civil liberties issues. Papers such as *The Times*, *Daily Telegraph*, *Daily Mail* and *Daily Express* regularly highlight the increase in state regulation over the lives of UK citizens. Part of this is an ideological opposition to policies across the public sector that they regard as political correctness 'gone mad'. However, they are also concerned over increasing central and local state power in areas such as the gaining of information on individuals for health and tax purposes or to promote environmental policies such as recycling. The concern of conservative critics is not with counter-terror powers but with the ever-expanding 'regulatory state' (Jenkins, 1996; Hitchens, 2004; for the regulatory state see Moran, 2001; 2003). Elsewhere other critics have focused on the growth of data collection/surveillance that is developing at an alarming pace in the private sector (Moran, 2007b).

Conclusion

The role of the United Kingdom in the 'war on terror' presents challenges on a number of levels. Indeed, the idea of such a 'war' is now contested in the United States, and the British government has distanced itself from the concept. The Gordon Brown government seemed to be using less apocalyptic language with regard to terrorism, although in other areas it continued with yet more terrorism legislation – the 2008 Counter Terror Bill proposes the extension of pre-charge detention. However the conflict is framed, the basic concept of a struggle against terrorism in the United Kingdom is the tip of an iceberg with regard to what it signifies about the threat and its control.

The period since 2001, and especially 2005, raises concerns about the clear threat from terrorist attacks, which seems now fuelled by 'neighbour terrorism', that is, from UK citizens who have been radicalized to plan acts of violence (Walker, 2007). The state's response has been to develop special powers, although the approach to terrorism is not unique but represents an application of the techniques used against other forms of crime that are seen as requiring specialist measures: sexual offences, organized crime, serious fraud and anti-social behaviour.

If terrorism requires special powers, a number of other questions arise. One is simply whether the measures are as effective as is claimed. Often they are nowhere near as effective. This is an important and under-researched area compared with the more general discussions about terror powers and civil liberties, but it clearly needs to be integrated with any analysis of the effects on civil liberties, which itself involves rigorous study of how the measures are controlled in practice. Accountability varies widely, from parliament and the courts to media and protest groups, from bureaucratic to 'watchdog' styles of oversight. There should be overlapping circles of scrutiny, with some circles (courts, judiciary, oversight bodies) constituting the professional examination of the operation and effectiveness of special powers, while outer circles (media, NGOs) examine these issues but also test the wider effects anti-terror measures may have on protest and expression, for example. These processes and actors are, however, *responding* to the increase in state power in the United Kingdom.

The debate over state power and civil liberties in counterterrorism will need to be a long campaign itself, if the prospect of controlling terrorism is a task that will take 15 years. The spread of powers in place by then might only be guessed at. Alternatively the threat may reduce. It may reduce partly through the continuing development of skills by counter-terror agencies, as occurred in Northern Ireland. This might be joined with an internal process in which jihadist terrorism is already 'maturing' and that the numbers of recruits may decline. It may be the case that jihadist violence will decline once the 'political conditions creating it have disappeared'. This was a classic refrain heard from the Provisional Irish Republican Army (PIRA) over its three decades of struggle. In fact the PIRA achieved relatively little in terms of its original aims, but the political context was vital to its eventual cessation of operations. In the current context, despite the fact that the government cannot admit it, the practical political conditions leading to a decline in terrorism surely include the United Kingdom's withdrawal from Iraq and Afghanistan.

Whatever the case, as the chapters in this volume argue, the connections between politics, security, law and policing require detailed and dispassionate analysis.

Notes

1. The term 'war on terror' is used in quotation marks throughout the volume to denote a critical approach to the idea that UK counter-terror policy constitutes a war and that any conflict can be realistically mounted against a term such as terror.
2. For example, Taylor argues, in light of the expansion of private security, that there is a sense of the private interest 'breaking free' of the constraints of the State, and of obligations to the public institutions of the police, the courts and the justice system, in its own specific commercial interest, looking after itself. There is a powerful sense of the emergence of a new feudalism, in which in effect, powerful private interests police the territory over which they have a commercial hegemony, whilst leaving huge tracts of residual territory...under generalized surveillance but substantially unattended. (Taylor, 1999, p. 218)
3. Toby Dodge compares the British (1920s) and US (2003–) led processes of state building in Dodge (2006).
4. According to some reports, Mohammad Siddique Khan, one of the 7/7 bombers had become radicalized by 2001 (BBC, 2006i).
5. This is not the sole argument of the sophisticated Three-part documentary, *The Power of Nightmares* broadcast on BBC2 in January 2005.
6. A survey by Control Risks Group before 7/7 showed that war, corporate scandal and terrorism were three main risks to major companies but underpinning this, the lack of trust between companies, governments and local communities was the most important factor likely to impinge on business (Mesure, 2002). After 7/7 see Glover and Milmo (2006). When asked in an ICM survey what should be the current priorities for the government, 71% chose health, 50% education and 28% terrorism (Adam and Wintour, 2006).
7. Home Office, *Facts and figures* http://www.homeoffice.gov.uk/security/terrorism-and-the-law/ (statistics last updated 31 March 2007).

8. In 2006, Dhiren Barot was sentenced to life in prison for plotting explosions on both sides of the Atlantic. The seven men in the 'sleeper cell' around Barot were sentenced to between 15 and 26 years. In 2007 the five men involved in the fertilizer bomb plot received life sentences with the judge warning them they might never be released. The men involved in the 21/7 attempted bombings received life sentences with a minimum of 40 years.

9. The Foreign and Commonwealth Office (n.d.) country survey seems to show that various states passed much less legislation than the United Kingdom, and a number of instruments were passed to conform to United Nations' inspired measures after 9/11.

10. For example see Lord Hoffman's comments in *A(FC) and others v Secretary of State for the Home Department* [2004] UKHL 56.

11. For information on its latest report into the police shooting of Jean Charles de Menezes in 2005, which criticizes Met Assistant Commissioner Andy Hayman, see Dodd, 2007c. With regard to the shooting of Jean Charles de Menezes, the Metropolitan Police did not face murder charges but were prosecuted under the Health and Safety at Work Act 1974. Generally, see Prenzler (2000).

2
In the Shadow of 9/11: Security, Intelligence and Terrorism in the United Kingdom

Mark Phythian

Introduction

Prime Minister Tony Blair's response to the terrorist attacks of 11 September 2001 (9/11) put the United Kingdom at the forefront of the embryonic 'war on terror'. That day he abandoned a prepared speech to the Trades Union Congress to tell delegates that:

> This mass terrorism is the new evil in our world today. It is perpetrated by fanatics who are utterly indifferent to the sanctity of human life and we, the democracies of this world, are going to have to come together to fight it together and eradicate this evil completely from our world. (White and Wintour, 2001)

'This is not a battle between the United States and terrorism', he later explained, 'but between the free and democratic world and terrorism' (Ibid.). Days later Blair had adopted the Bush Administration language of being 'at war with terrorism'. He vigorously supported the US war to remove the Taliban from power in Afghanistan. Far more controversially he supported the Bush Administration in making the case for the necessity of extending the 'war on terror' to Iraq, and then militarily in undertaking the war to remove Saddam Hussein from power. Later, British troops came to assume a prominent role in the NATO campaign in Afghanistan, in sharp contrast to the marked reluctance of most NATO members to commit forces there. This leading role in the 'war on terror' gave rise to a number of security and intelligence challenges by providing the background to a series of Islamist terror plots, most but not all of which were frustrated by the work of the security and intelligence agencies. Most notably, the Security Service, MI5, failed to recognize, yet alone prevent, the 7 July 2005 (7/7) suicide bomb plot of four young British Muslims – Mohammad Siddique Khan, Shazad Tanweer, Jermaine Lindsay and Hasib Hussein – which claimed fifty-two lives in addition to their own and injured several hundred in the first instance of suicide bombing in Europe's history. This chapter reviews the principal post-9/11 Islamist terror plots in the United Kingdom, analyses the nature of the terrorist threat, the challenges presented by the post-9/11 security environment and explores the question of whether the 7/7 bombings could be considered to represent an intelligence failure.

Intelligence and Islamist terrorist plots in the United Kingdom

The 7 July 2005 London bombings

The 7/7 attacks inevitably raised questions as to whether the bombings could have been prevented, and as to the exact status of MI5 knowledge and understanding of the potential threat posed by radicalized young British Muslims. These questions were fuelled by the revelation that, although politicians and intelligence officials had claimed at the time of the bombings that the perpetrators were 'clean skins' unknown to police and MI5, two of them, Khan and Tanweer, had in fact been monitored as part of a wider intelligence operation. Moreover, it subsequently transpired that on the day before the bombings, MI5 Director General, Eliza Manningham-Buller, had personally assured a group of senior Labour MPs that there was no imminent threat of a terrorist attack to the United Kingdom (Cobain, Hencke and Norton-Taylor, 2007).

When the parliamentary Intelligence and Security Committee (ISC) came to investigate the bombings, it concluded that the failure to prevent them arose primarily from resource constraints. There is no doubting the strain on MI5's resources by July 2005. At the time of the 9/11 attacks MI5 had approximately 250 'primary investigative targets' in the United Kingdom, but this number rose to over 500 by July 2004, and again to approximately 800 by the time of the London bombings. Consequently, by 2005 the Joint Terrorism Analysis Centre (JTAC) – the body set up in June 2003 to bring together counterterrorist expertise from across government, and responsible for determining the official threat level from international terrorism – had to deal with a high volume of intelligence on the potential terrorist threat, estimated at approximately 1000 pieces per week. Given MI5's limited resource base, the ISC reported 'difficult decisions have to be made as to what priority to accord a particular piece of intelligence, and whether that piece or another lead should be pursued in more depth' (ISC, 2006, para. 21). Underpinning this reality is the fact that continuous surveillance of targets is a highly labour-intensive process and, given MI5's resource base, could only be undertaken selectively. Indeed, the ISC revealed that at the time of the 7/7 attacks an intensive surveillance operation could account for almost 50% of MI5's operational and investigative resources. As a result intelligence officers, 'have to make difficult professional judgements as to where finite resources should be allocated and focus on those targets that appear to pose the most immediate threat to life' (Ibid.).

This narrative of resource constraint was used to explain why Khan and Tanweer were not investigated more thoroughly when, in 2003 and 2004, both were observed on what the ISC termed the 'peripheries of other investigations' (Ibid., para. 45) – a reference to Operation Crevice (see below). As MI5's own post-7/7 review revealed, both Khan and Tanweer had been 'among a group of men who had held meetings with others under Security Service investigation in 2004' (Ibid., para. 46). Khan was covertly photographed and the meetings recorded. MI5 also had a record of Khan's telephone number, which had been used to establish contact with an individual who had been under MI5 investigation since 2003. MI5 told the ISC that:

> The individual under investigation was not himself an 'Essential' target and there was no reason for his contacts, which we now know to have been with Siddique Khan, to have been identified as exceptional or worthy of further investigation above other priorities. (Ibid., para. 47)

Hence, a decision was taken not to place Khan or other unidentified individuals under surveillance. MI5 argued, and the ISC seemed to accept, that this was because they 'were not categorized as investigative targets because, on the basis of the available intelligence, there was no reason to suggest they should be investigated above other more pressing priorities at the time' (Ibid., para. 49). This decision meant that, despite various leads, MI5 was unable to identify Khan prior to the 7/7 bombings. The ISC was only mildly critical of MI5's performance in this respect:

> It is possible that the chances of identifying attack planning and of preventing the 7 July attacks might have been greater had different

investigative decisions been taken in 2003–2005. Nonetheless, we conclude that, in light of the other priority investigations being conducted and the limitations on Security Service resources, the decisions not to give greater investigative priority to these two individuals were understandable. (Ibid., para. 56)[1]

Operation Crevice

By the second anniversary of the 7/7 bombings, the attack had emerged as being, far from an isolated incident, one of a number of overlapping Islamist terrorist plots facing the United Kingdom. One of the potentially most lethal was that uncovered and prevented by Operation Crevice, a significant intelligence success, but one overshadowed by the spectre of possible intelligence failure. In April 2007, five men – Omar Khyam, Waheed Mahmood, Jawad Akbar, Anthony Garcia and Salahuddin Amin – were convicted of a plot to explode bombs at targets, including the Bluewater shopping centre in Kent and the Ministry of Sound nightclub in London, using ammonium nitrate fertilizer bombs. MI5 was able to monitor the site where the fertilizer was stored, bug conversations (including one between two of the conspirators in which one asks, 'Bruv, you don't think this place is bugged, do you?' and the other replies, 'Do you know, we give them too much credit, bruv' (*The Economist*, 2007a), and insert an agent to pose as a receptionist at the storage depot. There is no doubting the resource intensity of Operation Crevice. At its peak in February and March 2004 it accounted for 34,000 man hours of police and intelligence work as the suspects were placed under 24-hour surveillance (Ibid.). This involved police and MI5 officers bugging ninety-seven telephone lines, carrying out covert property searches on twelve occasions, and generated over 3500 hours of tapes from bugs planted in suspects' homes and cars and concealed video cameras (Cobain and Norton-Taylor, 2007).

However, the trial also raised again the question of the extent of MI5's prior knowledge of 7/7 suicide bombers Khan and Tanweer, and the extent to which the 7/7 suicide bombings represented an intelligence failure, in the process raising fresh questions about the ability of the ISC, which had faced criticism over its inquiry into pre-war intelligence on Iraq's weapons of mass destruction, to oversee the intelligence and security agencies. During the Crevice trial it emerged that surveillance of Khan and Tanweer may have been much more thorough than previously believed, and that the indicators that they represented a potential threat may have been far less opaque than MI5 had suggested to the ISC. Both had been under surveillance eighteen months prior to the 7/7 bombings, and Khan emerged as a close associate of lead Crevice plotter Khyam, further calling into question MI5's decision to discontinue surveillance on the grounds that it judged he did not pose a direct threat to the United Kingdom.

Through this trial, rather than the original ISC investigation, it now became publicly known that eighteen months before the events of 7/7:

> MI5 followed [Khan and Tanweer] as they drove hundreds of miles around the UK, photographed them and recorded their voices. They followed Siddique Khan to his mother-in-law's home, made inquiries about his telephone, and listened to bugged conversations in which he talked about waging jihad. Yet they failed to identify either man, and cut short their investigations into the pair after deciding that they did not pose as high a risk to the country as other suspects under investigation. (Cobain, Norton-Taylor and Vasager, 2007)

Moreover, it also emerged that only months before the 7/7 bombings investigations into Khan had been reopened, something about which the ISC seemed to have been completely unaware when conducting its inquiry (Dodd, Cobain and Carter, 2007), and which was difficult to square with the explanation that he was not regarded as a threat. In the context of these revelations, which could only be reported at the conclusion of the Crevice trial, the contemporaneous early retirement of MI5 Director General Eliza Manningham-Buller in April 2007 was interpreted by some as a pre-emptive move reflecting a tacit admission of failure on MI5's part (Leppard, 2006b), one about which it may not to have been completely frank with the ISC. Nevertheless, in the wake of the Crevice trial Prime Minister Tony Blair rejected calls for an independent inquiry into the 7/7 bombings, on the basis that it would divert resources from tracking potential terrorists and also 'undermine support' for MI5 (Branigan, 2007b). Instead, he asked the ISC to look again at the matter, putting the Committee in a Catch-22 situation that could only further undermine its credibility.

The 21/7 plot

Two weeks after the 7/7 suicide bombings, on 21 July 2005 (21/7), a failed attack on the London underground took place. Two years later, in July 2007, the four would-be bombers – Muktar Said Ibrahim, Yassin Omar, Ramzi Mohammed and Hussein Osman – were each sentenced to life imprisonment, to serve a minimum of forty years.[2] Once again, the spectre of intelligence failure hovered over the trial. The plotters had been under surveillance for over a year, yet they were still able to attempt to detonate bombs on the London underground. During the trial it emerged that lead plotter Ibrahim had travelled to Pakistan in December 2004. Ibrahim, who was on bail at the time of the attempted bombings on charges of distributing extremist literature, had been stopped by a Special Branch officer at Heathrow airport en route to Pakistan, but had been allowed to proceed even though he was carrying a ballistics manual, a military first aid kit and thousands of pounds in cash (Laville, 2007). As with Khan and Tanweer, whether MI5 correctly assessed how serious a potential threat Ibrahim represented prior to 21/7 is questionable (Morris, 2007). His trip to Pakistan overlapped with trips made by Khan and Tanweer, raising the prospect that they actually attended the same camps at the same time and the possibility that, as a consequence, the plots did not merely overlap, but were linked. Tanweer and Ibrahim certainly attended the same camp and the bombs prepared for the 7/7 and 21/7 attacks were almost identical and at the same time unusual.

The plot to kidnap and behead a Muslim soldier

In February 2008, Parviz Khan was sentenced to a minimum of fourteen years imprisonment after being convicted of leading a terrorist cell planning to kidnap and behead a serving British Muslim soldier and broadcast it on the Internet. Four co-conspirators were jailed between two and seven years (Dodd, 2008). The five had been arrested following January 2007 raids on houses in Birmingham in what was held to be an early success in the development of enhanced MI5-Special Branch co-operation post-7/7. It followed a six-month surveillance operation. Indicative of the problems of monitoring terrorist groups, the surveillance operation had been intended to go on for longer to gather further evidence for an eventual trial and to take in as wide a range of contacts as possible, but the raids were brought forward as the cell reportedly began its final preparations for the kidnapping.

The aircraft bomb plot

In August 2006, surveillance of a group of young British Muslims uncovered a plot to explode seven passenger aircraft as they flew from the United Kingdom to six cities in the United States and Canada, potentially the most lethal of the post-9/11 UK terrorist plots. They were to be exploded by combining explosive ingredients carried on to the planes by separate passengers so as to avoid detection. Twenty-four arrests were made in the United Kingdom, as well as several in Pakistan, resulting in a lengthy 2008 court case. The police-MI5 surveillance operation that uncovered the alleged plot had been in place for over a year, based on a tip-off from within the Muslim community shortly after the 7/7 attacks (Norton-Taylor, Laville and Dodd, 2006).

The doctors' plot

At the end of June 2007, an attempt to plant car bombs in London, imitating a tactic by then commonplace in Baghdad, failed. Over the same weekend the group responsible for this attempt drove a burning vehicle into the terminal of Glasgow airport in the first instance of an attempted suicide car bombing in the United Kingdom. All of the principals involved worked as doctors in the United Kingdom. By this time, twenty people had been convicted of terrorist offences in the United Kingdom during 2007.

The significance of Pakistan

In all of these plots, links to Pakistan emerged as a common thread, raising a number of questions, including how closely the traffic between the United Kingdom and Pakistan was monitored by the security and intelligence services prior to 7/7. Two of the 7/7 suicide bombers, Khan and Tanweer, had visited Pakistan from November 2004 to February 2005. Khan had made an earlier visit in July 2003, and may well have travelled to Afghanistan some time before this (ISC, 2006, para. 53). It is not clear that MI5 was aware of any of these trips prior to the 7/7 bombings and they seem to have been slow to appreciate the full significance of Pakistan to terrorist plots aimed at the United Kingdom.

As the government's official account of the bombings notes, extended visits to Pakistan by British Muslims are a frequent occurrence – for example, there were 400,000 visits by British residents in 2004 at an average length of forty-one days, posing a significant challenge in terms of monitoring, although profiling around age and gender alone would have made the task more manageable (UK Government, 2006a, para. 50). Given that Pakistan, in particular the border region with Afghanistan, represents the cradle of the 'war on terror' it would seem appropriate for the British security and intelligence agencies to attach a high priority to monitoring such visits. But despite the efforts of MI6 in Pakistan it was not, in hindsight, sufficient. Liaison with the Pakistani ISI seems to have yielded less than complete co-operation. Although there is evidence that co-operation improved post-7/7, for example, with regard to the August 2006 airliner bomb plot, it remained subject to periodic frustrations and raised clear ethical issues in relation to a number of cases of prolonged detention without trial in Pakistan, usually accompanied by allegations of torture.

Khan and Tanweer's visit emerged as being of central importance to the 7/7 plot. Reportedly, ISI officials believe that Khan spent time there liaising with one Mohammed Yasin, an al-Qaeda operative and explosives expert (Harnden and Ansari, 2005). Tanweer spent time at a training camp near the Kashmir border run by Harkat ul-Mujahedin ('Movement for Holy Warriors'), a group implicated in the kidnap and murder of American journalist Daniel Pearl in 2002 (Herbert and Sengupta, 2005). The precise detail of the visit is murky. According to the ISC: 'It has not yet been established who they met in Pakistan, but it is assessed as likely that they had some contact with al Qaida figures' (ISC, 2006, para. 37). It concluded it was likely that some form of operational training took place,[3] but that the extent to which the bombings were 'externally planned, directed or controlled by contacts in Pakistan or elsewhere remains unclear' (Ibid., para. 38). A mobile phone SIM card found on Tanweer's remains after the bombings contained a list of telephone numbers in Pakistan, investigation of which led to arrests there but without significant advances in the investigation. Nevertheless, it seems Khan and Tanweer had contacts amongst the milieu of extremist clerics and possibly even rump members of the Afghan-era al-Qaeda in Pakistan, an assumption reinforced by 'suspicious' contacts with an unknown individual in Pakistan after their return to the United Kingdom (UK Government, 2006a, para. 52).

As noted above, lead 21/7 bomber Muktar Said Ibrahim also made a visit to Pakistan, one that overlapped with those of Khan and Tanweer. In addition, lead Crevice bomber Omar Khyam was a regular visitor to Pakistan, his first trips to mujahideen training camps extending back to 2000. Following the 2003 US–UK invasion of Iraq he flew back to Pakistan to offer his services to a senior figure in the al-Qaeda network, from where he was encouraged to plan attacks in the United Kingdom. At least one of those involved in the doctors' bomb plot had visited Pakistan (Gardham and Bedi, 2007). The August 2006 airliner bomb plot also had a firm link to Pakistan. Indeed, it transpired that the immediate trigger for the arrests in this case was the apprehension in Pakistan of Rashid Rauf, an explosives expert who fled the United Kingdom following the 2002 fatal stabbing of his uncle and who had received training at an al-Qaeda camp and was linked to militant groups. Illustrative of the tensions involved in intelligence co-operation in the 'war on terror', the timing of Rauf's arrest seems to have been determined by the fact that US intelligence was prepared to 'render'

Rauf unless he was immediately arrested. British intelligence preferred to keep him at large to monitor the emerging plot for longer, presumably to gather further evidence against the British suspects to strengthen any future prosecution case (Doward and Townsend, 2006). A number of those arrested in the United Kingdom had visited Pakistan in 2005, their trips again overlapping with those of 7/7 bombers Khan and Tanweer, raising the possibility of some linkage. It was claimed by a Pakistani security source that al-Qaeda's chief ideologue, Ayman al-Zawahiri, had personally sanctioned the airline bomb plot (Campbell, 2006).

However, it is also important to note that, as a British official in Islamabad has pointed out, militants do not travel from Britain to Pakistan to be radicalized, they travel there because they have already been radicalized (Whitaker, Lashmar and Buncombe, 2007). The would-be jihadists who have made the trip have raised their own funds, sought out trainers, made connections and subsequently constructed their own bombs – a fact that accounts for the good luck of the failures of 21/7 and June/July 2007. Thus it is important to avoid the pitfall of assuming that the centrality of Pakistan is indicative of a highly organized and co-ordinated global conspiracy.

The nature of the threat

These plots raise the question of what al-Qaeda is. According to Jonathan Raban:

> The name al-Qaeda means something different practically every time it's used. Sometimes it's…intended to conjure shadowy legions of all the various militant Islamist groups around the globe…Sometimes it's held to be a transnational corporation, like Starbucks, with a spiderweb of sleeper-cell outlets spread worldwide, but controlled from a headquarters somewhere in Pakistan or Afghanistan. Sometimes it's described as a franchise outfit, like 7-Eleven, renting out its name to any small-time independent shopkeeper who's prepared to subscribe to the company program, and sometimes as a single store, or bank, owned and operated by Osama bin Laden (Raban, 2005).

And as Gilles Kepel has pointed out, by the time of Operation Enduring Freedom and the hunt for Osama bin Laden:

> Al Qaeda was less a military base of operations than a database that connected jihadists all over the world via the Internet. The US attack on Afghanistan and the elimination of the Taliban mistook a shadow for the prey. Even as bin Laden disappeared into the valleys and caves

of the Afghan–Pakistan border, he reappeared in cyberspace to claim responsibility for deadly attacks as far away as Indonesia. The sponsor of global jihad was at once everywhere and nowhere. (Kepel, 2004, 6)

For her part, former MI5 Director General Eliza Manningham-Buller distinguished between the 'core of al-Qaeda' and the 'many potential terrorists who have no linkage to al-Qaeda but are inspired by its ideology and actions' (Manningham-Buller, 2005). JTAC introduced its own three-tiered typology in early 2005. 'Tier 1' represented those thought to have direct links with 'core al-Qaeda'. 'Tier 2' represented individuals or networks more loosely affiliated, and 'Tier 3' those without any links but inspired by the ideology. Significantly, in May 2005 JTAC's definition of the threat to the United Kingdom was that it was essentially Tier 2 and Tier 3 in nature. Similarly, the March 2004 Madrid train bombers were assessed as belonging to Tier 3 (ISC, 2006, para. 98).

Reflecting the JTAC typology, the MI5 website is careful to distinguish between al-Qaeda, its 'associated networks' and 'those who share Al Qaida's ideology but do not have direct contact with them' (http://www.mi5.gov.uk/output/Page311.html). Elsewhere, however, MI5 somewhat bundles these together to provide an official explanation for Islamist terrorism that is as significant for what it omits as for what it says:

Al Qaida's networks comprise groups which previously conducted violent campaigns in pursuit of change in their own countries, plus individuals who have broadly embraced Usama bin Laden's view of the world. This means they are intent on attacking US and other Western interests, as well as replacing regimes that are not deemed pious enough.

Many of these networks are loose-knit, operating without a conventional structure and with connections across the world, bound by shared extremist views or experiences. Whilst some of these networks are centrally guided by Al Qaida, others are autonomous, but both work to carry out terrorist attacks, and are influenced by radical propaganda shared over the Internet.

The terrorists draw their inspiration from a global message articulated by internationally recognisable figures such as Usama bin Laden. The message is uncompromising and asserts that the West represents a threat to Islam; that loyalty to religion and loyalty to democratic institutions and values are incompatible; and that violence is the only proper response. (http://www.mi5.gov.uk/output/Page33.html)

Missing from here, of course, is any reference to the significance of the US and UK war in Iraq in the emergence of suicide bombers in the United Kingdom, despite the wealth of evidence that Iraq has been a significant factor in the radicalization of British Muslims. Consideration of the war in Iraq as a motivating factor also begs the question of how far the 7/7 attacks and the failed subsequent attacks are a consequence of intelligence failure and how far they are a consequence of policy failure – that is, the question of how far policy decisions have created a potential threat so widespread that existing security intelligence structures cannot be expected to cope with it, and have therefore created an environment in which intelligence 'failure' is inevitable.

While both the ISC report into 7/7 and the government's official account of events leading up to the bombings provide a clear account of *how* they were carried out, neither probe *why* particularly deeply. Hence, neither deals with the question of whether policy failure could be said to be a factor. As the ISC noted at the beginning of its report: 'Given our remit ... the Report does not seek to answer wider questions about the efficacy of the Government's counterterrorist strategy ... nor do we seek to establish whether any of these wider policies (foreign and domestic) might have made a difference to preventing the July attacks' (ISC, 2006, para. 6). Later, it explained that: 'We have not sought to investigate in detail ... who the group were, how they became radicalized, or how they planned and executed the attacks. This goes beyond our remit to cover the work of the intelligence and security Agencies and, in this context, what they knew about the 7 July group' (Ibid., para. 32).

However, a majority of the public believed that there was a link between the 7/7 bombings and British foreign policy towards Iraq. In a July 2005 *Guardian*/ICM poll, two-thirds thought so, while only twenty-eight per cent believed the two were not connected (Glover, 2005). Moreover, a range of commentators, experts and officials have openly linked the events of 7/7 with the war in Iraq. Peter Taylor argues: 'The common denominator in London and Madrid is undoubtedly Iraq. The Madrid bombers planned to force the Spanish government to withdraw its troops from Iraq – and succeeded. London has long been in jihadi sights because of Tony Blair's unswerving support for George Bush' (Taylor, 2005). BBC security correspondent Frank Gardner, himself a victim of an al-Qaeda attack in Saudi Arabia in 2004, when asked by BBC Political Editor Andrew Marr whether it was the 'very diversity, that melting pot aspect of London' that led Islamist extremists to kill members of the British public, replied: 'No, it's not that. What they find offensive are the policies of western governments and specifically the presence of western troops in Muslim lands, notably Iraq and Afghanistan' (Milne, 2005; Gardner, 2006, pp. 359–64). Former Foreign Secretary Douglas Hurd was equally clear:

> The likelihood of young Muslims, whether in Britain or elsewhere, being attracted to terrorism was increased by our action in Iraq. We attacked a Muslim country on grounds which turned out to be empty. We broke international law. We faced no serious threat from Saddam Hussein and received no authority from the Security Council. We brought about the deaths of thousands of innocent Iraqis... We created in Iraq a new base for terrorism, and the world including Britain is less safe because of that. (Hurd, 2005)

A September 2005 internal government working group report 'Working Together to Prevent Extremism: Tackling Extremism and Radicalisation', concluded that, 'British foreign policy in the world cannot be left unconsidered as a factor in the motivations of extremists', and that the Iraq war was 'undeniably a factor' (Woolf, 2005). By the end of July 2005 even the MI5 website was describing Iraq as 'a dominant issue' for extremists in the United Kingdom (Norton-Taylor, 2005b), although this was subsequently replaced by the account of terrorist motivation cited above, which brought MI5's explanation more closely into line with that offered by members of the Blair government.

Following the August 2006 airline bomb plot arrests, an open letter from leading British Muslims to Tony Blair, the signatories to which included Labour MPs Sadiq Khan and Shahid Malik, highlighted the link between Islamist terrorism in the United Kingdom and British foreign policy. By 2006 this referred not just to the presence of British forces in Iraq but also to the much increased British military presence in Afghanistan, the site of mounting civilian casualties, largely as a consequence of US bombing, and the Blair government's tacit support for Israel's summer 2006 invasion of Lebanon. The letter urged Blair 'to fight against all those who target civilians with violence, whenever and wherever that happens', and offered their view 'that current British government policy risks putting civilians at increased risk both in the UK and abroad' (Woodward and Bates, 2006). Transport Secretary Douglas Alexander called this suggestion 'dangerous and foolish', while

Foreign Secretary Margaret Beckett termed it the 'gravest possible error' (Temko, 2006). In the face of this pressure, Sadiq Khan explained:

> We have not said that there is a link between foreign policy and acts of terrorism but rather that there is a link with the sort of materials that are used to radicalise young people. Many of us feel that we are trying to address these issues but it seems that we are in a boat trying to empty out water and that the vessel has a massive hole in it which is our foreign policy. (Hencke and Muir, 2006)

Perhaps most significant of all is the testimony of the 7/7 suicide bombers themselves. A videotape of Mohammad Siddique Khan, broadcast on al-Jazeera on 1 September 2005, alongside a statement from al-Qaeda's Ayman al-Zawahiri, featured Khan warning the British public that

> Your democratically elected governments continuously perpetuate atrocities against my people all over the world. And your support of them makes you directly responsible, just as I am directly responsible for protecting and avenging my Muslim brothers and sisters. Until we feel security, you will be our targets. And until you stop the bombing, gassing, imprisonment and torture of my people we will not stop this fight. We are at war and I am a soldier. (ISC, 2006, para. 39)

The following year, to coincide with the first anniversary of the bombings, a video message from Shazad Tanweer was released in which he talked of 'a series of attacks that will continue... [until] you pull your soldiers from Afghanistan and Iraq' (www.cnn.com/2006/ WORLD/europe/07/06/london.bombings.newvideo/index.html). Both contained essentially the same message as that given to the peoples of Europe by Osama bin Laden himself in April 2004, the month after the Madrid train bombings, in which he claimed that

> Our actions are but a reaction to yours – your destruction and murder of our people, whether in Afghanistan, Iraq, or Palestine... In what creed are your dead considered innocent but ours worthless? By what logic does your blood count as real and ours as no more than water? Reciprocal treatment is part of justice, and he who commences hostilities is the unjust one... Therefore, stop spilling our blood in order to save your own. (Lawrence, 2005, pp. 234–5)

At the level of policymakers, how far was there evidence of any warning or advice that foreign policy decisions, particularly over Iraq, carried with them risks of this sort? In 2003, the ISC disclosed that five weeks before the March 2003 Iraq war, Tony Blair was warned by the Joint Intelligence Committee (JIC), in a report entitled *International Terrorism: War with Iraq*, that, 'al-Qa'ida and associated groups continued to represent by far the greatest terrorist threat to Western interests and that threat would be heightened by military action against Iraq' (ISC, 2003, para. 126). In his evidence to the ISC, Blair himself conceded that 'there was obviously a danger that, in attacking Iraq, you ended up provoking the very thing you were trying to avoid ... I suppose time will tell whether it's true or it's not true' (Ibid., para. 128). In advance of the Iraq war Blair's Cabinet colleagues also voiced concerns. Former Foreign Secretary Robin Cook's diaries record an April 2002 Cabinet meeting at which Patricia Hewitt argued that a unilateral US–UK invasion of Iraq would create 'a lot of tension among the Muslim communities in Britain' (Cook, 2003, p. 135).

In May 2004, a year after major combat operations in Iraq were declared to be at an end, but over a year before the 7/7 attacks, Michael Jay, the Foreign Office Permanent Undersecretary, wrote to Cabinet Secretary Sir Andrew Turnbull to warn that:

> Colleagues have flagged up some of the potential underlying causes of extremism that can affect the Muslim community, such as discrimination, disadvantage and exclusion. But another recurring theme is the issue of British foreign policy, especially in the context of the Middle East peace process and Iraq. Experience of both ministers and officials ... suggests that ... British foreign policy and the perception of its negative effect on Muslims globally plays a significant role in creating a feeling of anger and impotence among especially the younger generation of British Muslims. (Bright, 2005)

Attached to the letter was a strategy document, 'Building Bridges with Mainstream Islam', which outlined how Britain was now viewed as a 'crusader state' and hence on par with the United States as a potential target. Two months before the 7/7 bombings, a May 2005 JTAC report echoed this analysis, noting how 'events in Iraq are continuing to act as motivation and a focus of a range of terrorist activity in the UK' (ISC, 2006, para. 82).

Finally, in April 2006 a JIC report from April 2005, *International Terrorism: Impact of Iraq*, was leaked to the press. This report, circulated to Tony Blair and senior Cabinet colleagues, clearly stated that the war in Iraq 'has reinforced the determination of terrorists who were already committed to attacking the West and motivated others who were not.' It added that 'Iraq is likely to be an important motivating factor for some time to come in the radicalization of British Muslims and for those extremists who view attacks against the UK as legitimate' (Leppard, 2006a).

For obvious political reasons, Tony Blair and his Cabinet were unable to publicly accept this. Instead they characterized the motivation of the terrorists differently, with Blair arguing:

> We have got to be really careful of almost giving in to the perverted, twisted logic with which they argue. Of course these terrorists will use Iraq as an excuse. They will use Afghanistan. September 11, of course, happened before both those things and then the excuse was American policy on Israel. We have got to be very careful that we don't enter into a situation where we think if we make some compromise on some aspect of foreign policy, these people are going to change. They are not going to change.[4]

Then Defence Secretary Geoff Hoon suggested that;

> we have always been a target. I don't think that it has changed that. These people have an agenda to destroy democracy, whether that is in Iraq, US or the UK. That is why we have been warning since long before operations began in Iraq that people had to be vigilant because we were a target. In the aftermath of 9/11, there were serious concerns about the threat to the UK. It hasn't suddenly arisen. (Grice, 2005)

Similarly, the then Foreign Secretary Jack Straw asked:

> Would we have been safer had we not taken military action in Iraq? Now, no one can say for certain but it is my judgement that, because we were in any event a target, and so was the rest of the world, for this extremist terrorism well before Iraq, that there is no guarantee whatsoever that we would have been safer had we not taken military action in Iraq. (Russell, 2005)

These statements exemplify a line of argument that contends that the 7/7 attacks vindicated the Blair government's stand on Iraq because the events of 7/7 were the realization of the threat Blair had warned existed since 9/11. Hence, the attacks of 7/7 were not linked to Iraq, on the bizarre grounds that the 9/11 attacks preceded the war on Iraq,[5] or on the grounds that the bombers were 'Islamic fascists' who kill and die for nihilism. But they represent a credibility gap. As Seamus Milne has correctly noted:

> there were no al-Qaida-inspired attacks in Britain before the invasions of Afghanistan and Iraq. There were against the US – starting with the World Trade Centre in 1993 – triggered by the aftermath of the Gulf war, as well as jihadist campaigns in Kashmir, Chechnya and Bosnia. But Britain was not a target until it attacked the Muslim world. If the bombers' real focus was, say, sexually liberal western lifestyles, they would presumably be attacking cities like Amsterdam and Stockholm. (Milne, 2007)

Perhaps not surprisingly in view of the above, the government's official account of the 7/7 attacks is reluctant to openly ascribe a role to the impact of the war in Iraq. While a leaked draft of the report referred to Iraq as a key 'contributing factor', this phrasing was omitted from the final version (Townsend, 2006). Although conceding that the clearest statement of the group's motives was to be found in Khan's video, the published version restricted itself to observing that: 'The focus of the video is on perceived injustices carried out by the West against Muslims' (UK Government, 2006a, para. 39). The only other reference is hidden away in an annex, which refers obliquely to the impact of Iraq while avoiding use of the word (see Annex A, para. 11).

The current security intelligence challenge

In November 2006, MI5 Director General Eliza Manningham-Buller delivered a speech outlining MI5's understanding of the scale of the potential terrorist threat to the United Kingdom from radicalized British Muslims, revealing that it was contending with approximately 200 'groupings or networks', involving over 1600 individuals 'actively engaged in plotting, or facilitating, terrorist acts here and overseas' (Manningham-Buller, 2006), with almost thirty plots underway. While echoing the official government line that 'the international terrorist threat to this country is not new. It began before Iraq, before Afghanistan, and before 9/11', she also conceded that the 7/7 suicide bombers had been motivated by 'their interpretation as anti-Muslim of UK foreign policy, in particular the UK's involvement in Iraq and Afghanistan.'

There seems little other explanation for the exponential increase in the scale of the Islamist terrorist threat to the United Kingdom. As mentioned above, at the time of the 9/11 attacks, there were 250 'primary investigative targets' (arguably, most of which would have had an overseas focus), doubling to over 500 by July 2004, rising sharply to approximately 800 a year later, and doubling again less than eighteen months after that to the 1600 cited by Manningham-Buller. This scale of potential threat is too great to comprehensively guard against without a significant shift in the security–civil liberties balance. As one 'senior security official' reflected at the beginning of 2007:

> If the threat [today] was the same as in 2005 – that is, we were looking at 50 potential terror networks in the UK – we would have a better chance of picking up somebody like [Mohammad Siddique] Khan. But we are now dealing with some 200 potential terror networks in the UK and to be quite honest we wouldn't have a hope in hell. We can't put every person who expresses anger about British foreign policy under 24-hour surveillance, or we would be talking about a Stasi-style secret police force. (Barnett, 2007)

A number of challenges confront current counterterrorist strategy. One is how to combat the influence of Islamist websites, which does not just connect jihadists, it creates them. As Kepel put it: 'With the occupation of Iraq, the war for Muslim minds entered the global jungle of the Internet' (Kepel, 2004, p. 7). Jihadi Internet sites have become a key focus for the intelligence agencies in seeking to uncover future terrorist plots, a significance reinforced with the July 2007 conviction of three men, Younes Tsouli, Waseem Mughal and Tariq al-Daour, charged with inciting terrorist murder via the Internet, the first prosecution of its kind in the United Kingdom (Pallister, 2007; *The Economist,* 2007b, pp. 28–30).[6] The fluid nature of the Internet means that it is virtually impossible to permanently close down these sites. Infiltrating the tight-knit groups behind and within them, through the Internet and more physically, is a next key step for the security and intelligence agencies, one that is difficult but not impossible, as the Israeli experience with regard to Palestinian groups has shown.

There is also a clear need for an enhanced network of agents willing to report from within the Muslim community from where, police admitted, their level of intelligence was 'low' at the time of the 7/7 attacks. As a senior police officer put it: 'Deep knowledge of Muslim communities is rare in the service. If you are going to understand who is extreme and who is dangerous, which are different [concepts], you have to understand the community. Unless you know the subject well and what they are saying, often in Arabic or Urdu, and what the context is, you are not going to get a feel for it' (Dodd, 2005).

Towards this end, just two weeks after the bombings it was announced that intelligence units were to be set up to facilitate the collection of 'community by community' profiles of Muslim extremism. By early September 2005 it was being reported that MI5 would 'lower the surveillance threshold' for Muslim communities – in other words, extend the range of surveillance targets as part of an attempt to be more pro-active in identifying those who may be 'groomed' for terrorism (ISC, 2006, para. 134). The regionalization of MI5 and enhanced co-operation with regional Special Branches were an important dimension of this effort. Still, securing co-operation from within Muslim communities remained a challenge. As Metropolitan Police Deputy Assistant Commissioner Peter Clarke put it in April 2007: 'We must increase the flow of intelligence coming from communities. Almost all of our prosecutions have their origins in intelligence that came from overseas, the intelligence agencies or from technical means. Few have yet originated from what is sometimes called community intelligence' (Dodd, 2007b).

All of this helps explain the limited understanding of the nature of the threat prior to 7/7. It is not unreasonable to suggest that the examples of shoe bomber Richard Reid and would-be shoe bomber Saajid Badat, together with that of British citizens Omar Sharif and Asif Hanif, who attempted a suicide bombing mission in a Tel Aviv bar in 2003, should have alerted MI5 to the risk that British nationals were increasingly prepared to consider undertaking suicide bombings. Instead, the JIC judged that the terrorist threat came primarily from foreign terrorists entering the United Kingdom (ISC, 2006, para. 92) – the implication behind much alarmist media reporting in the 2001–2005 period. However, successfully disrupted plots and the example of Madrid demonstrated that the presumption in favour of foreign terrorists aiming to carry out 'spectaculars' against high-profile targets was some-what misplaced. By June 2005, the JIC judged that, given their impact in Iraq, suicide bombings could become a widely used tactic. However, it still did not think such attacks to be likely on the UK mainland (Ibid., para. 96). Indeed, in the days following the 7/7 bombings, in off-the-record briefings police and intelligence officials indicated that they believed the bombers had escaped – they did not think they were looking at a case of suicide bombing (Norton-Taylor, 2005a). In hindsight, analysis regarding the possibility of a suicide attack was poor. As the ISC noted, a different analysis could have contributed to greater alertness to the threat (ISC, 2006, para. 103). Further, as noted, an appreciation of the full significance of links to Pakistan only began to emerge post-7/7.

The radical Islamist threat is clearly an evolving one. The June/July 2007 doctors' bomb plots raised the spectre of direct Iraqi involvement, given that one of the doctors involved, Bilal Talal Abdulla, was an Iraqi and that individuals claiming to speak on behalf of the Iraqi variant of al-Qaeda have claimed to be planning attacks for the United Kingdom (Norton-Taylor and Cobain, 2007). Hence, a potential threat initially assumed to be external, exposed by the events of 7/7 as internal, may now, to an extent, be a combination of the two. Moreover, increased intelligence monitoring of individuals travelling from the United Kingdom to Pakistan for training is being countered by the rise in the number of individuals travelling instead to Bangladesh to undertake training, or travelling to Pakistan via South Africa to avoid detection (Norton-Taylor, 2007).

Learning to live with the limits of intelligence

At the same time as recognizing the possibility of a degree of intelligence failure in the cases discussed above, it is equally important to recognize the limits to intelligence. Historically, these have not been well under-stood, partly because of the secrecy that has attached to the agencies, and partly as a consequence of the agencies' own interest in promoting an image of intelligence omniscience. However, popular notions that intelligence can provide a fail-safe mechanism have created false expec-tations as to just what it can deliver. Intelligence cannot, and should not claim to, offer a crystal ball for seeing the future clearly. As Eliza Manningham-Buller put it: 'Some is gold, some dross and all of it requires validation, analysis and assessment. When it is gold, it shines and illuminates, saves lives, protects nations and informs policy. When identified as dross, it needs to be rejected: that may take some confidence' (Manningham-Buller, 2005). The Butler Inquiry into intelligence on weapons of mass destruction devoted an entire section of its report to the nature and limitations of intelligence, observing that: 'The most important limitation on intelligence is its incompleteness. Much ingenuity and effort is spent on making secret information difficult to acquire and hard to analyse... it is often, when first acquired, sporadic and patchy, and even after analysis may still be at best inferential'

(Butler, 2004, para. 49). The ISC itself highlighted the limits of intelligence in its 2003–2004 annual report, and its report into the 7/7 attacks. Readers of the government's *Response* to the ISC report will have been encouraged to see that a government that leapt at any incoming intelligence capable of bolstering its case for war in Iraq in the second-half of 2002 had, post-7/7, come to recognize that 'intelligence is generally fragmentary, of varying reliability and difficult to interpret' (UK Government, 2006b, para. D).

Finally, Manningham-Buller also acknowledged that, while some attacks had been thwarted by good intelligence and police work, MI5 was governed by the same high expectations as other Western intelligence agencies, and hence, 'we are judged by what we do not know and did not prevent' (Manningham-Buller, 2005).

This is not to say that there have been no failures of intelligence. A number of intelligence-led policing operations have turned out to have been based on faulty information. In one of these, the June 2006 police raid on a house in the Forest Gate area of London in relation to a suspected chemical bomb plot, and involving some 250 officers, one of the two unarmed and innocent (Muslim) men arrested was shot by raiding police officers. However, the high-stakes context in which such failures have occurred should be acknowledged. As a senior police source reflected at the time: 'In other crime you can take a risk to firm up the intelligence. The trouble with this new world of terrorism is that you don't have the time, you can't firm up the intelligence to the point you [would] like. The public may have to get used to this sort of incident, with the police having to be safe rather than sorry' (Norton-Taylor and Dodd, 2006).

The dilemma, of course, is that unless the intelligence underpinning such operations is always accurate, proceeding along these lines cannot but further alienate the very mainstream Muslim opinion that the government needs to win over to overcome the terrorist threat, and which the legislative climate of anti-terror laws already serves to alienate (Butt and Dodd, 2006). Even where the intelligence underpinning police raids on Muslim suspects is subsequently proven to have been accurate via successful prosecution in the courts, the period between arrest and trial is one in which rumour and conspiracy theories can flourish.

Still, the most significant failure to date may well have been in relation to the failure to prevent the 7/7 bombings. In giving evidence to the ISC, Eliza Manningham-Buller had asked:

> Could we, could others, could the police have done better? Could we with greater effort, greater imagination, have stopped it? We knew

there were risks we were running. We were trying very hard and very fast to enhance our capacity, but even with the wisdom of hindsight I think it is unlikely that we would have done so, with the resources available to us at the time and the other demands placed upon us. (ISC, 2006, para. 144)

This invited the resource constraint explanation for the failure to prevent the 7/7 bombings outlined above. However, in light of the information that emerged as a result of the Operation Crevice trial whether this represents a complete explanation appears open to question. So too does the adequacy of the ISC as an oversight arm. Having dispensed with its limited investigatory arm, it had little option but to accept such mitigating pleas.

To return to our distinction between intelligence and policy failure, the resource explanation should also beg the question of how far the current situation is a consequence of governmental policy choices. The Blair government was highly successful in discouraging any suggestion that its foreign policy choices over Iraq, and increasingly Afghanistan, had fuelled the Islamist threat, all too aware of the fate that befell the Spanish government of José María Aznar, Blair's ally in making the case for war in Iraq, in the aftermath of the March 2004 Madrid train bombings. Nevertheless, the Iraq war has created a significant blowback problem for Britain, with over 100,000 British Muslims believing that the 7/7 bombings were fully justified, and 18% of British Muslims telling pollsters that they feel little or no loyalty towards the country (King, 2005). In some cases, of course, the cases of Iraq and Afghanistan have built on the potentially fertile ground of Muslim alienation and identity issues affecting second- and third-generation immigrants (Malik, 2007; Burke, 2008). Nevertheless, they have been the necessary pre-condition transforming disaffected Muslim youths into bombers and suicide bombers, as the rich vein of evidence from the suicide bombers and those convicted in failed plots referred to above demonstrates. All of this – including the ongoing though reduced British presence in Iraq and the long-term military commitment in Afghanistan – means that the immediate future cannot be anything other than a challenging one for the security and intelligence agencies, and the public may well need to learn to live with the limits of intelligence. In the current climate further intelligence 'failure' may well be inevitable.

Notes

1. Nevertheless, it should be noted that the decisions were deemed 'understandable', rather than, for example, 'reasonable' or 'justified'.

2. In February 2008, five accomplices were convicted of failing to disclose information about terrorism and assisting an offender and jailed for between seven and seventeen years.
3. The government's *Official Account* cautions that training camps in remote areas of Pakistan and Afghanistan 'are sometimes little more than groups of people getting together on an ad hoc basis in places where their activities will be difficult to be detected' (UK Government, 2006a, para. 47).
4. 'Intelligence Report Forces Blair on to Defensive', FT.Com, 19 July 2005, www.nytimes.com/financialtimes/business/FT200550719_10334_58887. html?pa.
5. For example, the letter from Alan Johnson and Jane Ashworth, 'Labour Friends of Iraq', *The Guardian*, 9 July 2005; letter from Jim Poyser, *The Independent*, 11 July 2005. ('Before your correspondents rush to blame the invasion of Iraq for Thursday's atrocities, they might care to consider two things: firstly, 9/11 happened before the Iraq war; and secondly, there would have been no Iraq war if 9/11 hadn't happened.').
6. At their trial the prosecution explicitly linked their activities to the Iraq war, arguing: 'Particularly since the coalition forces entered Iraq, each of the defendants developed a particular interest in the application and promotion of ideology and the call to join it in Iraq and to some extent Afghanistan' (Dodd, 2007a).

3
The Pursuit of Terrorism with Intelligence

Clive Walker

Introduction

It is an article of faith in the world of security services that the gathering of intelligence is a 'crucial' strategy in dealing with terrorism (Wilkinson, 2000, p. 105). The proposition is now embodied within the official government strategy statement about international terrorism and known as 'CONTEST'. Within its four elements of Prevent, Protect, Prepare and Pursue, intelligence falls within the latter and is said to be 'vital to defeating terrorism' (Home Office, 2006a, para. 65). Many reasons can be given for its elevated importance, including the sophisticated, secretive and committed nature of terrorist groups, features which mean that they do not make as many crass errors as 'ordinary decent criminals'[1] and also that they are difficult to infiltrate or, because of their motives and commitment, to break down into a flood of confessions. The importance of intelligence has also been reflected in institutional terms with the growth in expenditure on the intelligence community (for resource allocation after 9/11 see Intelligence and Security Committee, 2006: para. 118) and the establishment, since September 11, 2001 (9/11), of specialist bodies which tend to cut across local or institutional boundaries. These include the development of the Joint Terrorism Analysis Centre [JTAC] (Intelligence and Security Committee, 2003: para. 62; Intelligence and Security Committee, 2004: para. 92; http://www.mi5.gov.uk/output/Page421.html.) and the setting up of regional offices by the Security Service (House of Commons, 2004). In addition, the National Counter Terrorism Security Office is a police unit funded by the Association of Chief Police Officers but located within the Centre for the Protection of the National Infrastructure (under the umbrella of the Security Service), which was established in 2007 (http://www.nactso.gov.uk/). Its role is to offer specialist advice regarding security, protective measures and business continuity, especially through specialist police advisers known as Counter Terrorism Security Advisers. Within policing, the regionalization of police Special Branches and ports policing has been imposed (HM Inspectorate of Constabulary, 2003) while the Metropolitan Police has merged the Special Branch with the more operational Anti-Terrorist Branch to form the Counter Terrorism Command (SO15) (http://www. met.police.uk/so/counter_terrorism.htm.). Its head, acting under the title of the National Co-ordinator of Terrorist Investigations will normally be invited by Chief Officers in order to deal with terrorist crime which has occurred within their locality. Corresponding Counterterrorism Units are being formed in some regions, building on the formation of anti-terror units in 2005. As between policing and the Security Service, the Police International Counter Terror Unit provides 'an advisory and interpretive conduit between the Security Services and police forces on matters relating to international terrorism...' (HM Inspectorate of Constabulary, 2003, para. 2.65).

Though the predominance of intelligence is asserted far and wide, it is often ignored in discussions about the anti-terrorism laws currently set out in the Terrorism Act 2000, the Anti-Terrorism, Crime and Security Act 2001, the Prevention of Terrorism Act 2005, and the Terrorism Act 2006. They embody two main approaches. There is first the strategy of criminalization, such as by special offences (often dealing with preparatory activity such as training or glorification) and, for Northern Ireland at least, special court processes (for this see the Justice and Security (Northern Ireland) Act 2007). The second purpose is 'control' – to prevent, disrupt and counter and in this way to engage in risk management in response to the threat of terrorism. Measures such as proscription, detention without trial, control orders, port controls, data mining and the forfeiture of assets have all figured in this category. The risk society is more and more motivated by anticipatory risk, and it is felt to be too dangerous to allow the terrorists to move towards their objectives if the results are mass casualties or the use of weapons of mass destruction.

In between criminalization and control are some powers which could legitimately be used in either strategy. But their tactical use tends to cohere towards the control strategy. This group includes arrest and interrogation and stop and search, and it is especially around these where confusion lies. The result of their deployment in pursuance of control is low charging rates, leading to criticisms of illegitimate use. Yet if control, in this case through intelligence-gathering and disruption, counts as a positive outcome, then the operations cannot necessarily be said to be a total failure.

Both criminalization and control are controversial in their design and in the ways they are carried out. For example, what might appear to be the more straightforward approach of criminalization triggers the danger of special laws undermining the legitimacy of the criminal justice system and producing 'political' offenders (Roebuck, 1978; Ingraham, 1979; Ross, 2002; Walker, 1984; Beresford, 1987; Williams, 2001). Equally, the techniques of control are widely viewed as corrosive of the rule of law. Individual rights are diminished or eliminated without the public spectacle of an affirmation of the evidence against them, moderated by venerated rules such as proof beyond reasonable doubt and confrontation of one's accusers in open court. Aside from the evils (denial of due process and possible miscarriages of justice) which may be visited upon the suspect, there are wider concerns about delivering a sensible balance between personal and public liberty and reassurance in ways which do not transform or disrupt legitimate activities, such as air travel, (Florence, 2006) foreign currency transfers, (Razavy, 2006; Donohue, 2006) or political dissent and association (Joint Committee on Human Rights, 2007).

The dichotomy just presented, between criminalization and control, is often rehearsed as forming not just a functional disjunction between policing and intelligence-gathering but also a structural fissure: 'the main difference between a police and a security agency is in their goals: the police aim to obtain convictions, the security agency aims to gather information and produce intelligence' (Gill, 1994: 210). It follows that shifts in their respective strength and influence have been reflected not just in legal changes but also institutional reforms. One occurred when the Security Service was given primacy in anti-terrorism operations in 1992 (Gill, 1994, p. 126).

But the purported bifurcation is far from clean cut (Farson, 1992; Review of the Northern Ireland (Emergency Provisions) Act 1991, 1995, para. 126). The prime aim of the police, even within anti-terrorism work, has in reality always been order preservation rather than crime conviction. According to the over-arching counterterrorism strategy set by the United Kingdom Government, 'CONTEST', (Home Office, 2006a) prevention and preparation could be said to outweigh pursuit as strategic aims. Furthermore, the advent of the National Intelligence Model (NIM) (HM Inspectorate of Constabulary, 1997; Ratcliffe, 2002; James, 2003; John and Maguire, 2004), building on themes of problem-oriented policing and risk management, is testament to the growing emphasis on intelligence-led policing as a core police activity outside of counter- terrorism. Equally, Security Service personnel have begun to appear in court as prosecution witnesses.[2] The broad acceptance of the importance of intelligence in the anti-terrorism field should at least allay concerns elsewhere in policing about whether reforms such as the products of the NIM are going to be marginalized as no more interest than 'wallpaper' in the action-seeking culture commonly associated with operational policing (Cope, 2004, p. 192). But its pervasive use is hugely controversial, not only in terms of legitimacy but also in terms of efficacy. Thus, two of the 7 July 2005 (7/7) bombers, Mohammad Siddique Khan and Shazad Tanweer, had come to the attention of the Security Service but were not seen as pressing priorities, a level of inattention described by the Intelligence and Security Committee (ISC) as 'understandable' (Intelligence and Security Committee, 2006, paras. 46, 49, 56), though perhaps without the full knowledge of the facts that later emerged in the trial of those caught by Operation Crevice (see O'Neill, Evans and Woolcock (2007) and Phythian, this volume).

What lessons can intelligence-gatherers, analysts and users learn about the uses and abuses of intelligence? If we rehearse the ways in which, in the anti-terrorism field, intelligence arises, there are at least four modes: to make strategic assessments, including the sources, nature and levels of threat, and the need for new resources or security measures; to feed into criminalization operations in which individuals may ultimately be dealt with through the courts; to feed into control operations such as disruption and surveillance; and to feed into control operations that restrain individuals by overt executive-directed legal measures. These modes are not exclusive to terrorism, save perhaps for the final option. This chapter will therefore concentrate on that option which, it might be said, is predominantly what gives intelligence a bad name. The inherent difficulties of intelligence as a basis for action cause problems for professional policing institutions at all stages of the intelligence cycle. The Bichard Report focussed on dissemination and storage (Bichard Inquiry, 2004; Home Office, 2004a; Bichard Inquiry, 2005; for the opposite problem of undue data retention see White, 1977; Robertson, 1987). But an equally fundamental problem is that the deployment of intelligence as the trigger for official action is unpersuasive, as it is not proven as 'evidence' or beyond reasonable doubt. These difficulties are compounded, it is suggested, when ultimate decision making is in the hands of less experienced and more politically motivated government ministers and not detached judges. In those cases, policy can overwhelm or determine the direction of intelligence. What the reports of the Butler (Committee of Privy Counsellors, 2004, ch. 4) and also Hutton (2004) inquiries have found to be errors in the grand strategy of war surely applies to the smaller skirmishes over the repression of individuals. Through these inquiries and earlier legislation codifying the existence of the security apparatus (Security Service Act 1989, Intelligence Services Act 1994), there has been an intrusion of the law into the intelligence field over the last few decades. But it is the intrusion of intelligence into the legal world – not so much through the doors of law's inner sanctum, a court of law, but at least through executive hearings and orders – which is the subject of this chapter.

There are several measures in United Kingdom law that could be considered as illustrative in this context, but this chapter will consider control orders asking why was it necessary to rely upon intelligence; what was the quality of the intelligence; what were the processes in which the intelligence was used and did they put the intelligence to a suitable test?

Control orders

The overall system

The Prevention of Terrorism Act 2005 provides for 'control orders' that differ from detention without trial under Part IV of the Anti-Terrorism, Crime and Security Act 2001 (which it replaced) in a number of important respects (for full details see (Walker, 2002, ch. 8; 2005; 2007a)). By 16 January 2007, eighteen control orders were in force, with increasing numbers against British citizens (House of Lords, 2007). Most notably, they can apply to citizens as well as foreigners, and they do not necessarily rely on a notice derogating from rights to liberty under article 5 of the European Convention on Human Rights (ECHR), as incorporated into UK law by the Human Rights Act 1998.

As for the first difference, one consequent effect is that the jurisdiction for application shifted under section 15 from the Special Immigration Appeals Commission (SIAC) to the High Court or Court of Session (for Scotland). Nevertheless, the process by which this court review is undertaken very much resembles the SIAC model (delineated in the Schedule to the Act) and therefore, because of the facility to withhold sensitive evidence from suspects, encounters the danger of breaching fair process standards.[3] At the same time, the more fundamental assumption that judges cannot or should not handle issues of anticipatory risk assessment should be rejected (House of Lords, 2005a). Judges are involved every day in risk assessment, as when taking bail and sentencing decisions, and are able to do so consistent with due process standards such as recognized by Article 6 of the ECHR.

As for the second difference, control orders that derogate from rights to liberty (within the terms of article 5 of the European Convention) do require a derogation notice and can only be made by the courts (section 4), while non-derogating orders (expected to be the norm) must still be confirmed by the courts (section 3). This distinction must be understood in light of the jurisprudence of the ECHR which does not treat every restriction on physical movement as a loss of 'liberty'.[4]

Contents and issuance

The essence of the legislation is to permit the government to issue 'control orders' that may regulate and restrict individuals suspected of being involved in terrorism. They fit the pattern of dealing with anticipatory risk, and so the basis for the orders is intelligence-led:

> Much of the information is derived from intelligence. The sources and content of such intelligence in most instances demand careful protection in the public interest, given the current situation in which there is needed a concerted and strategic response to terrorism (and especially suicide bombings). The techniques of gathering intelligence, and the range of opportunities available, are wide and certainly in need of secrecy. Human resources place themselves at risk – not least by any means those who offer unsolicited information out of disapproval of conduct and events at which they may have been and could continue to be present. (Lord Carlile, 2006a, p. 12)

A control order is defined under section 1 as 'an order against an individual that imposes obligations on him for purposes connected with protecting members of the public from a risk of terrorism' (for an analysis of its definition see Walker, 2007b, p. 331). Subsection (4) sets out a very lengthy and non-exclusive list of obligations that may be imposed pursuant to a control order. It ranges from restrictions on movement (including curfews) through to restrictions on meetings, activities and possessions such as mobile phones and computers. The controlled persons may be required to cooperate with practical arrangements for monitoring control orders, such as wearing and maintaining apparatus as directed. The controlled person may also be required to provide information, including advance information about his proposed movements or other activities.

While control may be a step down from detention without trial on international human rights scales, its impact should not be dismissed lightly. Just as part IV detention was damaging to mental health and to family life and personal privacy, as well as directly infringing political rights, so also control orders can produce the same damage (Liberty, 2006: annexes 2 and 3).

There are two ways to secure a control order under section 1(2). The institution of a 'non-derogating' control order is by the Home Secretary, but if an order involves obligations that are incompatible with the right to liberty under article 5 of the ECHR (or any other right), it can be made only by the court on an application by the Secretary of State.[5] If incompatible with article 5, the obligation will be a 'derogating obligation'. Such an order must be justified by reference to a designation order (an order under section 14(1) of the Human Rights Act 1998 by which a derogation under article 15 is designated).

The Home Secretary may make a non-derogating control order, lasting twelve months at a time, under section 2(1) if he:

(a) has reasonable grounds for suspecting that the individual is or has been involved in terrorism-related activity; and
(b) considers that it is necessary, for purposes connected with protecting members of the public from a risk of terrorism, to make a control order imposing obligations on that individual.

The two tests in section 2(1) are designed to elicit the factual bases for the issuance of a control order, and their strength will be later tested in court. Examining in further detail the meanings of the two tests in section 2(1), as set out above, the first test is expressly objective, though the proof threshold is set at a low level, consistent with the dynamic of anticipatory risk. In fact, the threshold is lower, for example, than that required for the issuance of a civil injunction (House of Lords, 2005b). The second test is apparently subjective and has no specific standard set, though the modern practice is to set an objective standard.[6] In assessing the actual level of proof, consideration may be given to the statement of Lord Hoffmann in *Secretary of State for the Home Department v. Rehman* (a deportation case arising before the provenance of control orders), in which he stated that

> ...the question in the present case is not whether a given event happened but the extent of future risk. This depends upon an

evaluation of the evidence of the appellant's conduct against a broad range of facts with which they may interact. The question of whether the risk to national security is sufficient to justify the appellant's deportation cannot be answered by taking each allegation seriatim and deciding whether it has been established to some standard of proof. It is a question of evaluation and judgment, in which it is necessary to take into account not only the degree of probability of prejudice to national security but also the importance of the security interest at stake and the serious consequences of deportation for the deportee.[7]

This position was echoed in cases decided under Part IV. In *Secretary of State for the Home Department v. M*, Lord Woolf stated

...SIAC has to come to an objective judgment. The objective judgment has however to be reached against all the circumstances in which the judgment is made. There has to be taken into account the danger to the public which can result from a person who should be detained not being detained. There are also to be taken into account the consequences to the person who has been detained. To be detained without being charged or tried or even knowing the evidence against you is a grave intrusion on an individual's rights. Although, therefore, the test is an objective one, it is also one which involves a value judgment as to what is properly to be considered reasonable in those circumstances.[8]

The Court of Appeal relied on passages in *A v. Secretary of State for the Home Department (No. 2)* (a sequel to the December 2004 case dealing principally with the admissibility of evidence of torture).[9] However, the Court did regard as 'unfortunate' a statement by SIAC that the formula was 'not a demanding standard'.[10] Nevertheless, Lord Justice Laws concluded that

The nature of the subject-matter is such that it will as I have indicated very often, usually, be impossible to prove the past facts which make the case that A is a terrorist. Accordingly a requirement of proof will frustrate the policy and objects of the Act. Now, it will at once be obvious that the derogation issue and the scrutiny issue run together here. In dealing with the former I have already said that the legislature's choice of belief and suspicion as the test for certification and thus detention tends to support the view that the target of the

Act's policy includes those who belong to loose, amorphous, unorganised groups. So it does; the choice is apt to strike the target. Proof would not be.[11]

In sum, it is clear that control orders are intended to operate at a relatively low level of proof, certainly lower than in criminal trials.

In the original draft of the bill, non-derogating control orders could be instituted by the Secretary of State without any involvement of the courts. This feature was one of the major bones of contention in Parliament. After much jousting on the issue, a compromise was eventually reached that there should be an early judicial check by way of an *ex parte* application for leave to make the order. This means that the Home Secretary, and not the court, remains the author of the order but only if he has been granted permission by the court under section 3(1)(a). If the court concludes that the relevant decisions are not 'obviously flawed', directions will then be given for a full hearing to take place to consider the order as soon as reasonably practicable.

The sensitive nature of these intelligence-led procedures in court is exemplified by section 3(5). The initial hearings in connection with non-derogating control orders, in which the court will decide whether to grant permission for the order to be made under procedure (a) may be made in the absence of, without the knowledge of, and without representation for the subject of the order under section 3(5). However, the court must ensure that the controlled person is notified of its decision on a reference under subsection (3)(a). Furthermore, as a result of a parliamentary amendment, when the court orders that a full hearing in connection with a non-derogating control order must take place, the court must under section 3(7) make arrangements for the individual in question to be given an opportunity to make representations *inter partes* about the directions already given or the making of further directions.

Assuming there is a full hearing on a non-derogating control order, the court will determine under section 3(10) whether the decisions of the Secretary of State were 'flawed' in terms of the grounds for the order or in terms of the necessity for every obligation in the order. Although the term 'flawed' rather than 'obviously flawed' is used here, there is no legal difference: section 3(11) defines both by reference to 'the principles applicable on an application for judicial review'. It must thereby be understood by the court that the full hearing is not a *de novo* consideration of the evidence. Although the courts have been willing to exercise a higher standard of scrutiny when basic rights are at stake,[12] in these cases, they must stick to the recognized grounds for review – irrationality, illegality, procedural error and proportionality. The courts may not substitute their own judgment on the merits for that of the minister.[13] In addition to highlighting the limits in the grounds for review under the 2005 Act, one should also bear in mind that the decision being reviewed only requires a 'reasonable suspicion' for the process to be set in motion.

If, despite the hobbled nature of the inquiry, the court decides in a full hearing on a non-derogating control order that a decision of the Secretary of State was flawed, it must under section 3(12): (a) quash the control order; (b) quash one or more of the obligations contained in the control order; (c) give directions to the Secretary of State for him to revoke or modify the order; or, under section 3(13), it must uphold the order.

Derogating control orders, which can derogate severely from rights to liberty, may be issued under section 4 of the Act for six months at a time. Reflecting the fact that 'the right to liberty is in play' (House of Lords, 2005c), the courts are more heavily involved in the issuance of derogating control orders and higher standards of proof are adopted, albeit still consistent with the need to deal with anticipatory risk and diverging significantly from the norms for a criminal trial. It is not intended here to go into greater detail since the government made it clear from the outset that derogating orders were an embellishment to the legislation that would typically be kept in reserve. The political and legal reasons for this reticence are based on the added forensic risks of proving an emergency, especially if apparently based on the threat from just one individual at a time, and the political bad publicity and rancour in Parliament that would flow from having to derogate explicitly from rights. Nevertheless, the government took the stance in February 2005 that the 'threat that we currently face' allows for a derogation (House of Commons, 2005a). It could be argued that the London bombings in July 2005 have strengthened the government's case since they illustrate that catastrophic-suicide terrorism is a clear and present danger.

Criminal prosecution

Despite the dynamic of anticipatory risk and the difficulties for criminal trials that it implies, the government claimed from the outset that prosecution is 'our preferred approach' (House of Lords, 2005d). Parliament deemed the Prevention of Terrorism Bill inadequate to reflect this aspiration. Therefore, section 8 was inserted. This section applies where it appears to the Secretary of State that (a) an individual's suspected involvement in terrorism-related activity may have involved the commission of an offence relating to terrorism, and (b) that the commission of that offence is being or would fall to be investigated by a police force. Subsection (2) requires the Secretary of State to consult the chief police officer of that police force (as defined in section 8(7)) about the evidence relating to the individual before he makes a control order to consider whether there is evidence available that could realistically be used for the purposes of a prosecution of the individual for an offence relating to terrorism. If a control order is then made, subsection (3) requires the Secretary of State to inform that the chief police officer, and, thereafter, subsection (4) requires the chief police officer to keep the investigation of the individual's conduct under review throughout the duration of the control order to see whether prosecution for a terrorism-related offence becomes feasible. Other ideas floated during parliamentary debates for the facilitation of prosecution were not adopted. Prominent amongst these has been the proposal that evidence from the interception of communications should be available in court, thereby amending the current exclusionary rule in section 17 of the Regulation of Investigatory Powers Act 2000 (JUSTICE, 2006). An array of other proposals for encouraging prosecution was examined by the Joint Committee on Human Rights in its report, *Counter-Terrorism Policy and Human Rights: Prosecution and Pre-Charge Detention* (2006b, pp. 14–32). They include: inter-agency protocols for the sharing of information, firmer judicial pretrial management and incentives for witnesses.

Despite this emphasis on prosecution, the intelligence basis of control orders apparently renders the authorities very reluctant to take seriously this alternative to control orders, and the courts have also been unwilling to enforce the primacy of prosecution.[14]

Procedures

Jurisdiction in relation to control orders is vested within the Queen's Bench Division of the High Court (in England and Wales or in Northern Ireland) or the Outer House of the Court of Session in Scotland. This contrasts with the engagement of the SIAC for detention without trial and is a logical distinction because control orders are not part of immigration law. Yet, the issues of intelligence and the sensitivity of handling such material again arise, and the Act seeks to carve out a process within the High Court that is equivalent to that pertaining to SIAC. Accordingly, section 11(1) provides that control order decisions and derogation matters are not to be questioned in any legal proceedings other than proceedings in the court or on appeal from such proceedings.

At the same time, there is the assurance under section 11(2) that the relevant court will be able to consider human rights issues with respect to control order procedures. But the scope of appeals otherwise is reduced by virtue of section 11(3), which states that appeals from any determination of the court in control order proceedings can only be on a question of law.

Additional procedural issues are addressed in the schedule to the Act. There are two general concerns set out in paragraph 2 of the schedule. The first is a general duty on persons exercising the relevant powers to have regard to the need to secure proper review of control orders. At the same time, and emphasizing once again the presence of sensitive intelligence, there is also a duty to have regard to the need to ensure that disclosures of information are not made contrary to the public interest.

The court rules of procedure under paragraph 4 may provide, for example, that proceedings may be conducted in the physical absence of the controlled person or his legal representative and that proceedings may be concluded without full particulars of the reasons for decisions. At the same time, under paragraph 4(3), all 'relevant material' must be disclosed on paper, though application may be made (always in the absence of the controlled person (or any other relevant party) and his legal representative) for 'closed' evidence that is disclosed only to the court and to a person appointed under paragraph 7 of the schedule (the 'special advocate'). The special advocate is seen as a key safeguard for the controlled person. Their role is 'to represent the interests' of a relevant party in control order proceedings where that party and his legal representative are excluded from the proceedings, though without disclosing that closed evidence to them. The special advocate is not, however, 'responsible' to the party whom he represents. This means that the advocate is not obliged to follow instructions from the person. There are doubts whether a lawyer placed in such a situation can effectively represent a client (Metcalf, 2004; House of Commons Constitutional Affairs Committee, 2005).

Further detailed rules are contained in Part 76 of the Civil Procedure Rules.[15] Rule 76.2 requires the court to give effect to the overriding objective in paragraph 2 of the schedule to 'ensure that information is not disclosed contrary to the public interest'. Rule 76.22 enables the court to conduct hearings in private and to exclude the controlled person and his representatives from all or part of the hearing. Rule 76.24 describes the functions of the special advocate. By Rules 76.28 and 76.29, the Secretary of State must apply to the court for permission to withhold closed material from the controlled person or their legal representatives and file a statement explaining the reasons for withholding that material. The material is then scrutinized by the Special Advocate who may challenge the need to withhold all or any of the closed material.

Rule 76.26 modifies the general rules of evidence by enabling the court to 'receive evidence that would not, but for this rule, be admissible in a court of law'. One controversy arising here was whether the rules should exclude evidence arising from torture. In the subsequent case of *A v. Secretary of State for the Home Department (No. 2)*,[16] the House of Lords directed that when the SIAC considered detention orders, it could not receive evidence obtained by the use of torture because evidence obtained by torture was inadmissible in judicial proceedings.[17] In terms of the burden and standard of proof for the exclusionary rule to apply, the majority of their Lordships held that the appellant should raise a plausible reason as to why evidence adduced might have been procured by torture.[18] At that point, the burden passed to the SIAC to consider the suspicion, investigate it and determine whether the evidence should be admitted. The majority felt that the standard to meet at that point was whether, in the view of the SIAC, it was established on a balance of probabilities, that the information being adduced was obtained by torture. A significant minority (Lord Bingham, Lord Nicholls and Lord Hoffmann dissented) would have preferred that it be established before the SIAC that the statement was not made under torture. The same rules can be expected to apply to control orders.

Review by Parliament and the Executive

So as to ensure future parliamentary review, section 13 provides that sections 1 to 9 expire after twelve months (from 11 March 2005). They may then be renewed annually by statutory instrument, subject to the Secretary of State consulting with the independent reviewer appointed under section 14, the Intelligence Services Commissioner and the Director-General of the Security Service. Only the views of the independent reviewer (Lord Carlile) are revealed in public.[19] The government rejected the further safeguard of the insertion of a sunset clause (an expiration date) on the basis of the disquieting interpretation that sunset clauses, rather than representing an affirmation of confidence in parliamentary democracy in the face of the provocation of political violence, would in fact 'send the message to terrorists...that we are uncertain' (House of Commons, 2005b). However, the government did concede that new anti-terrorism legislation would be forthcoming in the following parliamentary session and that the opposition could then table changes to the 2005 Act. In fact, when that new legislation appeared, in the shape of what became the Terrorism Act 2006, no changes whatever were made to the 2005 Act.

As mentioned under section 13, the Secretary of State must appoint an independent person to review the operation of the Act (including the use of urgent non-derogating orders) and to report back to the Secretary of State after nine months and every twelve months thereafter. These reports must then be laid before Parliament.

In his first annual review, Lord Carlile (2006a), the independent reviewer, accepted that the control orders existing at the time had been properly made but raised a number of important concerns, particularly the contents of the control orders actually issued, which in his view 'fall not very far short of house arrest, and certainly inhibit normal life considerably' (Lord Carlile, 2006a, p. 13), strongly hinting that the orders go too far to qualify as non-derogating orders. Regarding section 8, he argued that letters from chief officers of police in relation to each controlled person are woefully thin on reasons preventing prosecution. Accordingly, he asked for more detail and also suggested that the letters be disclosed to the suspects (Lord Carlile, 2006a, p. 19).

Lord Carlile's second annual report pointed to some progress (Lord Carlile, 2007a), arguing the obligations imposed under orders had become more tailored and less formulaic. Furthermore, the Control Order Review Group, set up after his first report, was meeting regularly to consider the justification for extant orders, though he felt it should give more attention to pro-active measures to achieve exit from the regime (Lord Carlile, 2007a, pp. 4, 15–16). However, he remained critical of the detail disclosed in police letters about the possibility of prosecution and sought a better audit trail of police, prosecution and security agency meetings (Lord Carlile, 2007a, pp. 15–16, 25).

This review process has been very thorough but relatively conservative, concentrating on the fine detail but withdrawing from some of the more radical issues, such as the availability of intercept evidence for the purposes of prosecution, whether the process could be made more judicial, and whether the Act actually meets the standards of the European Convention, aside from the strong hint that the actual orders were wrongly categorized as non-derogating.

Review by the parliamentary Joint Committee on Human Rights has been more policy oriented (Joint Committee on Human Rights, 2006c), covering compliance with article 5 and article 6 of the European Court of Human Rights (ECtHR), and calling for greater judicial involvement and for a higher standard of proof.

Judicial review

Control orders have been subjected to rigorous judicial review, and several judges have forthrightly condemned fundamental aspects of the legislative provisions and the execution of the Prevention of Terrorism Act 2005. Judicial concerns have focussed on the extent of the conditions imposed pursuant to control orders and the fairness of the processes by which they may be tested.[20] This chapter asked whether constitutionalism could be maintained in a non-criminal justice mechanism-like control orders. Judges have demonstrated that it is possible but not without substantial effort and a degree of courage in the face of political and media criticism.

In the first case, *Re MB*, a hearing took place pursuant to section 3(10) of the Prevention of Terrorism Act 2005, regarding a non-derogating control order that was made in September 2005 against a British citizen on the grounds that he intended to go to Iraq to fight against coalition forces. The material delivered to the court included an open statement and supporting documents and a closed statement and supporting documents. The open statement referred to specific allegations as follows:

> MB is an Islamist extremist who, as recently as March 2005, attempted to travel to Syria and then Yemen. ... MB attempted to travel to Syria on 1 March 2005 but was prevented from doing so by police officers at Manchester airport. ... The Security Service assessment is that MB was intending to travel from Syria onwards to Iraq. ... On 2 March 2005, MB was stopped before boarding his flight to the Yemen by the Metropolitan Police at Heathrow airport. ... The Security Service is confident that prior to the authorities preventing his travel, MB intended to go to Iraq to fight against coalition forces. Despite having been stopped from travelling once, MB showed no inclination to cancel his plans. ... However, given that SHAREB is an experienced facilitator with the ability to acquire false documentation, the Security Service assesses that his lack of passport will not prevent MB from travelling indefinitely.[21]

These allegations were admitted to be 'relatively thin.'[22] Neither the closed evidence nor a summary of it was served on the respondent.

In this case, the principal adverse finding of the High Court was based on the restricted grounds for challenge, which amounted to a breach of the requirements of a fair and public hearing within a reasonable time by an independent and impartial tribunal established by law under article 6(1) of the European Convention.[23] In its view, 'nothing short of an ability to re-examine and reach its own conclusions on the merits of the case (applying the higher civil standard of proof...) would be sufficient to give the court 'full jurisdiction' for the purposes of determining the respondent's rights under Article 8 in compliance with Article 6.1 of the Convention'.[24]

The Court of Appeal reversed the High Court on several points. First, the Court of Appeal viewed the legislation as allowing for a much more rigorous standard of review than indicated by Mr. Justice Sullivan.[25] Given that control orders affect basic rights and that section 11(2) envisages that the reviewing court can apply the standards of the Human Rights Act 1998, section 3 of the 2005 Act had to be 'read down'[26] so as to allow the court to consider whether the decision was flawed at the time of the court hearing and not just at the time of the making of the order.[27] Next, the Court distinguished the standard of review embodied within the two elements in the decision of the Secretary of State, namely reasonable grounds for suspecting involvement in terrorism and the necessity for the order. On the first ground, the court asserted that it would have to satisfy itself that the evidence met the standard but, if the first leg could be established, that greater deference would be shown on the second necessity question but it would still be subjected to intense scrutiny.[28] Although the result was less than a full merits review, the Court of Appeal considered that it went far enough to satisfy article 6.[29] Second, as regards the standard of proof, the Court of Appeal also felt that that there had been confusion between substance and procedure.[30] Third, the court held that the fact that statutory procedures allowed closed hearings did not necessarily breach article 6.[31]

The House of Lords in *Re MB* reached a more Delphic position.[32] The Home Office is allowed to keep secret sensitive material, but the extent to which it does so may breach article 6 of the Human Rights Act 1998. It is accepted at the outset that control orders are to be treated as civil proceedings and not criminal proceedings, and so are subject to less demanding standards under Article 6. The argument is that in control orders:

> there is no assertion of criminal conduct, only a foundation of suspicion; no identification of any specific criminal offence is provided for; the order made is preventative in purpose, not punitive or retributive;

and the obligations imposed must be no more restrictive than are judged necessary to achieve the preventative object of the order.[33]

The fairness of the process will then be judged in light of the extent of disclosure and suppression, the importance of the evidence withheld, the possibilities of challenge and the severity of the consequences of the proceedings. While the intervention of a special advocate helps, the device does not necessarily cure all potential unfairness. The defendant must be allowed to know the material that is 'necessary to enable him, with or without a special advocate, effectively to challenge or rebut the case against him' or which is 'crucial to demonstrating the reasonable basis of the Secretary of State's suspicions or fears'.[34] Whether the process has been fair will be judged at the end of the hearing. MB's case was remitted back to the High Court for reconsideration.[35]

In the second case to have considered control orders, *Re JJ*,[36] the Court of Appeal sustained a breach of the Human Rights Act. Here, the non-derogating control orders were made against asylum-seekers who had previously been detained without trial. The obligations imposed included, *inter alia*, that the controlled persons be confined for eighteen hours per day in designated domestic residences and be electronically tagged; that the residences be subject to random searches at any time; that all visitors must provide their name, address, and photo identification; that their sole means of contact with the outside world from that residence is confined to a single telephone connection; and finally that, outside of the periods of confinement, they may only meet persons by prior arrangement and must not attend any meetings or gatherings, apart from at a mosque chosen with the approval of the Home Office.[37] The totality of restrictions in these orders meant that the Secretary of State had made, in substance, derogating control orders, which he had no power to make under section 2 and the orders must therefore be quashed.[38] The House of Lords adopted much the same reasoning: the cumulative impact of the restrictions amounted to a breach of liberty that rendered the order a nullity.[39] This outcome raised the practical question, an answer to which was vital for Home Office administrators: what would be a legal period of curfew? Lord Brown ventured that up to sixteen hours would be acceptable to him,[40] and so the Home Office has since adopted sixteen hours as the outer limit.

The third important case was *Secretary of State for the Home Department* v. *E*.[41] The gist of the reasonable suspicion against E was that he had provided support to the leadership of the Tunisian Fighting Group involved in terrorist-related activity, such as sending recruits to Afghanistan, though it was not a proscribed organization and there was no evidence that E had directly engaged in violence.[42] The obligations imposed on E comprised electronic tagging; residence at a specified address and a requirement to remain within it for a period of twelve hours; reporting to the monitoring company by telephone on any trip away from the residence; restrictions on visitors to the residence except with the prior agreement of the Home Office and restrictions on pre-arranged meetings outside the residence; submission to police searches; submission to temporary prohibitions and restrictions on movement; restrictions on communications equipment, including any access to the Internet or a mobile phone; a requirement to notify the Home Office regarding any intended departure from the United Kingdom; restrictions on banking facilities and on the transfer of money, documents or goods.[43] The allegation that article 5 rights to liberty had been breached by the cumulative obligations of the order, the argument which proved successful in *Re JJ*, prevailed in this case at first instance.[44] The Court of Appeal reversed. It emphasized that 'physical liberty' was the central issue and concluded that during daytime hours, there was no geographical restriction on his whereabouts, while many of the remaining restraints were interpreted as affecting rights to private and family life rather than liberty when they affected the family home.[45] The House of Lords agreed with the Court of Appeal,[46] finding the extent and circumstances of the restrictions to be 'plainly distinguishable' from those in *JJ*.[47]

In addition to concerns about the combined impact of restrictions under a non-derogating control order, an additional fault was detected in *E*. The High Court received in evidence on behalf of the Home Office judgments of the County Court of Brussels, dated 30 September 2003, and of the Court of Appeal of Brussels, dated 21 February 2005, relating to cases in which associates of E were successfully prosecuted, and in which there are references to their association with E and to his activities. This evidence was sufficient to convince the Court that there were substantial grounds for suspecting E of terrorist involvement and for the necessity of a control order.[48] The Court also accepted that the renewal of the order was not flawed in that there had been sufficient consultation with the police for the purposes of section 8(2) of the Act before the renewal had been made.[49] On the other hand, the duty under section 8(4) to keep under review the possibility of prosecution had not been sufficiently observed because the impact of the Belgian judgments and the material referred to in them on the prospects of prosecuting E were not adequately considered when they became available after the order had been made in March 2005. That material had later been considered for the purposes of the litigation,[50] but no serious inquiry seems to have been made as to whether it could trigger a British prosecution, and E had not been interviewed at any stage by the police. This defect on the part of the police tainted the Secretary of State's decision to maintain the order, as well as more generally throwing into question the seriousness of the professed wish of the executive to prioritise prosecution over control.[51]

The Court of Appeal reversed on both grounds. It also concluded that the duty under section 8(4) was not a condition precedent to the making of a valid order.[52] The House of Lords again agreed with the Court of Appeal, and in doing so, it has arguably deepened the demarcation between criminal justice processes and administrative action.[53] It held that a duty to prosecute wherever possible under section 8(2) was not a qualifying condition under section 2(1) to the making of an order, and a failure to observe it did not make the control order invalid, though it is stated in strong terms and is to be taken seriously.[54] The Home Secretary has a statutory duty to consult the police but not to reach any clear decision. Expecting the Home Secretary to reach a clear decision on the prospects of prosecution and obtaining a clear answer would 'emasculate' what should be an effective and expeditious procedure.[55]

The lesson to be derived from these cases is that the judges will no longer be passive bystanders in the processes by which intelligence is assessed and applied to individuals. Past experiences of emergency laws suggest that Lord Pearce stated accurately their usual stance in *Conway* v. *Rimmer* when he argued that 'the flame of individual right and justice must burn more palely when it is ringed by the more dramatic light of bombed buildings'.[56] Thus, the ' "Presumption of Executive Innocence"…which has continued to embody the attitude of the judiciary to executive power in such cases' (Simpson, 1992, p. 30) has generally fostered a supine attitude in response to executive measures (Campbell, 2005; Dickson, 2006). However, the control order cases illustrate that the courts are now more alive to fairness both in process and in substance. Therefore, assuming that resort to derogation remains unattractive, the government must seek to apply with much greater care and precision the terms of the 2005 Act, having regard to the need to invite representations and to keep prosecution under more active review. Meticulous scrutiny of the judges should keep the executive authorities on their toes, though their examination does not pose an insuperable barrier to the persistence of control orders. The problem the government then faces is whether the level of control will be too weak to protect public security. The former Home

Secretary, John Reid, reportedly complained that control orders 'have got holes all through them' (Ford, 2007). The solution to that concern must lie in terms of bolstering prosecution and applying more effective resources to the monitoring of the handful of controlees. Subject to these points, the cases have shown that control orders can be consistent with constitutionalism in the context both of individual rights and of what is the clear and present scourge of terrorism.[57]

Getting ethically smart with intelligence as a basis for legal process

There appear to be no fundamental objections to the melding of intelligence into legal process – it is not anathema to the legal system in the same way that one might suggest that evidence obtained through torture is intrinsically tainted.[58] Intelligence is information with value-added analysis and no more. But there may be two observations arising from this initial finding.

First, intelligence must be tested as rigorously as evidence if it is to be the foundation for legal process. So, decision-makers should be able to see the original data, otherwise there could be legitimate complaints about the non-disclosure of material information and rubber-stamping of executive decisions.

Second, there are degrees of relevance and reliability of intelligence that must be weighed in the overall context of any infringement of liberty. But the idea that decisions should only be made on the basis of 'pure' evidence is belied by the fluidity of the meanings of 'evidence' and 'admissibility' in criminal proceedings such as brought about by Part XI of the Criminal Justice Act 2003. This issue must also be viewed in light of the laissez-faire attitude of the ECtHR, which, while accepting that pretrial and evidential rules can be relevant to fair process under article 6,[59] has continually emphasized that the primacy of national regulation.[60]

Having asserted that intelligence is a proper basis for action, the experience of control orders suggests that, at least in the context of executive orders based on intelligence, further regulation is both desirable and possible in the interests of both upholding constitutional values and also providing reassurance to the public. So the question arises, what sort of regulation of intelligence should the law provide where it is the basis for legal process? (compare Omand, 2006).

First, there should be legal guidance about invocation and targeting. Invocation should be proportionate to the threat, and operatives should be required to consider whether more overt policing methods would achieve the same results. As for potential targets, given the known dangers of skewing the objects of investigative attention through police cultures (Gill, 2000, pp. 130, 249), guidelines about the legitimacy of individual and collective targets should be devised.

Second, what is counted as 'intelligence' in the first place or 'valid' intelligence in the second place, or 'quality' intelligence in the third place is not sufficiently structured under current law. Taking each in turn, arguments about what is 'intelligence' surely raise similar issues to those pertaining to forensic evidence. In other words, if this information is to be considered, the decision-maker should be able to understand: what are the qualifications of the person who generated the intelligence; and were the methods used to generate analysis acceptable to a wider community? The forensic science world is rightly wary of 'junk science' (Huber, 1991; Foster and Huber, 1997). The intelligence world should likewise be vetted for the sake of its reputation. Next, what constitutes 'valid' intelligence begins to raise normative issues. Is it acceptable, for instance, to use intelligence where the data have been obtained by torture or even obtained by illegal means such as an unlawful search (MacDonald Commission of Inquiry, 1981, pp. 513–14) or unlawful capture into jurisdiction, such as by kidnap?[61] As for quality in intelligence, what standards should be applied? The U.K. police force use a 5×5×5 reliability test (National Centre for Policing Excellence, 2005a) and the Bichard Inquiry Report has recommended a new Code of Practice covering record creation, retention, and deletion, taking account the nature, seriousness, circumstances, reliability and the age of the allegations (Bichard Inquiry, 2004, p. 135–8). The Code of Practice on the Management of Police Information (National Centre for Policing Excellence, 2005b) made under sections 39 and 39A of the Police Act 1996 and sections 28, 28A, 73 and 73A of the Police Act 1997 have duly appeared, but at just thirteen pages long, it does little more than scratch the surface and fails even to mention the Data Protection Act 1998 Principles. The Home Office guidelines on the disclosure of criminal records under part V of the Police Act 1997 talk more vaguely about information being credible and clear and reasonably current (Bichard Inquiry, 2004, p. 153). No codes or other documents have appeared to regulate the quality of intelligence in control order cases.

Processes must next be considered. There should be a safeguard of internal oversight by way of pre-authorization where feasible. The level of authorization should be based on the intrusiveness rather than the sensitivity (MacDonald Commission of Inquiry, 1981, pp. 513–14).

The hierarchy of authorizations should include, towards the upper end, persons with legal training (those concerns about involving judges in the world of intelligence have been addressed). In addition to the qualifications of the decision-maker, consideration must be given to other procedural features such as the standard of proof, legal representation, disclosure, and so on. This focus on judges need not exclude politicians, since they can bring to bear expertise about, for example, public reactions or diplomatic consequences. But the claim that politicians alone are expert in national security matters must be rejected when there are consequences for individual liberty and other constitutional values.

Outcomes must next be delimited. The general principle should be one of proportionality to the threat. This test might be broken down into components such as seriousness, temporality, and certainty (Bottoms and Brownsword, 1983). Without a high standard of proof and full, open testing, which is common in the executive measures, there should be time limits on the persistence of orders which are built upon intelligence (whether to exclude, detain, control, or otherwise). For example, an executive order should not persist for more than twelve months, and without the possibility of renewal on the same grounds (Gil Robles, 2005, para. 25).

Finally there is a need for continuing legislative and executive oversight. A specialist standing committee which reports to Parliament and not just the Home Secretary would fulfill this need.

However, rather than moving towards more effective governance of control orders, the trend towards similar measures in other areas is evident, for example the ASBO-like Serious Crime Prevention Orders, introduced by the Serious Crime Act 2007.

Conclusions

The debate continues as to whether 9/11 amounted to a wholly new form of terrorism or a novel form of war (Tucker, 2001; Defence Select Committee, 2002; Home Office, 2004b; Picco, 2005). But the perception that there is an enhanced state of vulnerability, which deepens the preoccupations of the risk society, means that responses, such as control orders, which address anticipatory risk from terrorism will continue to have cogency. It is certainly preferable to face up to societal needs for safety than to resort to the blunter instrument of detention without trial[62] or to subvert other laws (such as deportation) (Walker, 2007c) to achieve the same ends as control orders.

Alongside the attempted assessment of future risk comes uncertainty (O'Malley, 2004) and unfair process (Ashworth, 2004), giving rise to the inevitability of unjust intrusions on the moral autonomy of the individual. Equally, the executive-based response may be seen to impinge upon the rule of law and separation of powers. In view of these inherent qualms about measures of 'control', societies such as the United Kingdom would be well advised to adopt a criminal justice approach as the core response to terrorism rather than resorting to exceptional or extraordinary measures (Gross, 2003; Ackerman, 2004). A criminal justice response carries the important moral platform of legitimacy and fairness (Zedner, 2005), while also offering a practical response to danger. Expedients such as control orders may be acceptable *in extremis* by providing short-term abeyances from criminal justice but should not be adopted as long-term solutions to troublesome friends or foes.

The view of the Bichard Inquiry is that 'the effectiveness of the police service in the 21st century depends upon the effective use of intelligence for prevention and detection of criminal activity' (Bichard Inquiry, 2005, p. iv). This statement is undoubtedly true, but it should be subject to two provisos. One is that the implication of a trend towards 'high' policing – policing by coercion rather than consent and with centralized rather than localized policy agendas (Brodeur, 1983, p. 513) – may be inevitable as applied to political policing but should not be seen as a model for all policing. Second, even within the realm of anti-terrorism policing, it is co-operation from the public that has been the fundament of many successful actions against terrorism. State operations that involve methods or outcomes that are publicly condemned as unfair and alienate the public will therefore cost dear.

Notes

1. The term was coined by the Review of the Operation of the Northern Ireland (Emergency Provisions) Act 1978 (Cmnd. 9222, London, 1984) para. 136.
2. See *R v Fintan O'Farrell, Declan Rafferty and Michael McDonald* (2002) *The Times*, 3 May, p. 3.
3. See *Secretary of State for the Home Department v MB; Secretary of State for the Home Department v AF* [2007] UKHL 46.
4. See *Guzzardi v. Italy*, App. no,7367/76, Ser. A, No. 39 (1981).
5. For the division between the two types of order see *Secretary of State for the Home Department v JJ and others* [2007] UKHL 45 and *Secretary of State for the Home Department v E and another* [2007] UKHL 47.
6. See *Youssef v. Home Office* [2004] EWHC 1884, [62] (Q.B.).
7. [2001] UKHL 47, [56].

8. [2004] EWCA (Civ) 324, [16].
9. [2005] UKHL 71 cited at [2004] EWCA (Civ) 1123, [34], [46]. See also Joint Committee on Human Rights, 2006a, 48.
10. [2004] EWCA (Civ) 1123, [49].
11. Ibid., at [231].
12. See *R v. Ministry of Defence, ex parte Smith* [1996] 1 Q.B. 517.
13. *Secretary of State for the Home Department v. MB*, [2006] EWHC (Admin) 1000, [79].
14. *Secretary of State for the Home Department v E and another* [2007] UKHL 47.
15. Civil Procedure (Amendment No. 2) Rules, 2005, S.I. 2005/656, pt. 76.
16. *A v. Secretary of State for the Home Department*, [2005] UKHL 71.
17. Ibid., at [52]. But note that the court refused to apply the same exclusionary rule to inhuman and degrading treatment or to the use of information derived from torture in operational decisions. Ibid., at [53], [70].
18. Ibid., at [56].
19. The author's application under the Freedom of Information Act 2000 (c.36) for the materials supplied by the other correspondents under s.13 was refused by the Home Office on grounds of national security in 2007 (ref.T90467).
20. [2006] EWHC (Admin) 1000.
21. Ibid., at [20].
22. Ibid., at [66].
23. Ibid. at [104].
24. Ibid., at [87].
25. [2006] EWCA (Civ) 1140, [47]–[48].
26. Ibid., at [46]. 'Reading down' is a canon of constitutional interpretation by which more general words can be narrowed in meaning so as to comply with constitutional requirements. Such use of section 3 of the Human Rights Act 1998 is, and should be, a relatively rare occurrence. See *Re S(FC)* [2002] UKHL 10, [39]; Department for Constitutional Affairs (2006).
27. [2006] EWCA (Civ) 1140, [46]; see also *Secretary of State for the Home Department v. E* [2007] EWHC (Admin) 233, [32].
28. [2006] EWCA (Civ) 1140, [60], [64], [65].
29. Ibid., at [48], [60].
30. Ibid., at [67].
31. Ibid., at [80], [86]. Compare *Tinnelly and McElduff v United Kingdom*, App. nos. 20390/92;21322/93, Reports 1998-IV; *A v Secretary of State for the Home Department* [2002] EWCA Civ 1202; *R v H* [2004] UKHL 3; *R (Roberts) v Parole Board* [2005] UKHL 45.
32. [2007] UKHL 46.
33. Ibid., at [24] per Lord Bingham.
34. Ibid., at [34] per Lord Bingham, [68] per Baroness Hale.
35. Ibid., at [44]. Lord Bingham expressed some doubt whether the Act should be read down under the Human Rights Act 1998 s.3, so that orders would take effect only when it was fair for them to do so on the basis that the clear language of the Act allowed procedures that would be patently unfairly.
36. [2006] EWCA (Civ) 1141.
37. [2006] EWHC (Admin) 1623 at [18].
38. [2006] EWCA (Civ) 1141, [28].

39. [2007] UKHL 45.
40. Ibid., at [108]. A period of fourteen hours was not struck down in *Secretary of State for the Home Department v AF* [2007] UKHL 46, a case heard alongside MB. The High Court (Mr Justice Ouseley) had developed a rule of thumb that once the period of curfew reached or exceeded, twelve hours a day (it was fourteen hours in this case), the scope for further restrictions during those hours of curfew without depriving someone of their liberty was very substantially reduced [2007] EWHC 651 (Admin) at [78].
41. [2007] EWHC (Admin) 233.
42. Ibid., at [60]–[63].
43. Ibid., at [49].
44. Ibid., at [226], [233], [242]. The same judge (Mr Justice Beatson) found a cumulative breach of 'liberty' in similar circumstances in a fourth case, Secretary of State for the Home Department v. Rideh [2007] EWHC 651 (Admin).
45. [2007] EWCA Civ 459 at [62]–[69].
46. [2007] UKHL 47.
47. Ibid., at [10] per Lord Bingham.
48. [2007] EWHC (Admin) 233 at [82], [96].
49. Ibid., at [266], [284].
50. Ibid., at [124].
51. Ibid., at [293].
52. [2007] EWCA Civ 459 at [105]–[106].
53. [2007] UKHL 47.
54. Ibid., at [15].
55. Ibid., at [16] per Lord Bingham.
56. [1968] A.C. 910, 982 (H.L.).
57. The courts afford an added degree of deference to the Executive in recognition of the dangers of terrorism. See, for example, *Klass v. Germany*, App. No. 5029/71, Ser. A, No. 28, (1978); *Brogan v. United Kingdom*, App. Nos. 11209, 11234, 11266/84, 11386/85, Ser. A., No. 145-B, (1988); *Fox v. United Kingdom*, App. Nos. 12244, 12245, 12383/86, Ser. A, No. 182, (1990).
58. See *A v. Secretary of State for the Home Department* [2005] UKHL 71.
59. *Murray v. United Kingdom*, App. No. 14310/88, Ser. A, No. 300-A, (1994); *Shannon v. United Kingdom*, App. No. 6563/03, (2005).
60. See *Schenk v. Switzerland*, App. no.10862/84, Ser. A vol.140 (1988).
61. See *R v. Horseferry Road Magistrates' Court, ex parte Bennett* [1994] 1 AC 42; *R v. Mullen* [2000] QB 520.
62. The Attorney General of England and Wales called Guantánamo Bay 'a symbol of injustice, a recruiting agent for terrorists' (Rose, 2006, p. 6). See further, Duffy (2005).

4
Counterterrorist Finance Policies in the United Kingdom: The 'Silver Bullet' for Terrorism?

Peter A. Sproat

Theoretically, there is no doubt that any country threatened by organised violent groups should consider counterterrorist finance (CTF) policies. Those who commit acts of violence and terrorism need to raise finance for a wide variety of purposes. These include recruiting, training and maintaining members; paying for travel, accommodation, bribes, forged documents, reconnaissance equipment (e.g. audio-video), weaponry and bomb-making materiel; staging attacks and providing for dependents of those operatives captured or killed. Funds are also required for a variety of higher-cost services, including political and social activities such as propaganda and welfare that provide a veil of legitimacy for such organizations. In sum, finance is required for a variety of payments ranging from the 'pre-crime' purchasing of small items of everyday life to larger payments, including those for illegal materials and specialist services (Clunan 2005; for a critique of these issues see Naylor, 2006).

The United Kingdom has incorporated extensive counterterrorist policies in the area of finance. Indeed its government prides itself in promoting the implementation of such efforts on the world stage (H.M. Treasury, 2007, p. 4). Yet despite its alleged importance, works that consider the effectiveness of the United Kingdom's CTF policies are rare. This chapter's evaluation of CTF measures is particularly timely in light of the Government's recent admission that it is considering adding to these policies. Prime Minister Gordon Brown's recent suggestion is that the Government will;

> create what some will call a modern 'Bletchley Park' with forensic accounting of such intricacy and sophistication in tracking finance

and connections that it can achieve, for our generation, the same results as code breaking at the original Bletchley Park did sixty years ago. (Brown, 2006b)

The quote above explicitly rests on the assumption that CTF is key to the 'war on terror'. This chapter will reveal the rationale for CTF policies, the relative importance of CTF policies within the United Kingdom's arsenal of anti-terrorist legislation and explain which of the CTF policies are the most useful in practice. CTF, while effective in certain areas such as the new investigatory powers granted to the police, is not the 'silver bullet' one might believe it would become given the hype surrounding the anti-money laundering (AML)/CTF regime. The financial reporting regime has produced a disappointing result in terms of identifying financiers of terrorism. This outcome echoes that presently resulting from the similar AML reporting regime designed to tackle drugs and organized crime (Sproat, 2007, p. 184).

The aim and nature of the regime

The Government presently views its CTF policies as an integral part of the PURSUE strand of the overall counterterrorist strategy known as CONTEST that has been applied since 2003. That is, the CTF policies help the authorities pursue terrorists and those that sponsor them through asset freezing or by prosecution reinforced by financial investigation which also contributes to the Government's wider understanding of the terrorist threat. The CTF regime also supports the Prevent strand of CONTEST by creating a more hostile environment for terrorists – for example, by forcing the reporting of suspicious financial activity. Such tools sit alongside non-financial measures such as Control Orders and deportation as part of the Government's armoury of measures against terrorists and their supporters discussed in Walker's Chapter 3.

This then begs the question: what policies, procedures and legislation constitute the United Kingdom's CTF policies? Here they are categorized into four themes: (1) offences, (2) investigative powers, (3) cash seizures, asset freezes and forfeiture, and (4) the Suspicious Activity Reporting (SARs) regime enshrined in the criminal justice system. It is by this thematic approach, but not necessarily this order, that the various elements will be described and then evaluated. It is to the first of these aspects – financing offences – that this chapter now turns.

The main offences relating to the financing of terrorists are contained in sections 14–18 of the Terrorism Act 2000 namely; 'fund-raising' (s15), 'funding arrangements' (s17), the laundering of such property (s18) and use or possession of terrorist property (s16). Before examining each offence in more detail it is worth noting that section 14 defines 'terrorist property' as including: 'money or other property which is likely to be used for the purposes of terrorism (including any resources of a proscribed organisation)'. The latter covers money or any other property made available to a proscribed organization, regardless of the particular use to which it is put. Here it is also worth noting that at the time of writing the British government had proscribed forty-six international groups under section 3 of the Terrorism Act 2000 (including two for glorifying terrorism under section 21 of the Terrorism Act 2006), along with fourteen domestic groups, all of which are connected to the conflict in Northern Ireland.

In more detail, section 15 states it is unlawful: to *invite* someone to give money or other property with the intention or belief that it will be used for the purposes of terrorism; or to *receive* money in the above circumstances; or to *provide* money or other property knowing or having reasonable grounds to suspect that it will or may be used for the purposes of terrorism. Section 17 makes it an offence to enter into or become concerned in an arrangement from which money or other property is made available, or is to be made available to another, when one knows or has reasonable cause to suspect that it will or may be used for the purposes of terrorism. Section 18 makes it an offence for a person to enter into, or become concerned in, an arrangement that facilitates the retention or control by or on behalf of another person of terrorist property by either concealment, removal from the jurisdiction, transfer to nominees, or 'in any other way.' Section 16 of the Terrorism Act 2000 makes it an offence to *use* money or other property for the purposes of terrorism or to *possess* such a thing intending that it should be used, or has reasonable cause to suspect that it may be used, for the purposes of terrorism.

It is also useful to realize that in addition to these main offences the CTF legislation also deals with 'sins of omission' as well as 'sins of commission'. That is, section 19 of the Terrorism Act 2000 made it an offence for anyone to fail to disclose belief or suspicion of any of the offences noted above to a constable when such belief or suspicion is based on information that has come from information gained in the course of a trade, profession, business or employment. The same section made it an offence for those only within the regulated sector (those financial institutions subject to the law), to fail to disclose knowledge or suspicion of terrorist money laundering to a constable via an existing reporting regime (which now means the SARs regime). This was amended slightly by section 3 of the Anti-Terrorism, Crime and Security Act 2001 (ATCSA) to allow reporting to the United Kingdom's Financial Investigation Unit (FIU) then at the National Criminal Intelligence Service (NCIS), now within the Serious and Organised Crime Agency (SOCA). It contains its own Terrorist Finance Team that liaises with the National Terrorist Finance Investigation Unit (NTFIU) based in the Metropolitan Police. Schedule II, Part III s21A of the ATCSA 2001 imposed another demand on the regulated sector, the result of which is that those who make suspicious activity reports must do so when they themselves hold such suspicion (a subjective belief) or when reasonable grounds for knowing or suspecting (an objective criterion) exist.

Here it is also worth noting that terrorists funded by illicit money might be identified by use of 'ordinary' SARs generated by the regulated sector under the Proceeds of Crime Act (PoCA) 2002. This is because the PoCA demands that gatekeepers of the financial sector to report their suspicions to the authorities that a client might be engaged in money laundering. The legal 'stick' to force the gatekeepers of this regulated sector to report actual suspicion of money laundering is the threat of up to five years imprisonment and/or a fine. The level and type of suspicion required are the same as that required in relation to the reporting of suspicion of terrorist finance by the regulated sector noted above.

In addition to describing the offences and SARs regime, any credible evaluation of CTF policies in the United Kingdom must make note of the investigative powers. Both the terrorist legislation and the PoCA give special powers to law enforcement agencies when investigating CTF and criminal offences, respectively. Under Schedule 6 of the Terrorism Act 2000, the police can require a financial institution to provide information on a named or described individual for the purposes of the investigation when the tracing of terrorist property will enhance the effectiveness of the investigation. These are formally known as Customer Information Orders (informally they are known as production orders) and Financial Investigation Orders, respectively, and require authorization by the Judiciary. Failure to produce such information can lead to six months imprisonment and/or a fine. The information that can be obtained in this way is limited to: whether a business relationship exists or existed between a financial institution and a particular person; the account numbers of any other accounts to which the individual is signatory and the details of the other account holders; a customer's account number, their full name and address (or

former address), date of birth and the date on which a business relationship between a financial institution and a customer begins or ends;
any evidence of a customer's identity obtained by a financial institution in pursuance of or for the purposes of any legislation relating to
money laundering; and the identity of a person sharing an account
with a customer. Such Orders cover all transactions in a period of up to
twenty-eight days and must be distinguished from Account Monitoring
Orders that enable the police to monitor the transactions in an account
for up to ninety days. As with Customer Information Orders the latter
require the person in possession or control of the material to allow the
appropriate officer access by a particular time, and in a time, place and
manner required by the Account Monitoring Order. They are also
obtained in the same way but are authorized by Schedule 6A of the
Terrorism Act (introduced by the Anti-Terrorism, Crime and Security
Act 2001).

Those investigating potential terrorists occasionally use similar, but
not necessarily identical, investigative powers found within other
legislation. This is likely to be the PoCA that can be used for money-
laundering investigations, but theoretically it could also be the Police
and Criminal Evidence Act 1984 or Drug Trafficking Act 1994, depending
on the primary offence under investigation.[1]

The final two aspects of the United Kingdom's CTF regime under
consideration here are cash seizures, asset freezes and the forfeiture of
these, which are grouped together here because their rationales are
almost identical. The Government sees asset freezes (if not cash seizures)
as: 'an integral part of the Government's financial tool-kit for tackling
the threat of terrorism', because the freezing of assets can deny terrorists
and their facilitators the ability to raise funds and to move them through
the international system. The latter constitutes 'the key disruptive effect
of an asset freeze – equivalent to turning off their financial pipeline'. In
addition, the Government suggests the freezing of assets creates a
cordon around any funds that are already in the financial system and
provides valuable information on connections between individuals and
groups and their activities (H.M. Treasury et al., 2007, p. 26).

In terms of the legislation that authorizes such activities, Part 1 and
Schedule 1 of the ATCSA 2001 enables the seizure and detention of
cash – defined as coins and notes in any currency, postal orders,
cheques of any kind, bankers' drafts, bearer bonds and bearer shares –
anywhere in the United Kingdom if the police have reasonable grounds
to suspect that it was earmarked to be used for terrorist purposes, or
was part of the resources of a proscribed organization. Schedule 1 also

enables the forfeiture of seized cash on the civil standard of proof of the balance of probabilities and places the burden of proof on the defendant. In practice the police aim to prove guilt beyond all reasonable doubt. The PoCA legislation also authorizes any constable to seize any cash if she/he has reasonable grounds for suspecting that the cash is recoverable property or intended for use in unlawful conduct and if the sum seized is in excess of £1000. It too places the burden of the civil standard of proof on the defendant in relation to their ownership of suspected criminal cash.

In contrast, the freezing of assets is achieved by use of one of three different legal routes. The first is the use of Part 2 of the ATCSA 2001. Its various sections allow the Treasury to direct financial institutions to freeze the assets of *foreign* individuals, groups and if necessary countries where there are reasonable grounds to suspect they are likely to take action that is of 'detriment' to any part of the UK economy, or the lives or property of UK nationals. Interestingly, it is the legislature rather than the judiciary that must approve the order within twenty-eight days of H.M. Treasury issuing it. Such a freezing order must be kept under review and can last up to two years. In July 2006, H.M. Treasury agreed to introduce a procedure for the appointment of special advocates to represent the interests of the applicant when 'closed source' evidence was used in asset freezing cases (H.M. Treasury et al., 2007, p. 26). In practice, the freezing of foreign assets is often undertaken in concert with other countries. According to the section of H.M. Treasury's website on terrorism and terrorist finance, this is because the second and third routes involve the use of United Nations (UN) and European Union (EU) legislation enshrined in UK law. In terms of the former, the legislation is the *Terrorism (United Nations Measures) Order 2001* (SI 2001/3365), as amended. It provides H.M. Treasury with powers to freeze accounts of suspected terrorists, pursuant to United Nations Security Council Resolution 1373 (2001) on the suppression of terrorist finance generally. It goes on to note there is a whole list of UN-related statutory orders relating specifically to freezing the assets of al-Qaeda and Taliban that had begun prior to this. *The latest of these is The Al-Qaeda & Taliban (United Nations Measures) Order 2006 (SI2006/2952).* It updated the provisions in the domestic legislation giving effect to the UNSCRs from 1267(2002) to 1617(2005) relating to al-Qaeda, Osama Bin Laden and the Taliban. These include provisions to give effect to an asset freeze, including a prohibition on the making available of funds and economic resources to individuals and entities designated by the UN Sanctions Committee or by the UN Security Council, and provided for breaches of the Order to be criminal offences in certain circumstances. H.M. Treasury's website notes that the United Kingdom also implements the European Union's Council Regulation (EC) No 2580/2001 that gives effect to UNSCR 1373 (2001) in Community Law. Targets listed by the EU are deemed to pose a 'community-wide' threat as the European Communities Treaty does not provide the EU with the legal competency to enforce measures against the 'domestic' terrorists of member states. The result is similar but not identical lists of assets frozen, reflecting the legislation that authorized them. A comparison of the legislation behind the freezing of assets can be found within the Statewatch website and a complete and consolidated list of all those whose assets have been frozen is available at the H.M. Treasury website (for details of all websites noted see the bibliography).

In sum, the United Kingdom possesses a formidable range of CTF tools and promotes the implementation of such initiatives around the world. These facts make evaluating their effectiveness particularly intriguing and it is to this that the chapter now turns.

Evaluating the CTF regime

In February 2007 a report on terrorist finance led by H.M. Treasury stated that:

> The litmus test for success, and the goal to which the Government's counterterrorist finance community sets itself, will be whether year on year, the financial aspects of the terrorist threat are better understood and whether financial tools are deployed increasingly effectively in tackling them. While much of the Government's work in this area will remain confidential, the Terrorist Finance Action Group will track progress against these goals as an integral part of the Government's 'PURSUE' strategy. (H.M. Treasury et al., 2007, p. 39)

Unfortunately, the problems in using this methodology as a 'litmus test for success' are numerous. For example, even, if one overcomes the incredibly low-performance indicator of understanding more about the 'financial aspects of the terrorist threat', this does not necessarily mean one can do anymore to combat it in practice. Similarly, this 'better' understanding may mean little in terms of success if it produces an understanding that is far from a near-perfect understanding of how terrorists are financed in the United Kingdom. As for measuring success against 'whether the financial tools are deployed increasingly *effectively*', the government provides no indication as to what the latter might be. Simply, showing that financial tools are increasingly deployed could be as much a sign of failure as it is of success, if this occurred at a time that many more people were financing terrorism.

An alternative mechanism is required that is based on more concrete indicators, and it is possible for academics to find enough data to construct a general evaluation of the use of CTF policies. If we examine the most basic sign of success, the number of terrorist finance offences, Donahue's work is useful in that it can be read as suggesting that an evaluation should include 'the number of convictions' for terrorist offences and 'the importance of individuals captured' (Donahue, 2006, p. 307). In this regard, it is assumed she was writing specifically about convictions for terrorist finance offences or any terrorist offence when CTF work helped produce information that aided the investigation, although strangely she fails to provide even an estimate for either of these measures, or an explanation of the problems of obtaining such information. Unfortunately, exact figures for the number of arrests, charges or convictions for CTF offences within the official or academic literature could not be found. However, from Lord Carlile's annual reviews of the operation of the Terrorism Act 2000 (Lord Carlile, 2002, 2004, 2005, 2006b, 2007b) and the 2005 edition of the Northern Ireland Offices' Northern Ireland Statistics on the Operation of the Terrorism Act 2000, it is possible to state that of the 435 charges laid anywhere in the United Kingdom, using any of the 13 or 14 relevant sections of the Terrorism Act 2000 made between 19 February 2001 and 31 December 2005, 75 were made using sections 15–18. During this period there have been no more than eight convictions for these terrorist finance offences on the British *mainland*. These constitute one-fifth of the forty convictions obtained under the Terrorism Act 2000 in total according to the Home Office website.

From this one can say that CTF convictions constitute a minority of the total number of convictions for terrorist offences. This is unsurprising in that not only is there a quite a large number of terrorist offences for the police to choose from, but in practice, the multi-skilled investigative teams tend to arrest using more general offences, especially those involving the commission or preparation of terrorism under section 40 of the Terrorism Act 2000. Specific charges for CTF offences tend to be used when there is little possibility of charging for offences that are more general, especially those carrying longer sentences. Similarly, it is often easier to charge those suspected of funding terrorism with ordinary legislation. Indeed, according to the Home Office website, there have been 180 convictions under other legislation, including fraud along with convictions for murder, grievous bodily harm, firearms, explosives offences and false documents.[2] Unfortunately, again it is extremely difficult to say how many of these could have been charged with CTF offences.

Despite these limitations, it is still possible to show both the number of terrorist convictions (40) and that the total number of *any* terrorist-related convictions (220) are low when compared to the 1166 people arrested under any terrorism legislation in the United Kingdom (excluding Northern Ireland) between 11 September 2001 and 31 December 2006. Likewise, it is relatively small when compared to the 2000 people currently under surveillance by Security Service (BBC, 2007k). The large gap between the number of arrests and convictions can be explained in various ways. The most favourable to the authorities is that they favour early disruption rather than to await sufficient evidence to secure conviction because the consequences of failure are so extreme. The disadvantage of many arrests and few convictions is that mere disruption of those described as 'fanatics' can look like incompetence to the general population or overenthusiasm against a 'suspect community' by critics. The more Muslims who see it in this latter way the more difficult it will be for the authorities to gain the active support they require from them. The more intense this feeling of being targeted the more it will aid the propaganda of those who support and recruit home-grown terrorists.

As for 'the importance of individuals captured' via CTF policies, this is an incredibly difficult standard to measure, never mind provide evidence for, which may explain why neither Donahue nor the government have made such claims, despite her suggesting it should be a measure of success, and they are not made here (Donahue, 2006, p. 307). Here it is worth noting that on occasion the police have known about the presence in the United Kingdom of an individual on the UN list but failed to charge the individual because the listing State either failed to reveal the evidence for it or failed to show they would be prepared to push for an extradition. The result was that the police merely seized the assets that the individual had with him. That said, examples of convictions for CTF offences include two Algerians linked with al-Qaeda convicted of 'entering into a funding arrangement for the purposes of terrorism' (BBC News, 2003b). Other examples of those convicted of CTF offences include five men who planned to kidnap and kill a British Muslim soldier (BBC, 2007h).

Despite all of this, there is little doubt that the CTF investigative *powers* have played an important role in countering terrorism in the United Kingdom. This is because once a person is deemed worthy of further investigation the Government's claim that '[a]ll terrorist investigations have a significant financial component' appears to be correct. The number of more detailed investigations appears to run into hundreds in recent years. An impression of the scale of such activities is gained by the fact that the number of terrorist finance production orders issued by the NTFIU increased by 694 between 2005 and 2006 (H.M. Treasury, 2007, p. 32). This is because production orders are the main investigative power used by those who counter terrorist finance in the United Kingdom from which the use of other more unwieldy powers tend to derive. The practical value of financial investigative powers stems from their relative low cost, ease of access, rapid results and the ability to transform financial information into legal evidence when compared to telecommunications or surveillance. In practice, this means that financial investigators often have a leading influence in those investigations that have not resulted from a crime scene. The result is that financial information is now 'routinely used' as part of the evidential case to hold criminals and terrorists to account. In addition, financial investigations have a 'key intelligence role', allowing law enforcement to look backwards by piecing together how a terrorist conspiracy was developed and the timelines involved (H.M. Treasury, 2007, p. 10). Thus the Security Service's website noted: '[e]nquiries following the attacks of 7 July [2005] and attempted attacks of 21 July [2005] demonstrated the critical role of terrorist finance investigation in progressing specific enquiries and establishing an enhanced intelligence picture'. Financial investigations also have a less important function in looking forward, in that the resulting typology of potential warning signs of financial activity related to terrorism is relayed to those in the regulated sector that are tasked with identifying such suspicious activity (H.M. Treasury, 2007, p. 10).

As for the seizing of cash and the freezing of assets, Donahue's work is useful in that it suggests that an evaluation that focussed on 'the percentage of overall terrorist assets seized' would be better than one that focussed on 'the number of entities blocked and the value of assets frozen' (Donahue, 2006, p. 307). Of course, it is easier to find figures on the latter, although making sense of them is not so easy. According to a parliamentary answer on 31 January 2007 by Ed Balls, the then Economic Secretary to the Treasury, since 2001: 'there have been cash seizures under the [Terrorism] 2000 Act totalling £469,000, forfeitures by those suspected of involvement in terrorism totalling £126,000, and seizure of £1.4 million of terrorist funds under the Proceeds of Crime Act 2002' (Hansard, 31 January 2007). Putting aside the fact that cash seizures are not authorized by the Terrorism Act 2000, the report on *The Financial Challenge to Crime and Terrorism* by H.M. Treasury et al. published in the following month, noted that law enforcement agencies had seized some £444,000 in thirty-three cases under the ATCSA and 'at least £650,000' in cash seizures in terrorism-related cases under PoCA. The uncertainty results from the fact that: 'In Scotland, there have been two major terrorist finance cash seizures since 2003, resulting in the total seizure of £72,252', but H.M. Treasury does not make it clear whether this is in addition to, or part of, the other figure (H.M. Treasury, 2007, p. 30). Whatever the correct figures, and assuming that the amount seized was awaiting a decision as to forfeiture, the most favourable total is just under £2m of terrorist cash taken out of circulation. Here it is worth noting that some of the critics of the United Kingdom's CTF laws, including Donahue (2006, p. 304) and Amoore and De Goede (2005, p. 159), have claimed that the policies that demand the regulated sector produce SARs undermine their aims as the terrorists respond and move out of the formal financial system and into systems that rely on cash, in particular, cash smuggling. Such criticism does not seem to cause great concern to those investigating terrorist finance in the United Kingdom. This is probably because such a move would enable the authorities to simply seize, and later forfeit, the cash unless the alleged terrorist cared to challenge the authorities who merely have to show on a balance of probabilities that it related to either terrorism or crime. In practice, the PoCA legislation is often preferred as it is easier to show or to protect the source of information.

In terms of assets frozen, as of October 2007 a total of 284 separate accounts and approximately £625,000 of suspected terrorist funds have been frozen in the United Kingdom since 2001 – the approximation resulting from the fact some of it was held in dollars (Hansard 11 October 2007). Figures from February 2007 show that the United Kingdom had frustrated the ability of 443 individuals (359 of whom are listed in respect of al-Qaeda) to raise, move and use funds via financial institutions within the United Kingdom. The same is true for 184 entities (126 of which relate to al-Qaeda) (H.M. Treasury, 2007, p. 30). Figures provided by the Bank of England and cited by Ed Balls can be used to illustrate the relative importance of each source of law. They show that between 2001 and October 2006, a total of eighty-five individuals had their assets frozen under the United Kingdom's Terrorism (United Nations Measures) Order 2001. Of these, sixty-eight were first designated domestically by the Treasury and seventeen first designated by the EU. Fifty-eight entities have had their assets frozen under the UN regime, fifty-one were designated domestically by the Treasury and seven by the EU. In addition, 359 individuals and 124 entities have been designated under the Al-Qaeda and Taliban (United Nations Measures) Order 2002 on suspicion of having links with al-Qaeda or the Taliban (Hansard, 19 October 2006).

When these facts are coupled to sentences, such as asset freezes, 'cut off the financial pipeline to suspected terrorists' they sound impressive, but unfortunately they are not. The reality is that in total by October 2007 only £625,000 linked to designated terrorist suspects remained frozen in the United Kingdom. Alas, it is impossible to identify the individual(s) or group(s) to which this belongs as the Government has stated that '[t]he legislation does not permit the disclosure of amounts frozen for individual entities' (Hansard, 27 February 2006).

Unfortunately, it is incredibly difficult, if not impossible, to find figures on 'the percentage of overall terrorist assets seized' as Donahue would like, and it may be this difficulty that explains why neither she nor the government have produced them. The difficulty stems from the fact that even the most established groups within the array of terrorists that threaten the United Kingdom do not issue financial statements – neither do those more fluid groupings of home-grown Jihadists inspired or instructed by the hard-core (or should that be remnants?) of the original organization. What one can do is compare the amount of monies seized or frozen and compare them to official estimates of the enemy's assets. The result is that even the most favourable figure of approximately £2.62m seized or frozen since the introduction of the recent acts looks tiny in comparison to the claim made by H.M. Treasury that al-Qaeda spent some $30m per annum prior to 9/11 (H.M. Treasury, 2002, p. 8). It even looks small when compared to the assets of groups still involved in the Northern Ireland conflict (Moran, 2008, ch. 8). That said, no estimates as to how much terrorist money could be seized or frozen in the United Kingdom appear to have been produced and so it is impossible to produce the answer Donahue correctly prefers.

Despite this, there are a number of other facts suggesting that the Government itself is not comfortable with the results of its CTF regime. The first is that in February 2006 the Chancellor was still announcing that 'since 2001, we have frozen assets of terrorists of nearly £80 million – including for over 100 organisations with links to Al Qaeda' (Brown, 2006a) despite the fact that almost all of this money had been returned to the Government of Afghanistan after the fall of the

Taliban years earlier (H.M. Treasury, 2002, p. 9). The second is the fact that the Government is setting up a dedicated Asset Freezing Unit, to 'increase the expertise and operational focus that the Government is able to bring to bear on asset freezing' along with strengthening further the linkages between asset freezing and its wider counterterrorism framework. The third is that at the time of writing the Government is giving consideration as to whether to make further changes in these areas, including introducing a more practical definition of cash and enabling the forfeiture of property in relation to all terrorist offences – not just terrorist finance offences (H.M. Treasury, 2007, p. 25).

The SARs regime

The final aspect of the United Kingdom's CTF policies and procedures that is considered here is the SARs regime. This systematic sifting through the daily financial transactions of all the population – rather than individuals reasonably suspected of any crime – in the hope of identifying those who might be funding a possible (terrorist) crime in the future is probably the most controversial part of the United Kingdom's CTF policies. The controversy derives from the fact that it is an extraordinary measure in terms of the United Kingdom's traditionally liberal approach to criminal justice, and it is one that forces those in the financial sector to become unpaid monitors of financial transactions and informants for the British State.

According to the Government 'SARs also play an important role in relation to terrorist finance enquiries' with 'just under 2,100 SARs ... noted as being of possible terrorist interest in 2005' by the nation's FIU (H.M. Treasury, 2007, p. 32). That said, less than one-third of these of these – 650 to be precise – resulted in more detailed investigations. One reason for this is that a substantial minority of the SARs that arrive at SOCA's Terrorist Finance Team are unusable in that they fail to provide either a postcode and/or the name of an individual. Despite this, the remaining 650 SARs resulted 'in not only the seizure of cash thought to be destined for terrorism in Iraq but the tracking down of individuals wanted for terrorist charges and not just here but overseas' (Brown, 2006b). The fact that the Government did not specify the amounts seized or the number of individuals tracked suggests either that the impact in terms of identifying new suspects is probably quite limited or that the Government is poor at illustrating the success of its policy. The number of 'useful SARs' is increasing because of recent changes within the FIU at SOCA which has meant better working relations between the recently created Terrorist Finance Team in SOCA and the NTFIU. Thus between August 2006 and the end of April 2007 there have been just under 700 'terrorist-related' SARs that have been of some use to law enforcement, with approximately one-third of these going to the NTFIU in relation to ongoing investigations, one-third to local police forces for further investigations and one-third having intelligence value. It is in this way and on this scale that SARs provide useful *additional* information to those investigating financiers of terrorists or any terrorists identified by other means. The author has yet to see any evidence that suggests SARs have *identified* new financiers of terrorism for investigations that have resulted in convictions.

The limitations of the present-day SARs regime in *preventing* terrorist atrocities and identifying the terrorists *before* the event by detecting the legitimate transmission of legal monies through the financial system can easily be illustrated. According to the official account of the 7 July 2005 bombings, the group behind the attack raised the necessary cash 'by methods that would be extremely difficult to identify as related to terrorism or other serious criminality' (House of Commons, 2006, p. 23). It is therefore no surprise that no one seems to have suggested that SARs were ever made against the terrorists and alleged terrorists responsible for the atrocities of 7/7. Nor has anyone suggested that they were made against the 21/7 bombers.

Undoubtedly, the efficiency of the regime will improve as more feedback is given to the gatekeepers of the financial system in the regulated sector. However, in all probability it will continue to fail to live up to the ambitions of those who see it as a technological shield to the suicide bomber, akin to the Star Wars project to deal with intercontinental ballistic missiles (ICBMs). There are a number of reasons for this. First, there are still areas of the economy such as charities and trade that are not subject to this illiberal surveillance, despite the frequent widening and deepening of the SARs regime that results from the 'What if?' or 'Worst Case Scenario' mentality of its advocates in the 'threat assessment industry', to borrow a phrase from Van Duyne (1998, p. 359). There are also areas of the existing regime – such as Money Service Bureaux – that are not carrying out the task as well as the Government would wish (H.M. Treasury, 2007, p. 47–9).

Second, the system itself has contradictions. Even if Gordon Brown's 'Bletchley Park' suggestion is far more focussed and merely consists of (re-)configuring technology to check for activities such as liquidating accounts as has occurred with some suicide bombers, or purchasing certain 'high-risk' materials, the likelihood is that the vast majority caught will be false positives whatever the profiling logarithm the human programmers type in. As *The Economist* put it:

> The heart of the problem, from the banks' point of view, is that the vast majority of financial transactions look (and are) so routine and prosaic. America's Federal Bureau of Investigation recently tried to design a profile of how terrorists might use a bank. It failed to come up with any more unusual activity than placing a big deposit and then withdrawing cash in a series of small amounts. That profile, the anti-money-laundering boss at a big American bank points out, fits a quarter of banks' customers. (*The Economist*, 2002, p. 226)

Indeed, in practice the regulated sector's increasing replacement of human beings with automated systems to spot SARs is likely to have a negative impact on their role in combating terrorism. This is because it is likely to result in a higher proportion of poorer quality SARs and fewer knowledgeable people with whom the NTFIU and others in law enforcement can necessarily interact on a daily basis.

Third, even if the SARs regime was working perfectly it is geared to identify financial activities that are suspected of being criminal in nature. While a perfectly functioning regime would undoubtedly identify those involved in such activities, presently most funding for terrorists in the United Kingdom comes from perfectly legitimate activities. This last point is particularly important given the fact that the amounts needed to mount specific terrorist operations can be small. Even in the United Kingdom where the standard of living is much higher than in places such as Bali and Sharm El Sheik it is estimated that the Baltic Exchange bomb in the City of London in 1992 cost the Provisional Irish Republican Army only £3000 to mount (approximately £4300 in today's money according to measuringworth.com). The London bombings on the 7 July 2005 are said to have cost 'less than £8000', according to the *Report of the Official Account of the Bombings in London on 7th July 2005* (House of Commons, 2006, p. 23), although Robinson suggests it 'probably didn't cost £100' (2006). Similarly, the bombs that failed to explode on London's transport system on 21 July were made from legal substances such as hydrogen peroxide purchased from high-street chemists (BBC, 2007i) and stored in cheap plastic containers (*The Economist*, 2005). The low cost means that a terrorist attack could be funded through legitimate sources such as savings, drawing money on a credit card or a bank loan without reneging on the credit as some of the 7 July bombers did. Unsurprisingly, H.M. Treasury has acknowledged that the 'amounts of money needed to finance individual terrorist operations may be small or concealed' and that '[d]etecting the transmission of such relatively small sums as they move through the financial system is challenging, especially before the event' (H.M. Treasury, 2002, p. 11).

Conclusion

In conclusion, academic works that discuss CTF policies in the United Kingdom are rare, and those that evaluate their use are rarer still. General pieces on CTF tend to examine the law and its potential (and potential problems) in theory. However, by using the limited academic literature, official documentation and some key interviews it is possible to attempt to identify a number of important points and evaluate the significance of CTF policies within the United Kingdom's counterterrorist strategy since the introduction of the Terrorism Act 2000. In terms of the former, it is possible to work out that there have been very few convictions for CTF offences, and relatively few convictions when compared to the numbers arrested for terrorist offences – never mind the number placed under surveillance by MI5. That said, there have been relatively few convictions for *any* terrorist offences when compared to either the number of people arrested for such offences or placed under surveillance by MI5. It is likely that more 'terrorist finance suspects' have been convicted using the legislation relating to fraud, deception or money laundering than the anti-terrorism legislation. This is suggested because there have been far more convictions in 'terrorist-related' cases using ordinary criminal law than anti-terrorism legislation.

It is also possible to state that relatively little money has been seized or frozen when compared to the figures frequently mentioned in relation to al-Qaeda or Osama Bin Laden's operations. In addition, the SARs regime has provided few new leads although it does provide far more information to support ongoing investigations. At the same time, it is difficult to say how many people could have been convicted for CTF offences or how much money is available for forfeiture, or how many terrorists SARs can identify. These facts raise awkward questions about the effectiveness of CTF policies.

If one measured the contribution to the Pursue strand of the Government's counterterrorist strategy solely by the amount of convictions or value of assets frozen and seized then the CTF policies would be deemed to contribute little to it. For example, freezing and seizing have not hampered terrorist operations because if official estimates of al-Qaeda wealth are accepted, the amounts seized have been too low to make a difference to the organization/franchise that is al-Qaeda. Alternatively, if the cost of a terrorist operation is examined, it is so low that such measures will not prevent every attempt to mount such attacks. Likewise, if a contribution to the PREVENT strand was measured solely by the deterrence effect produced by the number of convictions or value of assets frozen or seized, or new terrorists identified by SARs, then the contribution of CTF policies to this strand would also be low. That said, if convictions were the main assessment criteria in regard to the Pursue and Prevent strands then it would be difficult to claim that *any* terrorist offence on the books credibly contributed to either strand, since the total number of convictions for all offences is so low compared to the numbers of those arrested under them or those placed under surveillance.

Similarly, there have been a small number of convictions for CTF offences of individuals linked to al-Qaeda and other terrorist organizations, as a result of which it is possible to state that CTF initiatives have had some success in making a dent in terrorist operations; and that these programmes have harmed terrorist groups' ability to operate – albeit on a small scale.

However, such a quantitative analysis undervalues the role of CTF strategy within the United Kingdom's counterterrorist policies. Here it is helpful to realize that those who undertake counterterrorism investigations in the UK work within multi-faceted teams in which CTF investigators play an important role along with forensics, surveillance and intelligence specialists. That is, the importance of CTF policies derives from the fact that *any* terrorist offence provides a gateway for the CTF specialists to using their investigative powers to gather evidence and intelligence on suspected terrorists. In detail, the Production Orders and Account Monitoring Orders contained in the Terrorism Act 2000 and PoCA enable the financial investigators to establish links between those currently under investigation and/or to produce a picture of what happened after a particular terrorist incident that are helpful to the whole investigative team.

Moreover, once one accepts that the United Kingdom uses disruption by both arrest and seeking conviction by use of anti-terrorist (or for that matter *any*) legislation as the main method to Pursue and Prevent terrorists in the United Kingdom, then one can see the relative importance of the contribution of CTF policies to both these strands of its counterterrorist strategy.

In sum, asset freezing, cash seizures and the SARs regime have produced poor quantitative results, and they have not constituted the 'silver bullet' some advocates of counterterrorist finance policies hoped for. Nevertheless, the investigative powers – in particular the Production Orders that derive from terrorist offences – do provide a useful weapon in their own right and they facilitate the use of other armaments by other members of the teams that investigate suspects in the United Kingdom's 'war on terror'.

Notes

1. Interview with Marti Fleming, Principal Officer, the Serious and Organised Crime Agency.
2. These statistics are compiled from police records by the offices of the National Co-ordinator for Terrorist Investigations. Unfortunately they do not provide a more detailed breakdown. http://www.homeoffice.gov.uk/security/terrorism-and-the-law/ (as of 24 April 2007).

Part II

Civil Liberties and Counterterrorism

5
A Chilling Consensus: Political Protest in the United Kingdom and the 'War on Terror'

Christopher J. Newman

Introduction

It is perhaps axiomatic to state that the Government and those who make policy need to develop coherent and consistent policies to respond to acts of terrorism (Martin, 2006). That such policies need to operate within constitutional boundaries and conform to human rights conventions should be equally as self-evident. There is little doubt that the events of 11 September 2001 in New York and 7 July 2005 in London have fundamentally affected the central nervous system of the laws and customs that comprise the Constitution of the United Kingdom. One only has to look at the case of *A & Others* v. *SSHD* [2004] UKHL 56 to see the difficulties experienced by legislators in dealing with those foreign nationals believed by the intelligence services to pose a terrorist threat. The discussions surrounding the desire of the UK Government and the police to extend the period of detention without charge reinforce the impression that the relevance of human rights to counterterrorism legislation has become something of a negotiation between the Executive and the Judiciary (Strawson, 2002).

This chapter will examine the development of the legislative framework governing public order in the United Kingdom during the period that it has been an active combatant in the 'war on terror'. For the purpose of this discussion, the phrase 'war on terror' is being used to cover a whole range of activities. The breadth of scope of the 'War on Terror' was made explicit in the speech made by President George W. Bush on 1 May 2003 delivered from the deck of the *USS Abraham Lincoln* in which he declared that the military phase of the Iraq invasion had ended. In this speech he stated that overthrowing Saddam Hussein was 'one victory in a War on terror that began on September 11th 2001, and still goes on' (Martin, 2006, p. 25). It is, indeed, true to say that much of the popular protest that has occurred in the United Kingdom has been focussed on the military action in Iraq. It is tempting to view the government's recent legislative attempts to deal with anti-war demonstrations as radically politicizing the policing of protests. Reiner (2000) points out, however, that it is by no means novel to accuse a government of using the police to enforce an unpopular political agenda. The concerns raised within this chapter are of a twofold, insidious challenge to political protests. First, the regulation of protest is being unduly influenced by the 'normalization' of emergency laws to deal with specific emergencies. The provisions of s132–138 of the Serious Organized Crime and Police Act 2005 will be discussed in the following sections and are the latest in a series of laws passed since the commencement of the 'war on terror' that are being absorbed into the permanent regulation of protest. This 'normalization' is not a new fear (Hillyard, 1987), but the raft of new legislation, indicates an increasing incorporation of emergency powers as protests against the military action in Iraq continue to arise.

The second concern that this chapter seeks to discuss, and is perhaps of even greater concern, is the attitude of the courts to cases relating to protest. By virtue of s6 of the Human Rights Act 1998 a specific duty is placed upon all public bodies to act in a way that is compliant with the rights enshrined in the European Convention on Human Rights (ECHR). If there is a danger that an individual may lose her or his right to liberty or the right to a fair trial, how much more significant is the threat to those rights provided under Article 10 (Freedom of Expression) and Article 11 (Freedom of Association)? These rights do have legal limitations. Article 10(2) and 11(2) respectively incorporate qualifications that allow the state to restrict the rights of the individual in the interests of national security, providing the restrictions are proportionate and necessary in a democratic society. Cases such as *R* v. *SSHD ex parte Hosenball* [1977] 3 All ER 452 indicate that, historically, the judiciary are not usually willing to interfere (and in some cases even enquire) where national security issues are raised by the state and the threat to popular protest in the post-9/11 world becomes clear. Although some academics see the latest restrictions on protest as part of a historical 'see-saw' between restriction and more liberty (Waddington, 2005), there is currently an apparent consensus between the legislators and the judiciary as to the fulcrum point where the balance between liberty and security lies. This, in turn, begets legislation with ever-increasing proscription, resulting in a chilling effect on the freedom to protest. Either deliber-ately or unwittingly this apparent consensus gives the appearance of a state willing to suppress protest with which it does not agree.

Terrorism legislation and popular protest

A significant area of concern is the use of the arbitrary search powers, as laid down in the Terrorism Act 2000, and their operation within the context of a widespread protest. The relevant provisions, sections 44 to 47, were almost directly imported into the Terrorism Act 2000 from sections 13A and 13B of the Prevention of Terrorism (Temporary Provisions) Act 1989. The power is analogous to those provisions intro-duced in section 60 of the Criminal Justice and Public Order Act 1994 and as such, s44 (4) (b) of the Terrorism Act 2000 provides, *inter alia,* that a senior police officer can authorize extended powers of stop and search within a specific zone or place where that officer considers it expedient for preventing acts of terrorism. Within the Metropolitan Police District, this authorization may only be given by an officer of at least the rank of Commander. Section 44 (4) (a) provides, in relation to other police areas, that authorization may only be given by an officer of at least the rank of Assistant Chief Constable. This authorization must be confirmed by the Home Secretary within forty-eight hours of it being given and can remain in force for no longer than a total of twenty-eight days, after which it must be renewed. The legislation, as drafted by Parliament, did not place a limit on the number of renewals that can be made and it has been acknowledged by the Home Office that a series of rolling authorizations, covering the Metropolitan Police District, have been in place since the power first came on to the statute books.

   The extended powers of stop and search in accordance with ss44 to 47 of the Terrorism Act 2000 provide an illuminating analogue with the established powers of stop and search under section 1 of the Police and Criminal Evidence Act 1984. The requirement that an officer conducting a search under s1 of the 1984 Act has reasonable suspicion is seen as one of the key safeguards acting as a restraint on discriminatory and random stop and searches by police officers who are searching for prohibited arti-cles. By contrast, the power bestowed by s45(1) of the Terrorism Act does not require the officer to have reasonable suspicion that the persons or vehicles that have been stopped are connected with terrorism or are indeed carrying articles that could be used in connection with terrorism. The mere presence of an individual in a particular zone or place where the authorization is in force will be sufficient to render that individual liable to be searched. That this power is intended to be coercive is confirmed by inclusion of the offence under s47 (2) of failure to stop when requested or willful obstruction of a police officer carrying out such a search. Where an individual seeks to challenge police action in conducting a search, the only legal mechanism available is that of judicial review. Although searches may ultimately be subject to judicial oversight, such scrutiny will, of necessity, be *ex post facto* and as such will not provide any immediate remedy for those stopped (Davenport, 2005, p. 28).

The effect of the power of search under section 44 is to introduce random or blanket searching. It has been noted that, but for the aforementioned pre-conditions, the limited nature of the search and the fact that the legislation is part of the overall nexus designed to combat terrorism, these provisions would in all likelihood offend various provisions of the ECHR (Walker, 2002, p. 147). Such compatibility, however, is not immutable and it is true to say that the English courts have been statutorily compelled into adopting a guardianship role in respect of an individual's Convention rights. Section 3 of the Human Rights Act (HRA) 1998 provides that all Acts of Parliament and subordinate legislation must, so far as is possible, be read and given effect in a way that is compatible with Convention rights, even if there is contrary authority on the question. Section 3 of the HRA 1998 applies to all public authorities. By virtue of section 6 of the HRA 1998, Courts and the police will both be deemed to be public authorities for the purpose of the Act and as such are required to give effect to the Convention rights. It is, therefore, tempting to therefore that the additional bulwark provided by a human rights-conscious judiciary, on top of the safeguards outlined above, would provide adequate protection from the capricious exercise of this power. In the case of popular protest, however, it would seem that all branches of the State are willing to allow polymorphous national security arguments to trump this most fundamental of political rights: the right to object in public. The case of *R (on the application of Gillan)* v. *Commissioner of Police for the Metropolis [2006] UKHL 12; [2006] 2 A.C. 307 (HL)* provides an illustration of how, far from being an azoic statement of principles, terrorism legislation is being used in the post-9/11 world to bypass the regulatory framework that exists for dealing with threats to public order.

On 9 September 2003, authorization was granted by the Assistant Commissioner for the Metropolitan Police Service under s44 of the Terrorism Act 2000. This authorization, subsequently confirmed by the Secretary of State, permitted the police to exercise this extended power of stop and search within the whole of the Metropolitan Police district and thus covering the Greater London area. The same day that authorization had been granted, Kevin Gillan was involved in a protest against an arms fair that was being held in East London. As a result of this protest, Gillan had been stopped and searched by police and had various items of his personal property seized. Gillan applied first to the Divisional Court and then to the Court of Appeal seeking a judicial review of the lawfulness of the stop and search.

Both of these appeals were rejected. On each occasion, however, the Court in question granted leave to appeal on the basis that the case raised important issues relating to judicial scrutiny of national security issues. The resultant appeal to the House of Lords centred on two key areas. First, it was contended that the use of the word 'expedient' in s44(3) of the 2000 Act should be interpreted to mean that authorization would only be granted where there were reasonable grounds for believing that it was necessary and suitable for preventing terrorism. Second, the authorization contravened the right to liberty, private life and freedom of expression as guaranteed by the ECHR.

The appeal was rejected by the House of Lords. It was decided by their Lordships that in drafting s44(3) of the 2000 Act, Parliament had intended the word 'expedient' to be used in its normal context and the appellant was, in effect, asking the court to impose the criteria of necessity when Parliament had chosen the criteria of expediency. The Court felt that the legislation imposed sufficient regulation in respect of the authorization for the power under s44. It was held that Parliament had clearly appreciated the significance of using the word 'expedient' in that it was appropriate in a measure intended to protect the public from a terrorist threat.

Procedurally, their Lordships found that the Assistant Commissioner and the Secretary of State had both acted as per the requirements of the statute. In relation to the broader question regarding the interference with Convention rights, the Court stated that, providing the police officer conducted the search in line with the Code of Practice, the provisions under s44 would not interfere with an individual's right to liberty. Similarly, the Court found that these provisions were necessary in a democratic society and a proportionate response to the burgeoning terrorist threat. As such, and because they were regulated by a clear body of laws, which were freely accessible to the public, s44 came within the exceptions provided for by Article 8(2) and Article 10(2) of the ECHR.

When analysing the decision of the House of Lords in this case, commentators tend to focus upon issues of interpretation and the disproportionate impact on minority ethnic groups with all of the adverse effects that these have upon community relations (Walker, 2006a). While these issues undoubtedly represent (to coin a phrase) a clear and present danger and a wholly necessary area of enquiry, one of the more insidious effects of the decision is the potentially chilling effect that it could have on widespread popular protest. The current state of the law means that any individual taking part in a protest within the Metropolitan Police District, the subject of which involves any issue of national security, is liable to be stopped and searched under s44. The decision in *Gillan* means that providing the police officer carrying out the stop and search follows the correct procedure, the individual will have no redress other than a lengthy judicial review process.

Protesting around Parliament during the 'war on terror'

With the passing of the Serious Organized Crime and Police Act (SOCPA) 2005, the post-9/11 legal landscape suffered a further tectonic shift. The 2005 Act was part of an aggressive, pre-election agenda pushed through by the Blair government in April 2005 and has been criticized for the somewhat inadequate gestation period, with some noting 'that it was particularly disappointing that a more careful review was not undertaken in the White Paper' (Owen et al., 2006, p. 5). Although the Act was primarily administrative in its ambit, it also provided an illuminating example of the attitude of the government in relation to dissent aroused by the conduct of the 'war on terror'. Among the provisions creating an English-style FBI and changing the police power of arrest, there was a piece of legislation designed specifically to put an end to the protest of one individual citizen. Since 2001, Brian Haw had occupied a part of Parliament Square opposite the main gates of the Houses of Parliament, in a protest against government policy in Iraq and the general conduct of the 'war on terror' (Owen et al., 2006, p. 97). The case of *Westminster CC* v. *Haw* [2002] EWHC 2073 (QB) saw an unsuccessful attempt to remove Haw by means of an injunction. Accordingly, Part 4 of SOCPA 2005 'significantly curtails the right to protest within a one kilometre radius of Parliament' (Robbins, 2007, p. 22). Specifically, s133 (1) of SOCPA 2005 provides that any person who intends to protest or organize a demonstration in the vicinity of Parliament must apply to the police for authorization to do so. A specific offence of organizing, taking part in, or carrying on a demonstration in a public place in the designated area if appropriate authorization has not been given was provided by virtue of s132 to ensure that Haw could be arrested and removed.

The statute falls short of granting the Commissioner of Police the power to prohibit the demonstration if notice is given, but under s134 (3) he may impose conditions that he feels are necessary to prevent hindrance to the operation of Parliament or to prevent serious disorder. It is, perhaps, worthy of note that these elements echo the terms of the Public Order Act 1986 in relation to the general statutory provisions governing protests and assemblies and both of these statutory provisions can reduce or neutralise the impact of a procession or assembly. In order to combat the presence of existing protestors (specifically Haw), a Commencement Order (Article 4(2) Serious Organised Crime and Police Act (SOCPA) 2005 (Commencement No 1, Transitional and Transitory Provisions) Order (SI 2005 No. 1521 C66)) was also introduced to amend the provisions of section 132 (1) to include continuing demonstrations as well as new demonstrations.

The inevitable judicial challenge to this aspect of SOCPA occurred in the case of *R(on the application of Brian Haw) v. Secretary of State for the Home Department*, Commissioner for the Metropolitan Police Service [2005] EWHC (2061). This centred upon Haw's contention that his demonstration had started before the 2005 Act had come into force. The High Court ruled that as Haw's protest was underway well before the coming into force of SOCPA 2005, he did not require the authorization of the Police. Furthermore, the court pointed out that the Commencement Order not only failed to introduce transitional arrangements but did, in fact, contain substantive amendments to the original legislation. The Secretary of State was granted leave to appeal the decision. The subsequent hearing at the Court of Appeal overturned the decision by the High Court and ruled that Parliament, by virtue of s132 (6), had clearly intended to regulate all demonstrations within the designated area no matter when they started. However, the Court focussed not on the protest itself, nor indeed was there any substantive discussion surrounding freedom of expression. Instead, the Court chose to concentrate on the interpretative issues surrounding the legislation.

Dissatisfaction with the provisions of Part 4 of SOCPA 2005 was not limited to Brian Haw and his campaign. In August 2005, two separate protests within the designated area were conducted with the Divisional Court hearing consolidated appeals following the conviction of four protestors for conducting unauthorized protests in the case of *Blum* v. *Director of Public Prosecutions and other appeals* [2006] EWHC 3209 (Admin). Stephen Blum and Aqil Shaer were part of a demonstration organized by the 'Stop the War Coalition' specifically against the provisions of Part 4 of SOCPA. Somewhat more controversially, the legislation was used to disrupt the protest of Milan Rai and Maya Evans that occurred on 25 October 2005. Evans stood opposite Whitehall and read out the names of all British soldiers who had been killed in Iraq while Rai read out the names of Iraqi citizens who had died in the conflict. In both protests, each of the protestors admitted to knowing that authorization would be required, and were given the opportunity by police to end their protest. Indeed, it was noted that 'the demonstrations were peaceful and good-humoured. ... The demonstrations were as much as anything a demonstration against the requirement that authorisation should have been required to demonstrate in Parliament Square and/or in Whitehall' (per Waller LJ at para. 9).

The four protestors sought to argue, at first instance, that section 132 of the 2005 Act was not compatible with Articles 10 and 11 of the ECHR (Freedom of Expression and Freedom of Assembly) and, as such, the court should act according to section 3 of the 1998 Act and read down section 132 of the 2005 Act. It was also argued that under section 6(1) of the HRA 1998 it would be unlawful for the Court to convict the appellants. In each case, this argument was rejected, with the court finding that the relevant sections of the 2005 Act were indeed compliant with the Convention. In the subsequent appeal the protestors changed tack, arguing that all public bodies have to justify whether, at each stage of the criminal process, the decision to arrest, charge and convict was necessary and proportionate given that in each case the demonstrations had been both peaceful and good humoured. The appellants argued that the state, in its various public authority guises, should have looked not only at the failure to obtain the requisite authorization but also at the conduct of the demonstrators. This line of reasoning was rejected and the appeal was dismissed. The ECtHR in the case of *Ziliberberg* v. *Moldova* (Application no. 61821/00) held that member states do have a right to require authorization for demonstrations. Once it was accepted that the authorization procedures within SOCPA 2005 were compatible with Convention rights, it was not legitimate to ask the court to look at the unauthorized conduct. Similarly, Parliament must be entitled to impose sanctions for not seeking authorization otherwise the compatibility of the sections and their effect would be no more than illusory (*Blum*, per Waller LJ at para. 29).

The decision of the appellate courts in both *Haw* and *Blum* seem clearly to indicate that the courts will not interfere with the operation of sections 132–138 SOCPA. S4 of the HRA 1998 allows superior courts to make declarations of incompatibility if the Court feels that the legislation offends against any of the rights enshrined in the ECHR.

Although the judiciary have been imbued with a guardianship role in relation to Convention rights by virtue of s6 of the 1998 Act, they appear presently to be acting merely as sentinels, overseeing the laws that have been passed. It is to the legislature and the executive in the post-9/11 world that one must look for the promulgation of such laws. There is, however, concern that these appear to bestow exceptionally broad ranging powers on the police to deal with what many feel is legitimate protest concerning the 'war on terror' (Robbins, 2007).

Public Order, the Individual and the Post-9/11 World

Arguably, it is within the realm of public order law that the principal legislative tools engaged by the state to deal with undesirable expression are to be found. The offence of disorderly conduct, contrary to section 5 of the Public Order Act 1986, provides, *inter alia*, that it is an offence to use threatening, abusive, insulting or disorderly words or behaviour, or display any writing, sign or other visible representation that is threatening or abusive within the hearing or sight of a person likely to be caused harassment, alarm or distress. The words or behaviour need not be used towards another. From the outset it was recognized that section 5 of the 1986 Act, although a relatively minor offence, could have a significant chilling effect on protest and expression. Indeed, section 5 of the 1986 Act was originally intended to counter behaviour such as groups of youths persistently shouting abuse or obscenities and low-level football hooliganism (Card, 2000, p. 158–60).

It may be that a police officer decides that an essentially peaceful protest falls within the ambit of section 5 of the 1986 Act, due to the potential for that protest to cause harassment, alarm or distress. That protestor can then be arrested and her or his participation within that protest can be ended (Smith, 1987, p. 116). The breadth of interpretation available to the courts in relation to the terms 'harassment', 'alarm' or 'distress' means that a broad range of behaviour is prohibited under section 5 of the 1986 Act. This can potentially render an individual liable to arrest for promulgating their own deeply held expressions, beliefs and opinions. This is a significant area of concern; although it is true to say that such disquiet is not limited to the post-9/11 legal landscape (Newman, 2006). It has been noted that the problem caused by individual dissenters is not the primary mischief that section 5 of the Public Order Act 1986 is designed to counter; it just so happens that this falls within the general area of antisocial behaviour (Geddis, 2004, p. 873). These issues are ever more surprising when one considers the intended impact of s6 of the HRA1998 and the proposed guardianship role of the courts in relation to those rights enshrined within the ECHR.

When looking at the view taken by the Courts, the case law before 9/11 seemed to suggest that political protest would enjoy some protection. In *Percy* v. *DPP* [2001] EWHC Admin 1125, [2002] JCL 291 the group being insulted comprised American citizens working on a US Air Force Base, and the individual was protesting against the 'Star Wars' missile defence programme. In this case, the Divisional Court held that a criminal conviction was a disproportionate way of dealing with the circumstances of that case.

The decision in *Norwood* v. *DPP* [2003] WL 21491815 showed that the English judiciary were prepared to delineate between political opinion and unacceptable hate speech, a decision the ECtHR was willing to ratify by means of its judgment in *Norwood* v. *UK* (2005) 40 EHRR SE11. In this case, the appellant was convicted under section 31 of the Crime and Disorder Act 1998 for the racially aggravated version of the offence under section 5 of the 1986 Act. The appellant had displayed a poster, containing the words, in very large print, 'Islam out of Britain' and 'Protect the British people' with a reproduction of a photograph of one of the twin towers of the World Trade Centre in flames and a Crescent and Star surrounded by a prohibition sign. The appellant in this case was a member of the British National Party and he contended that his actions were reasonable. Lord Justice Auld stated that Norwood's conduct was unreasonable, and that in this case, section 5 of the Public Order Act 1986 was itself a statute that could protect the rights of others and/or prevent crime and disorder.

Individual protestors, such as Norwood and Percy demonstrate that it is not only the neoteric terrorism legislation that threatens to dissipate the rights of those who seek to offer contrary opinions post-9/11. One of the fundamental challenges facing the English legal system emanates from the utilization, by the state, of existing legislation to suppress speech and opinions. This, of course, is not a problem unique to issues relating to the actions of terrorist groups and the wider conduct of the 'war on terror' by the government. It is, however, indicative of a problem which the post-9/11 political landscape has highlighted. Lord Justice Sedley in his judgment in the case of *Redmond-Bate* v. *DPP* [2000] H.R.L.R. 249 stated that: 'Free speech includes not only the inoffensive but the irritating, the contentious, the eccentric, the heretical, the unwelcome and the provocative provided it does not tend to provoke violence. Freedom only to speak inoffensively is not worth having.' The reaction to government policy surrounding the 'war on terror' has encouraged individual and collective protest which, at times, has encompassed the entire range of reactions mentioned by his Lordship. The temptation when viewing such pronouncements is to direct the debate towards the law regulating hate speech and the implications for free expression. The purpose of this discussion, however, is to remain focussed on the public order implications of the 'war on terror'. Police officers are imbued with the same legislative guardianship role on Convention rights as the judiciary under s6 of the HRA 1998. Yet they are required to make decisions regarding free expression and liberty within society while at the same time remaining mindful of their duties to keep the peace and protect their own safety and that of members of the public.

Popular protest at Fairford

The conduct of the 'war on terror' and the subsequent invasion of Iraq have seen many expressions of dissension, some of which have been discussed herein. Perhaps the most profound effect upon the legal landscape comes from the activities of those who engaged in a number of demonstrations at Fairford, in Gloucestershire, an RAF base used by the United States Air Force. These protests tested the delicate but febrile relationship between popular protest and the need for regulation of such protest. The state, specifically the police, sought to use public order legislation and terrorism provisions, specifically s44–47 Terrorism Act 2000, to prevent a perceived threat of widespread disorder. The opposing view held by the protestors was of a state perpetrating an unlawful incursion into a foreign country and trying to silence any internal opposition. Fairford became the fulcrum upon which the English legal system would try and balance these two contrapositive viewpoints.

The first of the two significant demonstrations occurred at the commencement of hostilities in Iraq in the spring of 2003. A number of protestors, including Margaret Jones and Paul Milling, had broken into the RAF base and caused damage to fuel tankers and bomb trailers and attempted to damage the runway. Similar activities were undertaken by Benjamin Aycliffe and others at the Marchwood Military Port in Hythe, Hampshire a few weeks prior to this, where the protestors had chained themselves to tanks or reconnaissance vehicles. This successfully halted the work of the port, which involved loading ships bound for the Middle East. All of the protestors, at both sites, were charged and convicted at first instance of either aggravated trespass in contravention of section 68 of the Criminal Justice and Public Order Act 1994 or criminal damage, contrary to section 1 of the Criminal Damage Act 1971 respectively.

It was contended by those convicted of aggravated trespass that the activity of the military on the bases was contrary to customary international law, and that as such, the British and US governments were committing the crime of aggression against Iraq. The protestors argued that the crime of aggression was capable of being an offence within the terms of section 68(2) of the Criminal Justice and Public Order Act 1994, therefore, the activities on the military bases were not lawful and as such the offence under section 68(1) of the 1994 Act could not be made out. Those accused of criminal damage contended that they honestly believed that the force they used in causing the damage was reasonable to prevent a crime, namely the government pursuing the war in Iraq. As such, these protestors claimed that because of the assimilation of the crime of aggression into domestic law, their actions fell within the ambit of section 3 of the Criminal Law Act 1967 that provides *inter alia* that a person may use such force as is reasonable in the circumstances in the prevention of crime.

The protestors' appeals against their convictions were made to the Divisional Court and the Court of Appeal with both of these being rejected. Although the protestors were granted leave to appeal to the House of Lords, this appeal in the case of *R* v. *Jones & Others* [2006] UKHL 16 was also dismissed. The court held that it was a matter for Parliament, not the judiciary, to determine what types of conduct should attract criminal sanctions. The court also stated that there were compelling reasons in favour of the traditional reluctance of courts to review the exercise of prerogative powers in relation to the deployment of armed services and the conduct of foreign affairs. The House of Lords essentially feared that should it accept that the crime of aggression had been assimilated into domestic law, this case would then require the court to make a finding on the culpability in going to war either of the government of the United Kingdom or of a foreign government. In finding that the crime of aggression was not automatically incorporated into domestic law, the House of Lords was bound to conclude that the appellants had failed to show that the activity occurring on the military bases was unlawful, and as such the conviction for aggravated trespass was appropriate for this offence. As with those convicted under section 1 of the Criminal Damage Act 1971, the general defence under section 3 of the Criminal Law Act 1967 was unavailable.

In his judgment, Lord Hoffmann (at para. 39) recognized that the war in Iraq had caused deep divisions amongst the people of the United

Kingdom. However, his Lordship went on to equate the protestors' actions as akin to the actions of a sheriff in a lawless Western town, not appropriate within a democratic society with its own appointed law enforcement officers (Jones, per Hoffmann LJ at para. 74). It was felt that to legitimate the use of force where an individual or small group of citizens were dissatisfied with government policy would create a dangerous precedent (Jones, per Hoffmann LJ at para. 82). If successful, the appeal against conviction could have resulted in a judicial enquiry into the war in Iraq and, potentially, the 'war on terror'. Similarly, a successful appeal could have been interpreted as judicial authority for citizens to engage in direct action, potentially even terrorist activities, should the government be accused of an action that is contrary to international law. It is perhaps clear to see why this appeal was moribund from the start. It is of some interest to note that both Jones and Milling have subsequently been convicted of conspiracy to commit criminal damage at Bristol Crown Court on 6 July 2007 (BBC, 2007e). This contrasts with the acquittal of two other protestors, Pritchard and Oldditch, at Bristol Crown Court on 22 May 2007 on the same charges (BBC, 2007a). Both of these cases were trial by jury and as such of no real legal significance, but they do indicate the polarity of attitude to anti-war activists.

Following on from these protests, and as part of the wider campaign against government policy, a large number of demonstrators known as the 'Gloucester Weapons Inspectors' had travelled in three coaches from London to RAF Fairford to take part in a demonstration against the war in Iraq. The protest was designed to occur just a few hours before aircraft were due to take off to conduct military action against Iraq. The demonstrators had informed the police of the planned protest as required by section 11 of the Public Order Act 1986. This requirement of advance notice differs from the requirement for police authorization as seen under section 132 of SOCPA 2005 but was included in the legislation to allow the police time to consult with organizers and to formulate operational arrangements (Card, 2000, p. 212). Despite such consultation, the Chief Constable of the relevant police area does have the power to impose conditions on any protest march and subsequent assembly under ss12 and 14 of the 1986 Act, should he or she believe it necessary to do so.

Several conditions were imposed using this authority. The three coaches from London were stopped at a distance of 5 km from the perimeter of the fence. The coaches and occupants were then searched using authority granted under s60 of the Criminal Justice and Public

Order Act 1994. This was partly a result of the activities of earlier protests, such as the one undertaken by Jones and Milling, and partly due
to intelligence that members of an anarchist group called the WOMBLES
(standing for 'White Overall Movement Building Libertarian Effective
Struggles') were intending to travel with the group and disrupt the
protest.

This search resulted in the seizure by police of items, such as masks
and protective clothing, which potentially could be used to disguise the
identities of protestors. Also recovered were spray paint, scissors and a
smoke bomb. The police were not able to identify the owners of certain
items and one individual was arrested for an incident at a previous
demonstration. The police then directed that the coaches be turned
around and escorted back to London, a journey of some two and a half
hours. The police escorted the coaches on the whole route and did not
allow the coach to stop. Prior to escorting the coach back to London,
the police identified those who intended to speak at the demonstration
and they were allowed to proceed to the airbase, where the demonstration passed off peacefully.

A judicial review was sought of the police actions. In stopping the
vehicle, the police had taken action short of arrest. They did not draw
on any statutory provisions for this, instead relying on broadly defined
common law authorities such as *Albert* v. *Levin* [1982] AC 546, which
accepted that a police officer can take reasonable steps to restrain an
imminent breach of the peace. In light of this, the Court of Appeal in
R(on the application of Laporte) v. *Chief Constable of Gloucestershire* [2004]
EWCA Civ 1639 held that the police had acted lawfully in preventing
the passengers reaching the airfield where they had apprehended a
breach of the peace. They did find, however, as the breach was no longer
imminent, that the police had acted unlawfully by escorting the coaches
back to London.

Although lacking the potential constitutional impact of the *Jones*
case, the subsequent appeal to the House of Lords in *R(on the application
of Laporte) v Chief Constable of Gloucestershire* [2006] UKHL 55 was of no
less legal significance. Indeed, Lord Bingham stated that this case 'raises
important questions on the right of the private citizen to demonstrate
against government policy and the powers of the police to curtail
exercise of that right' (Laporte, per Bingham at para. 1). That the police
action was a direct interference by the state upon the rights of the individual under Articles 10 and 11 of the ECHR was not contested by either
of the parties. The House of Lords, however, found that all of the police
action was unlawful; with Lord Mance describing the police action as

being neither 'reasonable' nor 'proportionate' (Laporte, per Mance at para. 152). Instead, his Lordship found that police action had been 'general and indiscriminate' (Laporte, per Mance at para. 153). The police had not focussed on the potential anarchists who may have sought to disrupt the protest. Instead, by treating everyone as a potential threat to public order, they had interfered with the right to protest of those individuals who had acted lawfully by seeking to take part in a peaceful assembly.

The decision by the court in this case highlights the fact that police power to act to prevent breaches of the peace is now limited. The House of Lords has, in this case, limited the previously broad ambit of the common law powers to prevent and deal with breaches of the peace. It has been noted that the police believed they had sufficient legal powers to deal with any trouble that might have arisen (Davenport, 2007, p. 214). Instead of dealing with those who might have caused the trouble, the police took action that suppressed the entire protest and infringed the Article 10 and 11 rights of the demonstrators. Ironically, the court recognized that it would have been possible for the police to apply for a banning order under section 13 of the Public Order Act 1986, which would have been equally as indiscriminate in suppressing the peaceful protest (Laporte, per Lord Brown at para. 130).

Conclusions

At the start of this chapter two concerns were highlighted. In relation to the 'normalization' of emergency legislation, the decision in *Gillan* showed that random stopping and searching has already started to fall within the legislative mainstream. Legal practitioners, commenting in respect of another, non-terrorism, public order case have voiced concerns about the potential aggregation of pre-existing restrictions on protest with the stop and search powers under section 44 of the Terrorism Act 2000 (Robbins, 2007). In the case of *Austin and another* v. *Metropolitan Police Commissioner*, [2005] EWHC 480 (QB), a case currently subject to an appeal to the Court of Appeal, the High Court found that the police had acted lawfully in detaining protestors in the centre of London for over seven hours during an anti-globalization protest. By means of imposing conditions on the protest using the powers granted to police officers under Part 2 of the Public Order Act 1986, the police had shown that the detention had been necessary and proportionate to prevent the widespread disorder that had accompanied previous May Day celebrations. If this is combined with the power under section 44 of the 2000

Act, the state has placed a formidable array of discretionary powers at the disposal of police officers. There is little to assuage the fear of commentators that such legislation will lead to an enduring state of war denying rights to those accused of offences and the general population. It is fallacious to assume terrorism law exists in a legal bubble; it would perhaps be of less concern if it did. However, *Gillan* shows that the regulation of public order will utilize emergency provisions from the terrorism sphere to interfere with free expression and free assembly. That interference appears to be much easier when the protestors are part of a group agitating for change.

The second area of concern highlighted was the attitude of the judiciary to defending free expression and popular protest. At first sight, the case of *Laporte* does indeed provide 'a rare cause for celebration for civil libertarians' (Robbins, 2007). This judicial activism should perhaps be seen less as a triumph and rather more like a finger in the dyke. It was accepted by all parties that there was sufficient legislation in place for the police to have simply banned the demonstration at Fairford. The assertion made by Lord Hoffmann in *Jones* at paragraph 89 of his judgment, that it is a mark of a civilized community to accommodate protest and civil disobedience, seems somewhat dissonant when balanced against cases such as *Gillan, Haw, Blum* and *Jones*. It is the contention of this chapter that the connection between the two issues raised herein result in an insidious causal nexus. It may be that the 'war on terror' is destined to fulfil the Orwellian prophecy and become a perpetual war. If this is the case, then the longer that war continues, the easier it becomes for the emergency legislation to be accepted by the judiciary as normal tools for the policing of public order generally. Once emergency legal and practical measures are assimilated within the general criminal justice system, and accepted as such by the judiciary at all levels of the court hierarchy, they may prove extremely difficult to oust. Such a chilling effect on protest may not be the hardest hitting legacy of the 'war on terror', but may well prove to be one of the most enduring.

6
National Security, Religious Liberty and Counterterrorism

Ian Leigh

Introduction

On 7 July 2005 (7/7), fifty-two people were killed and around seven hundred injured by four bombs in central London, three of them on London underground trains and a fourth upon a bus. Investigations quickly established that the attacks were not the work of overseas terrorists targeted by the United Kingdom's post-9/11 legislation, but rather of British suicide bombers (Intelligence and Security Committee, 2006; Her Majesty's Government, 2006). On 21 July 2005 a further series of four small explosions on the transport system took place. This time, however, only the detonators exploded. Nevertheless, the attempts resulted in the largest investigation ever conducted by the Metropolitan Police, with four suspects under arrest within eight days. In January 2007, the trial began at Woolwich Crown Court of six defendants on charges of conspiracy to murder and conspiracy to cause explosions arising from the 21 July explosions. Four of the men were found guilty and given life sentences, with minimum terms of forty years (Milmo, 2007).

Since these bombings, preventing the radicalization of young British Muslims has become a major counterterrorism priority. This involves some delicate judgements in implementing policies targeting violent Islamist terrorism; for example, profiling in stop and search by the police, which has the potential to further alienate Muslim communities the more that it is focussed upon them. The whole question has become connected with wider concerns about multi-culturalism. There are signs also of an increasingly sharp conflict within British society between secularism and varieties of conservative religion (which is increasingly and indiscriminately seen as suspect in the post-9/11 climate). This chapter considers the issues raised by a number of the policies, both proposed and those implemented since July 2005, as directly targeted at British Muslims.

It could be argued that the government's counterterrorist response to the Islamic community has swung through a series of phases. Before 9/11 there was recognition of the problem of international Islamic terrorism (including amendments to the definition of terrorism, attempts to extend the law of conspiracy, and the extension of proscription to Islamic groups).

Post-9/11 the approach was ambivalent. On the one hand there was *the intensified use of facially neutral powers* (e.g. stop and search), resulting in the Muslim community feeling discriminated against and controversy over profiling. The second prong of the post-9/11 approach can be called 'balanced targeting', that is, measures addressed specifically at the Muslim community but 'balanced' to make them more presentable or acceptable and to protect the Muslim community from an Islamaphobic backlash. Foremost among these are the new offence of incitement to religious hatred (finally enacted at the third attempt in a much-diluted form in 2006), which was intended to placate moderate Muslims by seemingly giving them equal legal 'protection' to that enjoyed by other religions. Other aspects of balancing are the government's (initially very muted) criticism over Guantánamo Bay and the much-publicized official dialogue with the Muslim community (Home Office, 2005a).

The post-7/7 phase resolves some of the ambivalence of government policy. It is now clear that the official objective is to engage with moderates and therefore to isolate 'extreme' or 'radical' Muslims. The difference is that the government is now prepared, with less concern over balancing, to overtly target radical groups in a way that it was not before in the face of the unmistakeable evidence of a small core of home-grown violent radical Muslims (e.g. BBC News, 2007c). However, the inevitable difficulty is in setting the boundaries for state activity so as not to interfere with legitimate dissent, for example, concerning UK foreign policy or with religious freedom. The issues of young Muslims who attend madrassas in Pakistan (as had the 7/7 bombers), people who visit jihaddist websites, or Islamic bookshops stocking militant literature, or who raise money for the conflicts in Palestine or Chechnya, are all examples of the problem (BBC News, 2006d).

In his now famous 'the rules of the game are changing' speech of 5 August 2005, the then Prime Minister Tony Blair announced a series of proposals impacting on Muslim individuals and communities

(Blick et al., 2006). These included increased use of citizenship and immigration powers,[1] proscription of additional Islamist groups, renewing the effort to deport violent radical Muslims (by entering memoranda of understanding with other states designed to overcome the European Convention obstacles by giving guarantees against torture),[2] proposed new police powers to hold terrorist suspects for up to ninety days before charge, and to close a place of worship used as a centre for 'fomenting extremism', and a new offence of justifying or glorifying terrorism anywhere in the world. Some, but by no means all, of these proposals were included in a draft Terrorism Bill published in September 2005 and enacted as the Terrorism Act 2006.

Among the new offences created by the 2006 Terrorism Act are offences of encouragement (glorification) of terrorism (section 1), relating to bookshops and other disseminators of terrorist publications (section 2), preparation of terrorist acts (section 5), and further terrorist training offences (section 6). The Act also extends the powers of the Secretary of State relating to proscription, to allow for the proscription of groups that glorify terrorism or the activities of which associate them with acts that glorify terrorism, and to deal with proscribed organizations that change their names (sections 21–22). Controversially, it also allows the extension of detention of terrorist suspects (with judicial approval) for up to twenty-eight days (sections 23–24).

This chapter seeks to assess a number of these measures against their impact on human rights – in particular their effect on religious liberty. For that reason the legal context for protection of religious liberty is first explained. Subsequent sections discuss the question of profiling in use of stop and search, the proscription of Islamist groups, legislation and powers concerning the so-called preachers of hate, the proposals for powers to close places of worship and the new offence of glorification of terrorism.

Human rights and religious freedom

Before considering the question of limitation of religious liberty a common objection should be discussed. It is often said that 'Radical' Muslims or fundamentalists (or Wahabbists, etc.) are not representative of 'true' Islam. Islam is tolerant and peace-loving and suicide bombers and those who encourage, praise and defend them are not Muslims: such people put themselves beyond the right of religious liberty. Similar statements have been made repeatedly by political leaders since 9/11 and their implication appears to be that we should therefore be unconcerned about restrictions aimed at people and groups with religious beliefs such as these (e.g. BBC News, 2001).

Whatever the theological merits of this argument about Islam may be, they are irrelevant to the present discussion. It is not for me to adjudicate on what represents true Islam, any more than it is for the Prime Minister, the Home Secretary, or the courts. Transparent shams apart, claims of religious liberty have to be taken at face value in the legal arena and the labels that religious practitioners give themselves have to be treated as authentic self-definitions. Only brief reasons can be given here, but among several reasons for this are the lack of competence of the courts to adjudicate theological disputes, the interference with the autonomy of religious groups of them doing so and – most important of all – that none of various international human rights documents contain limitations on which *beliefs* may be held (Ahdar and Leigh, 2005, chs 4 and 6).

The case in 2005 of the Muslim schoolgirl, Shabina Begum, illustrates the point. The Court of Appeal found that a school acted unlawfully in excluding her because in wearing the jilbab she failed to comply with the school's uniform policy (*R (on the application of SB)* v. *Headteacher and Governors of Denbigh High School* [2005] EWCA Civ 199). Lord Justice Brooke found that the school had failed to consider the girl's right to manifest her religion at all since it had taken a fixed position that in allowing Muslim pupils to wear the shalwar kameeze (a form of dress satisfying less strict moderate Muslim opinion) it had done all that was necessary to accommodate religious feelings (Ibid., paras. 76–8). However, the House of Lords found (by a majority) that, in view of the other choices of school open to Shabina Begum, there was no interference with her right to manifest her religion and, in any event, that if there was, it was justified (*R (on the application of Begum)* v. *Headteacher and Governors of Denbigh High School* [2006] UKHL 15). Despite these differences in approach, the point for our analysis, as all the judges accepted, is that whether *some (other) Muslims* would be able to manifest their beliefs within the school's policy was irrelevant, since Shabina Begum was unable to do so. The issue of religious belief and the practical manifestation of that belief became even more critical in the period after the 7/7 attacks in London.

Every major religion has so-called extreme minorities. But those groups are no less entitled in law to freedom of belief than the majority 'acceptable-to-liberals' face of the religion concerned. Groups and individuals espousing extreme beliefs based on their understanding of the Qu'ran are entitled to have their claims of religious liberty recognized, rather than defined away as not involving religion in the first place.[3] Government rhetoric that denies this is best understood as part of the politics of engagement with moderate Islam and the prevention of radicalisation.[4]

In considering religious freedom, Article 9(1) of the European Convention on Human Rights (ECHR) is of immediate relevance:

> Everyone has the right to freedom of thought, conscience and religion; this right includes the freedom to change his religion or belief and the right either or alone or in community with others and in public or in private to manifest his religion or belief in worship, teaching, practice and observance. (Evans 2001; Martínez-Torrón, 2002)

This Convention right is recognized in English law under the Human Rights Act (HRA) 1998. Under the Act courts are under a duty to interpret legislation 'as far as possible' to give effect to it (section 3) and public authorities (e.g. the Home Office, the police and the Crown Prosecution Service) must act in a way compatible with this right (section 6). Once domestic remedies have been exhausted, individuals also have the right to petition the European Court of Human Rights to complain of violations of Article 9.

Whereas belief *per se* is unlimited under Article 9 (1), the right to manifest one's religious beliefs is qualified. As Article 9 (2) states:

> Freedom to manifest one's religion or beliefs shall be subject only to such limitations as are prescribed by law and are necessary in a democratic society in the interests of public safety, for the protection of public order, health or morals, or for the protection of the rights and the freedoms of others.

Unlike the Articles dealing with the right to respect for private life, freedom of expression, or freedom of association (Arts. 8, 10 and 11), national security is *not* one of the justified grounds of restriction. As Professor Silvio Ferrari has remarked, most human rights treaties and domestic constitutions were not drafted with religiously motivated terrorism in mind and, consequently, contain no provision enabling the limitation of religious liberty on grounds of national security, although in the current climate there is likely to be pressure to change that (Ferrari, 2004, p. 370ff.).

There are some signs from Strasbourg that the European Court of Human Rights (ECtHR) may be tempted to follow the approach criticized above and put radical Islam outside the protection of Article 9 entirely. In the *Refah Partisi* case from Turkey, the Court upheld the banning of a political party whose policy was that the (overwhelming) Muslim majority would be governed by private law founded on religious principles (*Refah Partisi (The Welfare Party)* v. *Turkey* (2003) 37 EHRR 1). The Court found that neither Articles 11 or 9 had been breached: it found that Sha'ria was itself incompatible with the Convention because of divergences 'from Convention values, particularly with regard to its criminal law and criminal procedure, its rules on the legal status of women and the way it intervenes in all spheres of private and public life in accordance with religious precepts' (Ibid., para. 123).

Recently, the House of Lords in *Williamson* (concerned with corporal punishment in independent Christian schools) affirmed Strasbourg case law (see especially *Campbell and Cosans* v. *United Kingdom* (1982) 4 EHRR 293, 304–05) that had set a minimum threshold or filter for belief (religious or philosophical) deserving of protection under the Convention. Lord Nicholls of Birkenhead stated:

> When questions of the 'manifestation' arise…a belief must satisfy some *modest, objective minimum requirements*. These threshold requirements are implicit in Article 9 of the European Convention and comparable guarantees in other human rights instruments. The belief must be consistent with basic standards of human dignity or integrity. Manifestation of a religious belief, for instance, which involved subjecting others to torture or inhuman punishment would not qualify for protection. The belief must relate to matters more than merely trivial. It must possess an adequate degree of seriousness and importance… (*R* v. *Secretary of State for Education and Employment, ex p Williamson* [2005] UKHL 15, para. 23, italics added).

This approach would allow a Muslim group espousing violence to be treated as outside the protection of Article 9 altogether. In the same case, however, Lord Walker admitted to some misgivings:

> …the court is not equipped to weigh the cogency, seriousness and coherence of theological doctrine. … the requirement that an opinion should be worthy of respect in 'democratic society' begs too many questions. (Ibid., para. 60)

It is submitted that Lord Walker is correct and that in fidelity to the text of the Convention even violent beliefs must be treated as within the scope of freedom of religion. The claim of right to *manifest* such beliefs (through teaching, organizing, and so on) may be limited under Article 9 (2) for 'public safety, for the protection of public order, health or morals, or for the protection of the rights and the freedoms of others'. The advantage of this approach is that it allows consideration to be given to the important questions of whether restrictions on rights are 'prescribed by law' and 'are necessary in a democratic society'. The latter standard in particular under Convention jurisprudence imports notions of proportionality, that is, weighing the state objective against the limitation on religious freedom.

Racial/religious profiling and stop and search

The debate about racial profiling that has gone on since 9/11 in North America has a UK parallel. The intensified use of facially neutral powers (e.g. stop and search by the police under sections 44–45 of the Terrorism Act 2000) has resulted in the Muslim community feeling discriminated against. In one respect the powers have been extended in a way that is clearly aimed at the Muslim community: the Anti-Terrorism, Crime and Security Act 2001, passed in response to 9/11, allows (subject to certain conditions) the police to require any person to remove any item which the constable reasonably believes that person is wearing wholly or mainly for the purpose of concealing their identity (ATCSA 2001 s.94 (inserting s.60 AA into the Criminal Justice and Public Order Act 1994)). The Home Office has issued guidance about the use of this power with regard to police instructions to remove Muslim veils (Home Office, 2002).

That amendment apart, it is clear that these powers have been used to a greater extent against Muslims than other members of the community (Liberty, 2004). This was officially acknowledged by Hazel Blears (a junior Home Office minister) in evidence to the Home Affairs Select Committee:

> ... the fact that at the moment the threat is most likely to come from those people associated with an extreme form of Islam, or falsely hiding behind Islam, if you like, in terms of justifying their activities, inevitably means that some of our counter-terrorist powers will be disproportionately experienced by people in the Muslim community. (Home Affairs Select Committee, 2005a)

A survey of approximately half of all police forces by the BBC in October 2005 found significant variations in the use of the stop and search power but that some (e.g. Hampshire and Humberside constabularies) had used the anti-terrorism powers on several thousand occasions in the preceding three months (BBC News, 2005e).

Use of stop and search powers gave rise to a major legal challenge in the case of *R (Gillan)* v. *Commissioner of Police for the Metropolis*[5] in which the House of Lords found that the stopping and searching under the Terrorism Act 2000 of a protester and a journalist in the vicinity of an arms fair in London did not violate their Convention rights. It was note-worthy that the power expressly did *not* require the police officer to have reasonable suspicion of the presence of articles connected with terrorism (section 45(1) Terrorism Act 2000), that the power extended to the whole Metropolitan Police area (all of London in effect) and that, despite procedural safeguards, it had been renewed monthly for more than two years. Nevertheless, their Lordships found that that there was no breach of Articles 5 (the right of liberty) or 8 (right to respect for private life) in detaining and searching in this way: the power was authorized by law and necessary in a democratic society. Reliance was placed on the fact that the applicants had made no attempt to contradict evidence based on intelligence material of the value of such searches, despite an invitation to do so through a closed hearing process.[6]

Although, not directly in issue, in *Gillan*, Lord Brown used the occasion to pronounce on public concerns over racial and religious profiling in the face of evidence that the powers were used substan-tially more frequently to stop and search people of Asian appearance. He concluded that:

> Ethnic origin accordingly can and properly should be taken into account in deciding whether and whom to stop and search provided always that the power is used sensitively and the selection is made for reasons connected with the perceived terrorist threat and not on grounds of racial discrimination.[7]

Moreover, he added:

> ... not merely is such selective use of the power legitimate; it is its *only* legitimate use. To stop and search those regarded as presenting no conceivable threat whatever (particularly when that leaves officers unable to stop those about whom they feel an instinctive unease) would itself constitute an abuse of the power.[8]

Gillan suggests that in the face of an open-ended 'war on terror', the senior judiciary has accepted that minor restrictions on liberty (by comparison, that is, with indefinite detention) do not infringe human rights (BBC News, 2005e). The latest figures reported by the Home Office (for 2005) show, however, that the proportion of people of Asian ethnicity stopped and searched under these powers is in fact declining (Home Office, 2006c, ch. 4).

Proscription

Under the Terrorism Act 2000, groups can be proscribed by the state, that is, designated as terrorist groups. Following these activities such as membership in proscribed groups, or providing financial and other support to proscribed groups are serious criminal offences. Before 9/11 there was a recognition of the problem of international Islamist terrorism. This included amending the definition of terrorism in 2000 to include religiously motivated violence and the extension of proscription to Islamic groups (al-Qaeda was proscribed in February 2001). Of the forty-two international terrorist organizations proscribed in May 2007 some twenty-five were radical Islamic groups whose aims include fighting for the establishment of hard-line Islamic states in Algeria, Bangladesh, Egypt, Lebanon, Libya, Pakistan, Palestine, Somalia, South East Asia, Uzbekistan, and Yemen (Terrorism Act 2000 (Proscribed Organisations) (Amendment) Order 2005). In his 5 August 2005 statement the Prime Minister announced the government's intention to ban a further two Islamic groups the Hizb ut Tahrir ('Party of Liberation') organization and Al-Muhajiroun. Hizb ut Tahrir is a radical organization that aims to establish an Islamic state across the Middle East. It has been banned in a number of Central Asian states and in Germany because of alleged links to terrorism and anti-Semitism (BBC News, 2005c). Al-Muhajiroun, a group founded by Omar Bakri Mohammed, proposed the creation of a Muslim state in Britain. The Prime Minister's statement provoked wide condemnation in the Muslim community and by May 2007 neither group had in fact been proscribed. Al-Muhajiroun has disbanded since 2005, although in July 2006 the Home Secretary announced the proscription of two of its alleged offshoots – Al-Ghurabaa and the Saved Sect (BBC News, 2006c).

Under section 21 of the Terrorism Act 2006 proscription powers have been extended to organizations that 'glorify' terrorism (which includes any form of praise or celebration) by statements of any description, pictures or film or a poster or website, and organizations associated with such 'glorification'. Consequently groups that, for example, commemorate suicide bombers as religious martyrs may find that they are proscribed. Proscription of a group whose purpose appears religious may run the risk of violating Article 9 or Article 11 of the ECHR, dealing respectively with freedom of thought and belief and of association.

There is also a question about whether proscription is fit-for-purpose as a measure against all forms of international terrorism. It was first introduced in Northern Ireland (initially in the 1920s and then under the Prevention of Terrorism (Temporary Provisions) Act 1974). In the context of close-knit single-issue groups espousing political violence, a prohibition on membership makes not just symbolic but also practical sense. It is questionable though whether it can be so effective against looser umbrella 'franchise'-type groups and movements such as al-Qaeda. It is also a measure that can be easily evaded if a group splinters into new groups or merely changes its name. The Terrorism Act attempts to deal with this in section 22 which allows the Secretary of State to also proscribe any organization through which a proscribed organization is operating.

Do measures of this kind comply with the ECHR? The ECtHR has held that the discriminatory denial of legal personality to some religious associations, so that they are unable to litigate unless registered with the state, violates Articles 6 and 14 of the Convention (*Canea Catholic Church* v. *Greece* (1999) 27 EHRR 521). The proscription proposals (which will make it illegal to belong to a proscribed group) involve much more than denial of legal personality. However, as we saw earlier in the *Refah Partisi* case from Turkey, the European Court has taken a weak line on the banning of political groups with a radical Islamic agenda because of inconsistency of Sha'ria law with Convention values. A number of the proscribed organizations have as their objective the introduction by violent means of an Islamic state in various countries, based on Sha'ria law. A challenge from a group that celebrated violent martyrdom would be virtually certain also to meet the same fate under the Convention.

Preachers of hate

The government has taken a variety of measures to combat the spread of violent Islamist teachings because of the clear link (described below) to terrorism. There have also been attempts to strengthen the appeal of more moderate approaches to Islam. Working groups convened by the Home Secretary came forward in September 2005 with proposals for a

National Advisory Council on Imams and Mosques, a forum against extremism and Islamaphobia, and a 'roadshow' of populist speakers to expound 'the concept of Islam in the West' and to condemn extremism (Home Office, 2005c). The initiatives are underwritten with a £5m 'capacity building fund' from the Home Office 'to support all faith communities to play an active role in building a cohesive society'. Accompanying these measures has been recourse to new legislation covering speech. Among those discussed in this section are prosecution for public order offences, use of immigration and deportation powers, proposals to close places of worship, and the new offence of glorification of terrorism.

A number of radical Islamist teachers have been prosecuted for various offences connected with their preaching. Notoriously Abu Hamza was convicted in February 2006 and sentenced to seven years' imprisonment for soliciting murder and inciting *racial* hatred, as well as possessing a 'terrorist encyclopaedia' (BBC News, 2006a). Sheikh Abdullah el-Faisal had been similarly convicted in February 2003 of using threatening words to stir up racial hatred against Jews and Hindus (BBC News, 2003a).

Following 9/11, and faced with mounting evidence of 'Islamaphobia' and a rise in religiously motivated violence, the government proposed the introduction of an offence of incitement to religious hatred. The idea seemed only tenuously related to counter-terrorism – although radical Islamic preachers could certainly have been one target – and more calculated to balance the pressures on the Muslim community and to win over their support for the other anti-terrorist powers.

The offence was intended to placate moderate Muslims by seemingly giving them equal protection to that enjoyed by other religions. The common law offence of blasphemy does not apply to attacks on Islam (*R* v. *Chief Metropolitan Magistrate ex p. Choudhury* [1991] QB 429) and the Public Order Act 1986 offence of incitement to *racial* hatred covers some but not all religious groups: for example, Jews but not Muslims. This is a by-product of the interpretation of the definition of 'racial group' and the fact that Muslims are not a mono-ethnic group. There was widespread concern about the effect on freedom of speech of the proposed offence, and critics argued that ministers were using the opportunity of an international crisis to legislate on matters considerably wider than terrorism. Consequently, the House of Lords vetoed its inclusion in the 2001 anti-terrorism legislation (Ahdar and Leigh, 2005). Following this defeat, however, the proposal came back before Parliament twice: it was rejected in the 2004 Criminal Justice and Public Order Bill, only to be re-introduced after the 2005 election. In a substantially modified form, it became law (limited to threatening speech and with a strong free speech defence) in the Racial and Religious Hatred Act 2006.

Under the Racial and Religious Hatred Act 2006 it is an offence to use words or behaviour or to display written material that are threatening and that are intended to stir up religious hatred. The new offence applies to a range of existing public order offences under the Public Order Act 1986. These cover not only spoken words and behaviour, but also printed words, plays, recordings, and broadcasts and possessing such material with a view to publication and so on.[9] The government had wanted a much wider measure dealing with insulting and abusive words and behaviour merely *likely* to result in religious hatred. Many critics were wholly opposed to the law or concerned about its impact on freedom of speech or of religion. In the House of Lords they succeeded in amending the Bill by inserting a key provision:

> Nothing in this Part shall be read or given effect in a way which prohibits or restricts discussion, criticism or expressions of antipathy, dislike, ridicule, insult or abuse of particular religions or the beliefs or practices of their adherents, or of any other belief system or the beliefs or practices of its adherents, or proselytising or urging adherents of a different religion or belief system to cease practising their religion or belief system. (new section 29J, inserted in the Public Order Act 1986)

The new offence has not yet been brought into force and the Attorney-General has speculated that it may never be, because the restricted terms in which it was enacted mean that it adds little to the existing public order law (Goldsmith, 2007).

What has been the attitude of the ECtHR to offences of incitement to religious hatred? The Court has considered a law of this kind in one case only (*Gündüz* v. *Turkey*, below), although such offences exist in a number of countries. Clues as to its attitude can be gleaned, however, by considering its approach to 'hate speech' more generally. The Court of Human Rights has stated that:

> tolerance and respect for the equal dignity of all human beings constitute the foundations of a democratic, pluralistic society. That being so... it may be considered necessary in certain democratic societies to sanction or even prevent all forms of expression which spread, incite, promote or justify hatred based on intolerance (including religious intolerance), provided that any 'formalities',

'conditions', 'restrictions' or 'penalties' imposed are proportionate to the legitimate aim pursued.[10]

In a number of instances, therefore, applications from people convicted of racial hate speech or holocaust denial have been declared inadmissible.[11] The most fully reasoned decision was, however, the finding of a violation of freedom of expression in the case of a journalist convicted in Denmark in respect of a television documentary containing racist interviews (*Jersild* v. *Denmark* (1994) 19 EHRR 1).[12] The Court noted that the programme was a serious attempt to inform the public rather than to propagate the views of the interviewees. While restrictions on racist speech could be justified under Art. 10.2, here the limitation was not necessary in a democratic society.

Similarly, in the *Gündüz* decision the Court recognized that although expressions that seek to spread, incite or justify hatred based on intolerance, including religious intolerance, do not enjoy the protection afforded by Article 10 of the Convention. However, the Court considered that the mere fact of defending Shar'ia, without calling for violence to establish it, cannot be regarded as 'hate speech'.[13]

It appears, then, that expressions of points of view antithetical to Convention values will be protected under Article 10 depending on the context and provided they do not incite violence or hatred. This draws the line in much the same place as the 2006 Act.

When the religious hatred proposal was under discussion, the Parliamentary Joint Committee on Human Rights concluded that it would probably be compatible with the Convention, even before the Lester Amendment. The Committee drew an analogy with cases in which the European Court has found that laws prohibiting racist 'hate speech' do not violate Article 10, because the restrictions on freedom of expression can be shown to be necessary in a democratic society (citing *Jersild* v. *Denmark* (1994) 19 EHRR 1). It also pointed out that on one occasion the European Court has invoked Article 17 of the Convention (which prevents abuse of rights), declaring an application alleging violation of Art. 10 to be inadmissible because the Convention prevented the use of free speech in a way incompatible with the values of 'tolerance, social peace and non-discrimination' (*Norwood* v. *UK, Appl 23131/03*, ECtHR, 16 November 2004).

In order to qualify to meet this objective the Committee concluded:

> legislation would have to be shown to be clearly aimed at it and proportionate to the goal. The proportionality test in this case should be

a fairly strict one: if restrictions are wider than is reasonably necessary, they could threaten the freedom of public debate and religious expression and undermine the tolerance of other points of view which are essential foundations of our democratic and multi-faith society. (Joint Committee on Human Rights 2004–5, para. 1.128)

It seems likely that these tests are met and that the 2006 Act is Convention-compatible.

Apart from criminal sanctions, other steps taken since 7/7 aimed at 'preachers of hate' include amendments to immigration and deportation policy. The new 'Code of Unacceptable Behaviours' is intended as a public statement of the Home Secretary's policies on his use of 'public good' powers to refuse entry to or deport non-nationals (Home Affairs Select Committee, 2005b). In the words of the Home Office:

> It covers any non-UK citizen whether in the UK or abroad who uses any means or medium, including: writing, producing, publishing or distributing material; public speaking including preaching; running a website; or using a position of responsibility such as teacher, community or youth leader to express views which foment, justify or glorify terrorist violence in furtherance of particular beliefs; seek to provoke others to terrorist acts; foment other serious criminal activity or seek to provoke others to serious criminal acts; or foster hatred which might lead to inter-community violence in the UK. (Home Office, 2005b)

In a linked move the Foreign Office expanded the 'warnings index' of people who might come to the United Kingdom to foment terrorism and who could be prevented from entry under the Home Secretary's powers. The first target of this new approach was the radical preacher Omar Bakri Mohammed. After he left Britain for Lebanon in August 2005, the Home Secretary announced that he would not be allowed back. Control over the entry of imams amounts to a form of state entanglement in religious communities, although the proposed approach is essentially negative (unlike, for example, the Netherlands that employs a system of state licensing).[14]

In light of an earlier case involving denial of entry to the controversial Nation of Islam leader, Louis Farrakhan, it is likely that the courts will be deferential over the use of these powers (*R (Farrakhan)* v. *SSHD* [2002] QB 1391). The Secretary of State's decision in 2001 to prevent Farrakhan from entering the United Kingdom, because of the anticipated effect on racial, religious or ethnic tensions between the Muslim and Jewish communities, was upheld by the Court of Appeal. The court stressed that in law the decision was a personal one for the Home Secretary, that he was better placed than the court to weigh the competing factors, and was democratically accountable for his actions (Ibid., paras. 72–4, *per* Lord Phillips MR). On this basis it is unlikely that a successful challenge could be brought against the use of deportation or refusal of entry powers against radical Islamist preachers.

Powers to close mosques

There has been clear evidence also in some cases of a link between radical teaching in certain mosques and the recruitment of terrorists. The notorious Finsbury Park mosque (the North London Central Mosque Trust) was attended by a number of those who later came to prominence for planning or executing terrorist attacks, including Richard Reid (the 'shoe-bomber') and his associate, Saajid Badat who both appear to have been 'radicalized' by the teaching there (BBC News, 2004a; Bennetto, 2005). For others, such as Zacarias Moussaoui (the so-called twentieth hijacker from 9/11) and Kamel Bourgass (convicted of murdering police officer Stephen Oake during the search of a house for suspected ricin poison), and a group of Islamic extremists convicted in France in March 2005 of plotting to attack the US Embassy in Paris (Rotella, 2005; BBC News, 2005b; 2006b). There is evidence that they fell under the influence of extreme teaching at radical mosques from imams such as Abu Qatada or Abu Hamza.

The difficulties at the Finsbury Park Mosque came about because of the rise to dominance of Abu Hamza (the khateeb) over the trustees of the mosque (BBC News, 2004a). A dispute between him and the trustees resulted in an out-of-court settlement in which his preaching was limited to two out of the regular four Friday sermons and the trustees regained control of the building. The Finsbury Park mosque was searched by police in January 2003, in an operation involving some 150 police officers. Entry was effected at 2 am by battering down the front door of the mosque (*The Guardian*, 2003). Seven people were arrested under the Terrorism Act 2000 and in the search a chemical weapons warfare suit was reportedly found. The police's action in searching the mosque and sealing it off for several days also had the effect of ejecting Abu Hamza and his supporters and returning occupation of the mosque to the trustees, which was promptly closed by them for repairs. Abu Hamza continued to preach to his supporters in the street outside, however (BBC News, 2004a). When the mosque reopened under new leadership in 2005, Hamza's supporters attempted to protest during prayers and some services took place with a heavy police presence to prevent further disruption (BBC News, 2004b, 2005a).

In the meantime the Charity Commissioners had conducted an investigation under the Charities Act 1993 and concluded that Hamza's political activities and use of the building for him and some supporters to live in were inconsistent with the mosque's charitable status. The Commissioners had suspended Hamza from playing a part in the running of the mosque in April 2002, although that order was effectively ignored. In July 2003 the Commission used its powers to remove Hamza from his position because of mismanagement and misconduct in the administration of the trust (Charity Commission, 2003). The Commission concluded that this would not infringe Abu Hamza's rights to practice his religion and to freedom of speech under the ECHR, but if that if it did it was 'a reasonable, proportionate and necessary step to take to secure the proper use or application of the North London Central Mosque Trust's property' and was therefore compatible with the HRA and with convention rights.

This explains the background to a proposal for the police to be able to close places of worship canvassed by the Home Office in October 2005 (Home Office, 2005d). This consultation paper set out proposals for 'requirement orders': a court order to compel those controlling a place of worship (such as the trustees) to 'to take steps to stop certain extremist behaviour occurring in a place of worship'. 'Extremist behaviour' would be 'that which the police reasonably believe amounts to support for a proscribed organization under section 12 of the Terrorism Act 2000, or encouragement of terrorism'. Failing to take reasonable steps to comply with the order would have been an offence. Moreover (and regardless of prosecution) if the activity were still taking place a 'restriction order' might then be made by the court: this could order the temporary closure of parts or all of the premises.

This proposal would certainly have attracted close scrutiny on human rights grounds, not least because of its breadth – it was not confined to mosques, perhaps to avoid suggestions of discrimination. The opportunity to establish and operate a place of worship is a well-recognized aspect of communal religious liberty. Article 6 (a) of the UN Declaration of the Elimination of All Forms of Discrimination states that religious freedom includes the freedom 'to worship or assemble in connection with a religion or belief, and to establish and maintain places for these purposes'. The Supreme Court of Canada recently affirmed that '[g]enerally speaking, the establishment of a place of worship is necessary to the practice of a religion' and is 'an integral part of the freedom of religion' (*Congrégation des témoins de Jéhovah de St-Jérôme-Lafontaine* v. *Lafontaine (Village)*, 2004 SCC 48; (2004) 241 DLR (4th) 83, at para. 73 per LeBel J.). The ECtHR has taken an equally negative view of restrictions. In *Manoussakis* v. *Greece*,[15] the applicants, Jehovah's Witnesses, were prosecuted and convicted for having established a place of worship without obtaining the requisite prior authorizations from the recognized Greek ecclesiastical authorities and the Minister of Education and Religious Affairs. While registration requirements *per se* may not be contrary to the Convention, and licensing (e.g. for planning purposes: *ISKCON* v. *United Kingdom* (1994) 76-A Dec & Rep 90; Application No. 20490/92 (8 March 1994)) may be justified, the Court in *Manoussakis* v. *Greece* concluded that here the state was using the registration provisions 'to restrict the activities of faiths outside the Orthodox church' (para. 48).

This proposal was, however, dropped following consultation and did not find its way into the Terrorism Act 2006. It would be naïve, however, to assume that this signals the end of official interest in radical mosques. If the history of the treatment of 'subversive' groups in the Cold War gives any clues to the *modus operandi* of the Security Service and Special Branches, it can be expected that a number of mosques will be infiltrated either through the recruitment of existing worshippers or through introducing new members. There are clear risks to trust, religious fellowship and confidentiality within these religious communities. Again, however, the record of protection under the Convention is mixed. In an analogous case from Greece, complaints of systematic surveillance by the Greek National Intelligence Service of Jehovah's Witnesses were not treated as a religious liberty issue at all. They were addressed by the majority of the European Commission on Human Rights under Article 8 (the right to respect for private life), six members of the Commission finding that this provision embraced the right to hold and practise religious beliefs (*Tsavachidis* v. *Greece* (1999) 27 EHRR CD27).

Glorification of terrorism

The glorification offence was the government's response to the public disquiet caused by some radical Muslims clerics condoning the 7/7 bombings. Abu Uzair (of the Saved Sect) had reportedly claimed that the bombings were 'magnificent' and Abu Izzadeen (of the al-Ghurabaa group) described the bombers' actions as 'completely praiseworthy' (BBC News, 2005d). These remarks prompted a bizarre excursion into legal history when in, August 2005, the Attorney-General's office confirmed that the Crown Prosecution Service was considering whether prosecutions could be brought for treason. When that proved to be a blind alley attention turned to the creation of a tailor-made offence under the Terrorism Act.[16] The new offence is committed if a person publishes a statement likely to be understood to give direct encouragement or other inducement to other people in the commission, preparation or instigation of acts of terrorism (Terrorism Act 2006, sections 1(1)–(2)). It is enough that the maker of the statement intends or is reckless whether this will be the result. The breadth of the provision is demonstrated by subsection (3):

> ...the statements that are likely to be understood by members of the public as indirectly encouraging the commission or preparation of acts of terrorism or Convention offences include every statement which–
> (a) glorifies the commission or preparation (whether in the past, in the future or generally) of such acts or offences; and
> (b) is a statement from which those members of the public could reasonably be expected to infer that what is being glorified is being glorified as conduct that should be emulated by them in existing circumstances.

Furthermore, it is irrelevant whether the statement relates to any specific act of terrorism or indeed whether anyone else is in fact encouraged or induced (section 1(5)).

Strong reservations were expressed in Parliament over the vagueness and possible chilling effect on free speech of this provision (Joint Committee on Human Rights, 2005–6). Critics (including Cherie Booth, QC) argued that many forms of support for freedom fighters against repressive regimes would become an offence. The wording referring to indirect encouragement produced a sharp conflict between the two Houses of Parliament in which the Commons finally prevailed, although the Lords for its part insisted (amending the government's original proposal) that gross negligence alone would suffice by way of intention.

Conclusion

Professor Silvio Ferrari fears that post-9/11 security concerns 'will legitimize the increasing mistrust of some religious minorities in

Europe' and that they may be abused 'to stop religious practices that have little to do with religiously motivated violence' (Ferrari, 2004, pp. 376–7). Some aspects of recent British experience would seem to bear out those fears: the attempt to use the Anti-Terrorism, Crime and Security Act 2001 to legislate against incitement to religious hatred in general, the government proposal of a power to close places of worship, and the self-conscious promoting by current Minister of Justice Jack Straw of a public debate about the veil,[17] all being clear instances.

In the current British context ministers, of course, repeatedly argue – correctly – that the steps taken or proposed are not an attack on Islam *per se*. As with many other states' attempts in the past to counter home-grown terrorism, nevertheless, the legal measures have to be understood in the wider context of engagement with the community from which political violence emanates. The case has been advanced in this chapter that post-9/11 UK government counterterrorism policy has developed through different phases, at first attempting to placate moderate Muslim opinion by 'balancing' increased legal measures with other pro-Muslim reforms and, since 7/7, by a more sustained attempt to isolate radical Muslim preachers and to support and engage with the more acceptable face of Islam. Whether this broader 'hearts and minds' strategy can ever succeed while UK foreign policy on Iraq and Afghanistan remains a major cause of radicalization of young British Muslims is highly questionable, of course.

Even within the more limited sphere of the legal measures against terrorism, there are three clear risks. First that religious behaviour, expression and association will be restricted more than is necessary or justifiable. Second that necessary measures restricting other civil liberties such as privacy or free speech will have a discriminatory impact on Muslim groups in the way these are enforced. Third, because of the imprecision of terms such as 'glorifying terrorism' and 'unacceptable behaviours' there will be a chilling effect. Moreover, the perception that any of these is occurring may itself further radicalize the Islamic community in the United Kingdom in precisely the way that the government is seeking to avoid.

Notes

1. Extending the powers to remove citizenship to naturalized citizens 'engaged in extremism'; reviewing the threshold requirements for citizenship and establishing in consultation with the Muslim community a Commission on better integration; in consultation with Muslim leaders in respect of those clerics who are not British citizens, to draw up a list of those not suitable to preach who will be excluded from Britain.

2. A strategy that succeeded when the Special Immigration Appeals Commission (SIAC) accepted a memorandum of understanding with Jordan as satisfying Article 3 concerns in proceedings concerned with the deportation of Abu Qatada: *Abu Qatada* v. *Secretary of State for the Home Department* [2007] UK/SIAC 15/2005.
3. The religious motivation of Mohammed Siddique Khan, one of the July 2005 bombers, was clear from a video recorded by him as his will and last testament: see Her Majesty's Government, 2006, para. 39.
4. For example:
   I want to make it clear yet again that this is not in any way whatever aimed at the decent law-abiding Muslim community of Great Britain. We know that this fringe of extremism does not truly represent Islam. We know British Muslims, in general, abhor the actions of the extremists. We acknowledge once again the Muslim contribution to our country and welcome it. (Blair, 2005b)
5. [2006] UKHL 12. See also the chapter by Newman in this volume.
6. See, for instance, Lord Scott's speech at paras. 63–4.
7. Ibid., para. 81.
8. Ibid., para. 92.
9. Section 18 (use of words or behaviour or display of written material); Section 19 (publishing or distributing written material); Section 20 (public performance or play). Section 21 (distributing, showing, or playing a recording); Section 22 (broadcasting or including programme in programme service); Section 23 (possession of inflammatory material).
10. *Gündüz* v. *Turkey* (2005) 41 EHRR 59, para. 40 (holding that the applicant's conviction for inciting religious hatred violated Art. 10).
11. These range from *Glimmerveen and J. Hagenbeek* v. *the Netherlands*, nos. 8348/78 and 8406/78, (DR) 18, p. 187 to *Garaudy* v. *France* (dec.), no. 65831/01, ECHR 2003-IX and *Witsch* v. *Germany*, no. 7485/03, 13 December 2005.
12. And see *Lehideux and Isorno* v. *France* (2000) 30 EHRR 665. Contrast the admissibility decision in *Garaudy* v. *France*, Appl. 65831/01, 24 June 2003.
13. *Gündüz* v. *Turkey* (2005) 41 EHRR 59, para. 51.
14. See de Graaf for an examination of the Netherlands generally.
15. (1996) 23 EHRR 387. See also *Metropolitan Church of Bessarabia* v. *Moldova* (2002) 35 EHRR 13.
16. The Lord Chancellor dampened speculation, however, in a radio interview, making clear that he thought treason prosecutions unlikely: BBC Radio 4, 2005.
17. Straw stated that when they visited his office for advice he asked his Muslim constituents to remove their veils (BBC News, 2006e).

7
The Torture Debate: A Perspective from the United Kingdom

Philip N.S. Rumney

Introduction

Since the events of 11 September 2001 (9/11), the efficacy of torture as an interrogation tool in the 'war on terror' has become a mainstream topic of discussion and debate, involving policymakers, journalists, pressure groups and various disciplines within the Academy. Although much of the academic debate has taken place in the United States (Greenberg, 2005), increasingly attention has been paid to these issues in other countries including the United Kingdom (Evans, 2006; Brecher, 2007) and Australia (Bagaric and Clarke, 2005; O'Rouke, 2005). In the context of the United Kingdom, the attention given to this issue parallels attempts by the government to undermine, by a variety of means, the absolute prohibition against torture, inhuman or degrading treatment contained in the European Convention on Human Rights (ECHR). Some scholars are aghast that the efficacy of torture is being considered. Others predict terrible consequences if torture were legally regulated (Gearty, 2005). However the proponents of a legalized system of coercive interrogation have engaged in a sustained attack on current legal prohibitions and for some, consideration of torture has become a marker for determining issues of personal judgement. Richard Posner, for example, has suggested that anyone who questions the permissibility of torture in any circumstances 'should not be in a position of responsibility' (Posner, 2004, p. 295).

At first sight, there would appear to be little to connect the opposing sides in this debate, other than the topic of their discussion. Personal insults are casually lobbed at opponents, along with allegations of 'intellectual dishonesty' (Bagaric and Clarke, 2006). The proponents of a legalized system of coercion and the critics of this position make competing, and in some instances, irreconcilable claims about such issues as the effectiveness of coercive interrogation and the consequences of its regulation. In the midst of these claims, this chapter aims to draw some conclusions regarding some of the policy, legal and ethical arguments within this debate.

At its best, the torture debate has raised fundamental questions regarding the approach of liberal democracies to the rights of terrorist suspects, the protection of society from terrorist violence and the appropriate response of state institutions to such violence. It has also identified areas of weakness and inconsistency in the case for absolute prohibitions against torture, as well as its regulation. At worst, this debate appears to be guided by an ignorance of both historical and contemporary sources, selective citation and suspect claims. These are matters for all the participants in this debate to be concerned about. Defective scholarship is hardly the foundation for building a case that will convince others. Consequently, this chapter will critically evaluate some of the arguments made by those participating in this debate. Specifically, it will examine the issue of slippage as an argument against the use of coercion and the effectiveness of coercion as an interrogation tool. This will include analysis of the use of coercive interrogation in Northern Ireland in the 1970s.

Torture and the UK government's counterterrorism dilemma

Anthony Lester and Kate Beattie recently argued that the United Kingdom government is attempting to dilute its commitment to Article 3 of the ECHR's absolute prohibition on the infliction of torture and inhuman or degrading treatment (Lester and Beattie, 2005). Human Rights Watch has also accused the government of a 'dangerous ambivalence' towards torture, arguing that 'the British government has severely undermined its own work by chipping away at the international torture ban. It has even begun a direct assault on existing jurisprudence' (Human Rights Watch, 2006). These governmental efforts are the recognition of a dilemma wherein torture is an 'unqualified evil', yet it may also 'yield up information capable of saving lives, perhaps many lives' (*A and others* v. *Secretary of State for the Home Department*, UKHL 71 [2005]: para. 160). This dilemma has been implicitly recognized by Helen Fenwick who has briefly considered the possibility of a judicial reinterpretation of Article 3 to allow for the use of torture in emergencies to save innocent life (Fenwick, 2002, p. 44) and has led some members of the general public to support the use of torture to counter terrorism. An opinion poll run by the BBC World Service in 2006 found that of 27,000 people in 25 countries asked whether they would support 'some torture' to combat terrorism, 59% said 'no' and 29% said 'yes'. The poll found a clear majority of those questioned from the United Kingdom were against the use of torture: 72%, with 24% in favour (BBC, 2006g).

The United Kingdom's response to the threat of terrorism challenges the absolute prohibition in two broad ways. The first is by providing those who allegedly carry out acts of torture in the 'war on terror' with material assistance. It has been claimed, for example, that the UK government has allowed planes used by the US Central Intelligence Agency (CIA) to land at British airports. These planes have been implicated in the CIA's rendition program whereby terrorist suspects are flown to other countries for the purposes of interrogation. It has also been alleged that some of these 'rendered' detainees have been tortured (Committee on International Human Rights, 2004; Amnesty International, 2006a). A recent report of the European Parliament suggests that Prestwick airport in Scotland has been used as a 'stopover' point for aircraft associated with rendition flights (Marty, 2006, para. 43; Joint Committee on Human Rights, 2006d, para. 152) and the House of Commons Foreign Affairs Select Committee has noted the government's reluctance to inquire about the use of British airports by rendition flights (UK Foreign Affairs Committee, 2005, para. 51). It has been claimed that CIA rendition flights have landed at Belfast International airport (BBC News, 2006f) and the government has admitted that such flights have landed at British military airports (Norton-Taylor, 2006). It has also been alleged that British intelligence led to the abduction of at least one UK citizen to Guantánamo Bay as part of the United States' rendition programme (Rose, 2005; Grey, 2006).

The second means by which the absolute prohibition is being challenged is via the legal process. Article 3 of the ECHR has also been subject to two recent court decisions that illustrate government attempts to circumvent the Article 3 prohibition. In *A and others* v. *Secretary of State for the Home Department,* UKHL 71 [2005] the Crown unsuccessfully argued that it should be able to use evidence derived from torture in court proceedings. The second case concerns Article 3 jurisprudence that makes it unlawful for the UK government to deport any person to another country where it is likely that they will face torture or inhuman or degrading treatment (see *Chahal* v. *United Kingdom* [1996] 23 EHRR 413). To circumvent this restriction the UK government has secured what it refers to as 'memoranda of understanding' with certain countries that are known to use torture. These memoranda set out an agreement that any person deported there from the United Kingdom will not face torture on their return. Human rights groups have condemned such diplomatic arrangements as being inadequate to safeguard the rights of those deported and amounting to a breach of national and international law (Human Rights Watch, 2004; Amnesty International, 2006a).

In a recent decision of the Special Immigration Appeals Commission, it was decided that a Jordanian national, Abu Qatada, could be deported to Jordan and that *inter alia* diplomatic assurances could be recognized as valid by the courts and did not breach Article 3 of the ECHR (see *Omar Othman (aka Abu Qatada)* v. *Secretary of State for the Home Department* (2007). In addition to these developments, a newspaper report suggested that former Home Secretary John Reid was considering the introduction of legislation that would remove Article 3 protection from terror suspects in court proceedings where there are 'overriding considerations of national security' (Peppard, 2005; Al-Skeini, 2007; Verkaik, 2007).

While the government is looking for ways to circumvent the absolute prohibition contained in Article 3, since 9/11 it has not gone so far as to suggest that an exception should be created to allow for the coercive interrogation of terrorist suspects within the United Kingdom. The purpose of what follows is to examine the reasoning and use of evidence regarding such an exception. The next section will consider the implications of debating such a controversial topic.

Debating a 'previously undiscussable topic'

Eric Posner and Adrian Vermeule have argued: '[a]mong legal academics, a near consensus has emerged: coercive interrogation must be kept "illegal," but nonetheless permitted in certain circumstances' (Posner and Vermeule, 2005, p. 2; Posner and Vermeule, 2006, p. 673). While earlier criticism of this view can be found (Greenberg, 2005), in the last three years a growing number of scholars have rejected the regulation of torture in any circumstances (Roth, 2005; O'Rourke, 2005). In the United Kingdom the use of illegal coercive interrogation methods has been repeatedly rejected (Hope, 2004; MacMaster, 2004; Gearty, 2005, 2007; Evans, 2006; Kassimeris, 2006; Plaxton, 2006; Walker, 2006b; Spicer, 2007).

A starting point for analysis of this body of work is what should be a core aspect of scholarly endeavour: 'In a liberal intellectual system, the primacy of evidence, reason, and fair argument in pursuing knowledge and free speech in rectifying error is widely accepted' (Hamilton, 1998, p. 3). It would appear that in a number of aspects the torture debate departs from this standard.

First the suggestion by some scholars that torture is an illegitimate topic for discussion must be challenged. George Kassimeris claims: '[a]t the start of the twenty-first century we should not be debating the use of torture' (Kassimeris, 2006, p. 14) and Robert Spicer states: '[t]here is not, and should not be, any such debate' (Spicer, 2007, p. 1761). It has also been suggested that until recently the use of torture was 'undiscussable' (O'Rourke, 2005, p. 86). Yet, such a claim lacks historical awareness. The use of torture as an intelligence-gathering technique has for decades been considered by state officials and policy makers in many democracies, including: France (Vidal-Naquet, 1963, pp. 169–79; Horne, 2006, p. 197), Israel (Commission of Inquiry, 1987), the United States (McCoy, 2006) and the United Kingdom (Parker Committee, 1972; McGuffin, 1974; Taylor, 1980). Rather than seeing the use of torture as 'undiscussable', one of the few UK-based academics to consider this specific issue has argued that:

> It is a lack of debate which would be more worrisome since this would threaten to condemn the prohibition to obscurity. The idea that serious discussion of the legal questions surrounding the realisation of the absolute prohibition of torture as a matter of international law somehow has the effect of weakening the normative force of that prohibition is difficult to fathom. (Evans, 2006, p. 105)

Indeed, not engaging in the torture debate leaves the arguments of the proponents of a legalized system of coercive interrogation unchallenged. In addition, those who refuse to debate do not suffer the inconvenience of having their own assumptions and ideas challenged. Stanley Fish emphasizes this particular point when he warns of the 'attractions of premature judgment' and suggests that: '[The individual] must be protected from his own tendency to assume that the opinions he holds now are the right ones' (Fish, 2001, p. 85). Whether people need to be 'protected' from this tendency is open to question, but scholars need to be aware of the dangers of assuming their opinions are the correct ones. The scholarly resistance to the questioning of 'correct' ideas in effect assumes that the reasoning that underlies the absolute prohibition against torture requires no intellectual defence and that arguments in its favour are all of equal persuasiveness, supported by compelling evidence and rational argument. As will be seen in later sections, this is not always the case – precisely why scholarly analysis of this and other counterterrorism policies is essential.

As argued by Oliver Wendell Holmes, free speech is important so as to allow for the 'correction' of weak ideas (White, 1992, p. 440; Menand, 2001, p. 431). Failure to debate may therefore result in scholars avoiding any consideration of the weaknesses inherent within their own arguments. Through discussion and analysis, the case for an absolute prohibition on torture might well be strengthened. By contrast, what is implicit within the argument that torture should never be discussed is that those who want to retain the absolute prohibition have little confidence that their arguments will persuade others. The reality is that in a 'liberal intellectual system' the discussion and exchange of ideas is essential to testing their resilience (Rumney and O'Boyle, 2007, 2008). Bagaric and Clarke provide a good example of how intellectual exchange can lead to the revision of an argument. Their initial claim that torture was an 'excellent' means of intelligence gathering was subjected to detailed analysis and they have subsequently brought their view on this issue more into line with the literature by arguing that torture 'sometimes' works (Bagaric and Clarke, 2005, p. 588, 2006, p. 719).

The second troubling aspect of this debate is the way in which it is seen as an opportunity to expound a wider agenda and personalize issues. For some critics, the torture debate is an opportunity to condemn US society in general. Neil MacMaster, reflecting on support for torture by some American liberals, argues: 'That liberals and civil libertarians could go down such a road is symptomatic of the depth of the moral rot that has set into American society' (MacMaster, 2004, p. 4). In a recent article, Simon Cottee points to the way in which some on the Left have used the 9/11 attacks 'as a pretext for clarifying the depravity and exorbitance not of those who carried it out, but of the American Empire' (Cottee, 2006, p. 152). There is something equally objectionable in the way in which MacMaster takes the views of *some* American liberals and civil libertarians as reason not only to attack American policy, but American society in general. Likewise, the adopted tone of some of those who defend current practices by US agencies in the 'war on terror' is one of inaccurate generalization, rather than any serious attempt to deal with the substantive objections to current policy (e.g. MacDonald, 2005, pp. 95–6).

The tone of this debate has also clearly suffered due to the personalization of issues. Joshua Dratel, when discussing policymakers who favour the use of coercive interrogation, states: 'they should be compelled to watch the application of "aggressive interrogation" techniques or "counter resistance" measures on a human subject, or, better yet, perform such techniques themselves – or, even better still, be subjected to them' (Dratel, 2005, p. 116; Gearty, 2005a), an observation which gets the debate nowhere. Personalization is often accompanied by wholly inappropriate and unnecessary comparisons, as when Slavoj Žižek argues that Alan Dershowitz's style of argumentation in favour of a legalized system of torture is akin to the arguments used at the Wannsee conference in which senior Nazis planned the Final Solution (Žižek, 2002, pp. 105–6).

Analysis of two key issues in the torture debate

Since 9/11, the debate over the use of coercive interrogation has covered much ground in terms of the practical, ethical and philosophical justifications and objections to its use. Given the breadth of this debate it is not possible here to engage with all these arguments. Rather, this section will highlight some of the recurrent issues that arise in the torture debate, drawing on a range of historical, scientific and legal sources.

The problem of slippage

One of the main arguments cited against the regulation of torture is that its use cannot be adequately controlled within a legal framework (O'Rourke, 2005). Posner and Vermeule observe that: '[s]lippery slope arguments identify a possible unintended negative consequence of a particular policy; if this consequence is likely enough, then it ought to count as a cost in the cost-benefit calculus used to evaluate the rule' (Posner and Vermeule, 2007, p. 200). It is clear, however, that some of the leading proponents of a legalized system of coercive interrogation deny that 'unintended negative consequences' are a problem. Bagaric and Clarke claim that 'there is no evidence to suggest that the lawful violation of fundamental human interests will necessarily lead to a violation of fundamental rights where the pre-conditions for the activity are clearly delineated and controlled' (Bagaric and Clarke, 2005, pp. 615–16). Likewise, Posner and Vermeule argue that there is no evidence that the use of coercion leads to a 'culture of torture' and the 'purposes for which officials use coercion will expand' to *inter alia* 'extracting confessions from suspects in routine criminal cases' (Posner and Vermeule, 2007, p. 200). They appear to define slippage primarily in the context of coercion being used for 'purposes' other than intelligence gathering. This is a very narrow definition of slippage. There are other forms of slippage, where, for example, interrogators circumvent rules that are designed to regulate their conduct or where coercion is used against people who are believed to be terrorists, but who are, in fact, innocent.

The problem of 'unintended negative consequences', where officials circumvent the rules governing coercive interrogation, has a long history and is well recognized within the literature (Roper, 2006, pp. 65–6). More recent examples of this type of 'rule breaking' slippage include the operation of coercive interrogation in Israel (Rumney, 2006, pp. 502–4), Northern Ireland (Taylor, 1980) and some of the recent interrogations taking place in Iraq and Afghanistan (Rumney, 2006, pp. 504–5).

The 'unintended negative consequence' of wrongly targeting people as terrorists in the 'war on terror' is also in evidence. Recent research suggests that the factual basis for the continued detention of many Guantánamo detainees appears weak (Denbeaux and Denbeaux, 2006a, pp. 5–6, 2006b). For example, the US government defines someone as being 'associated with al-Qaeda' as applying to 'anyone who the Government believed ever spoke to an al-Qaeda member. Even under this broad framework, the Government concluded that a full 60% of the detainees do not have even that minimum level of contact with an al Qaeda member' (Denbeaux and Denbeaux, 2006a, p. 9). These findings have been supported by analysis of 132 prisoner files, along with a review of 'heavily censored' Combatant Status Review Tribunals transcripts for 314 Guantánamo detainees. Corine Hegland found that:

> Many of them are not accused of hostilities against the United States or its allies. Most, when captured, were innocent of any terrorist activity, were Taliban foot soldiers at worst, and were often far less than that. And some, perhaps many, are guilty only of being foreigners in Afghanistan or Pakistan at the wrong time. And much of the evidence – even the classified evidence – gathered by the Defense Department against these men is flimsy, second-, third-, fourth- or 12th hand. It's based largely on admissions by the detainees themselves or on coerced, or worse, interrogations of their fellow inmates, some of whom have been proved to be liars. (Hegland, 2006)

There is also evidence that some of those who have been 'rendered' from US custody to other countries for questioning, detained for long periods and allegedly tortured, have in fact been innocent of terrorist activity (Preist, 2005; Risen, 2006, pp. 34–5), a particularly serious problem given that those rendered to third countries are supposed to be terrorists known to and specifically targeted by intelligence services, who one would assume should be readily identifiable.

In judging the issue of slippage, it is also worth examining some of the specific examples used by participants in the torture debate. Posner and Vermeule reject the slippery slope argument, claiming *inter alia* that:

> In the context of torture, there have been many examples of Western countries adopting coercive interrogation and similar aggressive practices as temporary measures to deal with a particular emergency – France in Algeria, Britain against the Irish Republican Army – and then abandoning them when the emergency is over. (Posner and Vermeule, 2007, p. 202)

However, there is evidence of slippage in Algeria and Northern Ireland. In Algeria it has been claimed that torture took place well before the so-called Battle of Algiers, where in 1957 French authorities responded to an upsurge in terrorist violence. This is presumably the emergency to which Posner and Vermeule refer (Vidal-Naquet, 1963, pp. 30–1; Horne, 2006, pp. 197–8). In addition, the use of torture was accompanied by the killing of many detainees by the police and army (Vidal-Naquet, 1963, ch. 6 and p. 137). Indeed, it is claimed that murder was used to silence detainees who complained of torture and that: 'Children were known to have been murdered because their brothers or fathers had laid a complaint of torture' (Vidal-Naquet, 1963, p. 77). McCoy states that 'the systematic French torture of thousands from the Casbah of Algiers in 1957 also entailed over three thousand "summary executions" as "an inseparable part" of this campaign, largely, as one French general put it, to insure that "the machine of justice" not be "clogged with cases" and free terror suspects to launch other attacks' (McCoy, 2006, pp. 195–6). There are also allegations that some of those who were tortured had no link to terrorism, but were seen as a danger to French rule in Algeria for other reasons. For example, it is claimed that a young Muslim, Saadia Mebarek, was arrested and then tortured to death by members of the French army. She had allegedly encouraged Algerians not to take part in local elections (Vidal-Naquet, 1963, pp. 130–1).

The Algerian example has also been cited by one critic who suggests another form of slippage. Kassimeris states: 'Numerous recent studies on the Algerian war show that French violence in Algeria was designed to terrify, subdue and exhibit power rather than to extract information' (Kassimeris, 2006, p. 15). If true, then this is slippage in terms of the motives behind the use of torture. There can be little doubt that the French used brutal methods in suppressing terrorist violence. However, from one of the sources that Kassimeris cites, it is clear that torture was used for the purpose of intelligence gathering. When discussing the 'Battle of Algiers', Wall states: 'the elite paratroops under General Massu, who entered the Casbah, routinely applied torture in order to break the terrorist infrastructure' (Wall, 2001, p. 68). Other scholars come to a similar conclusion (Horne, 2006, pp. 204–5), along with some prominent victims of the French use of torture (Alleg, 1958). Thus, contrary to Kassimeris's assertion, torture was used to gather intelligence to fight terrorism. It may not have been the only motivation for its use, and indeed, its role in the French victory is in dispute (Rumney, 2006, pp. 498–500), but it cannot be doubted that torture was used for the purpose of intelligence gathering.

In Northern Ireland in the early 1970s the use of 'interrogation in depth' by British authorities involved the use of five 'disorientation' techniques: wall standing, hooding; subjection to noise; sleep deprivation; and deprivation of food and drink (see *Ireland* v. *United Kingdom* [1978] 2 EHRR 25: para. 96). These interrogations appear to have been governed by the *Joint Directive on Military Interrogation in Internal Security Operations Overseas*, 17 February 1965 (as amended 10 February 1967) which prohibited physical coercion, torture, along with humiliating and degrading treatment. While the Directive made some implied reference to sleep deprivation ('disruption of the normal routine of living'), it did not specifically prohibit any of the five techniques (Compton Committee, 1971) and there were repeated allegations that interrogators went beyond the techniques permitted as part of 'interrogation in depth'. A subsequent report found that many of these allegations could not be substantiated (Compton Committee, 1971, ch. 8). However, this report was very limited in that it only involved investigation of abuse on *one* single day. In addition, there is a problem with Posner and Vermeule's claim regarding the official abandonment of coercive methods. Even after the 'five techniques' were officially withdrawn in March 1972 (*Ireland* v. *UK*, 1978, para. 101), allegations of physical coercion and the use of techniques such as sleep deprivation continued (Taylor; 1980). The significance of these findings is not that they are based solely on the allegations of detainees, whom, it is acknowledged, at times gave entirely false or exaggerated accounts of brutal treatment (Bennett Committee, 1979, ch. 8; Taylor, 1980, p. 11).

Rather, the compelling evidence comes from doctors in the interrogation centres who examined the detainees. This medical evidence strongly suggests that some detainees were beaten with fists, burnt with cigarettes, slapped and choked. Some detainees were allegedly subjected to the officially withdrawn 'five techniques', while others suffered a range of injuries including, cuts, bruising, broken bones, perforated eardrums and concussion (Parker Committee, 1972, paras 27–42; Taylor, 1980). These findings are supported by an official government report published in 1979 which concluded, on the basis of medical evidence, that some injuries suffered by detainees 'were not self-inflicted and were sustained during the period of detention at a police office' (Bennett Report, 1979, para. 163). In other words, some coercive methods continued to be used long after they were officially withdrawn and violence was also a continuing feature of interrogations. Taylor also notes that the police and army were subject to rules on the conduct of interrogations, but '[t]hey made little difference' (Taylor, 1980, pp. 26–8).

The relevance of slippage to this debate is that it counts 'as a cost in the cost-benefit calculus' (Posner and Vermeule, 2007, p. 200). Because they define slippage so narrowly and deny that it is a problem, the proponents ignore the reasons underlying the existence of 'unintended negative consequences'. Slippage can result from poor training and ill discipline (Human Rights Watch, 2005), error (Priest, 2005; Risen, 2006), failures by superiors or the legal process to control or prevent rule breaking (Vidal-Naquet, 1963, chs 5 and 8; Taylor, 1980; Schmitt and C. Marshall, 2006; Shamsi, 2006) and crucially, slippage can occur because of the pressures on state officials to gather intelligence during times of emergency (Mackey, 2004; Schmitt and Marshall, 2006; Goldsmith, 2007, ch. 5). Many of the proponents of a legalized system of torture argue that it should only be used in cases involving the 'ticking bomb' scenario, which may help to limit some of these pressures. However, if absolute legal prohibitions on the use of coercion do not prevent abuse, it is difficult to see how a system of regulation is going to restrain desperate state officials who wish to save innocent life: mistakes or excesses are highly likely.

On the other hand, we cannot assume that the types of slippage discussed here will occur, or to the same extent, in all situations where coercive interrogation is used. There are clearly variations in how such systems might operate. For example, the regulatory system suggested by some proponents of a legalized system of coercive interrogation, such as Alan Dershowitz (2002), are different from the way in which individuals have been linked to al-Qaeda at Guantánamo Bay. Likewise, while interrogations in Northern Ireland in the 1970s were subject to general rules against abuse, there was no system whereby specific techniques had to be legally authorized on an individual basis (Compton Report, 1971; Parker Report, 1972; Bennett Report, 1979). However, the proponents still need to give serious consideration to this evidence in order that their proposals reduce the risk of slippage. Simply denying that such a problem exists is not helpful in formulating an appropriate system of safeguards.

The question of effectiveness

The question of effectiveness is clearly a key issue in the torture debate. While some commentators claim that we cannot know whether coercive interrogation works in gaining access to timely, reliable information (Levinson, 2004); increasing efforts are being made to examine this specific issue (Bell, 2005; Rumney, 2005, 2006). Within the torture debate, views as to the effectiveness (or otherwise) of coercion are often stated in confident language. George Kassimeris claims 'torture does not actually work: prisoners treated like those in Abu Ghraib will confess to anything' (Kassimeris, 2006, p. 14). Likewise, Harold Koh has stated: 'To be sure, there is abundant evidence that torture is not effective either as an interrogation tactic or an information-extracting device' (Koh, 2005, p. 653). Michael Plaxton notes: 'Whatever one thinks of torture, one cannot seriously dispute its utility. Coerced confessions do not possess a high degree of reliability – commentators have, at least since ancient Greece, remarked upon the manifest unreliability of admissions gleaned through torture' (Plaxton, 2006, p. 206). On the other side of the argument, Bagaric and Clarke have claimed that torture is 'an excellent means of gathering information' (Bagaric and Clarke, 2005, p. 588). Richard Posner claims that 'torture *is* often an effective method of eliciting true information, which is also the common sense of the situation ...' (Posner, 2006, p. 81) (emphasis in original) and others claim that torture 'sometimes' works as an intelligence-gathering tool (Dershowitz, 2002, p. 137).

In judging these various claims one has to consider a wide body of evidence to discover whether there are any recurrent patterns running through the literature. In such an analysis one has also to take account of sources of information, verification and the distinct possibility that in some cases the information released may be self-serving and inaccurate (Rumney, 2006, p. 499). In addition, in the 'war on terror' there is increasing evidence that the value of intelligence gained from coercive methods in some prominent cases has been exaggerated

(Froomkin, 2007). While some of the examples of successful coercion to be found in the literature are impossible to verify, it would be foolish and indeed contrary to more convincing evidence to suggest that we cannot make any determination. It may also be the case that some techniques are more productive than others, though this is often difficult to discern. Clearly, there are circumstances when coercion does work to produce reliable and timely results and indeed, there are ongoing claims that in Iraq, for example, the beating of detainees has led to significant disclosures of intelligence concerning insurgents (Rubin, 2007).

It is also crucial that we judge effectiveness by some criteria. Given the influence of the 'ticking bomb' hypothetical on this debate, it would appear that any intelligence gained from the use of coercion would need to be reliable *and* timely. If intelligence gathered by coercion fails to meet either of these measures, it might still be of some use, but in the context of the 'ticking bomb' hypothetical, it has probably failed. Another aspect of the question of effectiveness is whether torture is as effective as other methods of intelligence gathering. In the context of coercive interrogation in Northern Ireland it has been suggested that other methods might have been equally, or more effective (Rumney and O'Boyle, 2007, p. 1567). The trouble with such arguments, however, is that they are not relevant to situations where other methods have been tried, time is of the essence, and coercion is the last remaining option for interrogators.

The Northern Ireland experience also gives an indication of some of the complexities that exist in judging effectiveness. The Parker Committee considered the use of 'interrogation in depth' in Northern Ireland and the majority report concluded that the coercive techniques used against fourteen terrorist suspects had yielded very significant intelligence gains, including the identification of '700 members of both [Irish Republican Army] factions' who were responsible for '85 incidents on police files' and that the seizure of arms, ammunitions and explosives 'increased markedly' after 9 August (which is when the use of 'interrogation in depth' officially began) and 'resulted either directly or indirectly from information obtained by interrogation in depth' (Parker Committee, 1972, paras 20–1). The majority report was unequivocal that coercion did result in crucial disclosures: 'There is no doubt that the information obtained by [interrogation in depth] directly and indirectly was responsible for the saving of lives of innocent citizens' (Parker Committee, 1972, para. 24). The majority also noted that interrogation 'sometimes had the effect of establishing the innocence of both other wanted people and of the detainee himself' and that incorrect information was given 'in a few cases' (Parker Committee, 1972, paras 18, 22). However the minority report, while acknowledging that a 'considerable quantity of intelligence information was obtained' (Parker Committee, 1972, para. 14) did raise several important qualifications. One of these was that after 9 August 'there was a sudden and considerable increase in the number of people arrested and questioned so that a dramatic increase in intelligence information was in any case to be expected.' Taylor also notes: 'There was a limit to how many rounds of ammunition, pounds of explosives and piles of weapons fourteen men could reveal, especially when some had only the slightest IRA connections. But the "guinea pigs" were only fourteen of the 3,000 suspects interrogated by the RUC in the year that followed internment' (Taylor, 1980, pp. 20–1). Other questions remain unanswered. The intelligence leading to the seizure of arms and explosives is clearly significant, but it is less clear whether the disclosures relating to hundreds of people identified as belonging to the IRA, or the '85 incidents' were ever actually verified as being true. Having said that, these findings are significant and suggest 'interrogation in depth' did assist in gaining valuable intelligence, although it is impossible to judge the issue of effectiveness of these measures with any degree of precision.

It has been argued that the value of intelligence gathered by illegal interrogation methods in Northern Ireland was exaggerated (Parker, 2005, p. 123). John McGuffin, in *The Guineapigs*, describes both the Parker Committee's majority and minority report claim that interrogation 'in depth' saved lives as 'grotesque and ludicrous' and that it was 'not so' that detainees 'cracked' and disclosed 'valuable information' (McGuffin, 1974, pp. 106–7). However, as a point of contradiction, he admits that the use of coercive methods or their threatened use resulted in some of the detainees cracking 'hence the rise in the arrest figures and arms hauls' (McGuffin, 1974, pp. 107–8).

There are a number of inherent uncertainties in any assessment of the effectiveness of the coercive methods used in Northern Ireland. Commenting on a period long after the formal withdrawal of interrogation in depth, but when allegations of abuse during interrogations continued, Taylor notes: 'By the summer of 1977, the Provisionals were in a desperate position. Castlereagh [interrogation centre] was beginning to destroy their organization...The organization was vulnerable to infiltration and provided ready fodder for Castlereagh' (Taylor, 1980, pp. 20–1). In judging the effectiveness of coercive methods, whether they were the 'five techniques', physical violence or the infliction of injury, one can only speculate as to how much other intelligence-gathering methods such as infiltration also contributed to the pressure on the IRA described by Taylor. Yet, in making an assessment of relative effectiveness, such comparative data are essential. Further, there are some questions that can probably never be authoritatively answered. In questioning the efficacy of coercive methods some have noted that during the time interrogation in depth was used, acts of terrorist violence in Northern Ireland actually increased (Parker, 2005, p. 123; Rumney, 2006, p. 500). The problem, however, is that this is not necessarily an accurate measure of efficacy for the simple reason that we do not know what would have happened without the use of coercive methods. Indeed, if the increase in violence is evidence of failure, then it is also a failure for traditional policing methods that were being used.

Posner and Vermeule raise the issue of whether coercion 'works' in the sense of producing 'information that prevents harms, in a non-trivial range of cases' (Posner and Vermeule, 2007, p. 195). They cite examples from Israel of the successful use of coercion in thwarting terrorist attacks. They also lend support to their claim that torture 'works' by arguing 'it is hard to believe that many governments would use it if it were really ineffective' (Posner and Vermeule, 2007, p. 197). Similarly, Bagaric and Clarke also suggest: 'If the considered view of the CIA was that torture was not effective in most cases, it seems incredulous that President Bush and Vice President Cheney would have so vigorously lobbied Congress to exempt the CIA from legislation ... that bans "cruel, inhuman and degrading treatment of prisoners in the detention of the US Government" and allows the CIA to torture suspects where it is necessary to prevent a terrorist attack' (Bagaric and Clarke, 2006, p. 718). This is a curious point. Although there can be little doubt that coercion sometimes works, Bagaric and Clarke appear to be projecting their own view on the Bush Administration by suggesting that lobbying is evidence that it works 'in most cases'. This is a claim for which they provide absolutely no evidence. In a recent newspaper article Bagaric has also claimed: 'George Bush and Vice-President Dick Cheney are well versed on the effectiveness of various interrogation techniques' (Bagaric, 2007).

The problem with such statements is that they draw specific inferences from behaviour. A significant amount of the torture that goes on in the world exists as a means to instil fear, to persecute and oppress. Although torture may work as a tool of oppression, that has nothing to do with its utility as a tool for reliable and timely intelligence gathering. However, as a matter of official policy, the United States is not using coercion as a tool of oppression, but that does not mean that the decision-making process that led to its use is informed by a consideration of evidence. Decisions are sometimes driven by fear and the need to act. In the context of coercive interrogation, decisions may be made in the hope that they might produce some positive result. Indeed, there is evidence that the Bush Administration's use of 'extraordinary rendition' in the wake of 9/11 was not the result of detailed analysis of evidence or debate. Bob Woodward quotes President Bush two days after 9/11, in a conversation with Prince Bandar of Saudi Arabia, thus: 'If we get somebody and we can't get them to cooperate, we'll hand them over to you' (Woodward, 2006, p. 80).

On one level one can entirely understand the temptations of such a response. On 9/11 the United States had been the victim of a horrific attack and it was unlikely that it would be the last unless the Administration took preventative measures (National Commission on Terrorist Attacks upon the United States, 2004, chs 4, 5, 6). President Bush and his advisors would have realized quickly that there was a need for intelligence to prevent further attacks. The use of rendition, which actually began under the Clinton Administration, was undoubtedly motivated by the wish to obtain intelligence. In circumstances of high stress and with the need to take steps to prevent further attacks the decision to use coercive methods, on that level, is not difficult to fathom. But such decisions cannot be equated with evidence that torture works 'in most cases'. McCoy explains the decision to use torture thus: 'the powerful often turn to torture in times of crisis, not because it works but because it salves their fears and insecurities with the psychic balm of empowerment' (McCoy, 2006, p. 207). Likewise, Ackerman agues that: 'Security services can panic in the face of horrific tragedy. With officials in disarray, with rumours of impending attacks flying about, and with an outraged public demanding instant results, there will be overwhelming temptations to use indecent forms of interrogation. This is the last place to expect carefully nuanced responses' (Ackerman, 2006, pp. 108–9).

Dratel claims that the Bush Administration, prior to its decision to employ coercion as an interrogation tactic, did not provide any 'evidence that would justify the conclusion that torture would produce more, and more accurate, information more promptly than would ordinary methods of interrogation' (Greenberg, 2005, p. 112), although as Suskind notes, there were 'months of interdepartmental exchanges over the detainment, interrogation, and prosecution of captives in the "war on terror"' (Suskind, 2006, p. 111). Dratel also claims that there is a consensus amongst intelligence, military and intelligence investigators that the intelligence coming from Guantánamo 'has been minimal and of little value' and that the Administration has 'not provided a single piece of information gleaned from Guantánamo Bay detainees' (Greenberg, 2005, p. 114). These respective claims need to be disentangled. It would certainly appear to be the case that many of the released documents and memoirs that detail the decision making of the Bush Administration do not appear to consider the effectiveness of coercion as an interrogation technique (Greenberg and Dratel, 2005; Yoo, 2006). Some military personnel have also claimed that the Bush Administration has exaggerated the importance of the Guantánamo intelligence (Bright, 2004; Saar and Novak, 2005). However, the Bush Administration has released details of specific intelligence disclosures from Guantánamo. For example, the Department of Defense has released information regarding disclosures made under interrogation by Mohamed al Kahtani who, it is claimed, was one of the 9/11 conspirators (US Department of Defense, 2005a). In addition, the US government also provided more general information arising from disclosures made at Guantánamo in 'more than 4,000 reports [that] capture information provided by...detainees' (US Department of Defense, 2005b). Disclosures have included information about terrorist financing, the identity of al-Qaeda operatives at large, explosives trainers, details of bomb-making and the training of operatives. The report claims that 'much' of the information disclosed is 'corroborated by other intelligence reporting'. Assuming this assessment is accurate, it is worth noting that one cannot assume that these disclosures indicate that coercion 'works', or indeed, does not, because it is impossible to know how many disclosures resulted from the use of coercive methods. It is evident from the testimony of people who have worked at Guantánamo that interrogation methods vary significantly (Saar and Novak, 2005).

To support their arguments that torture works as an intelligence-gathering tool, Bagaric and Clarke attempt to distinguish examples of ineffectual coercion from their own proposal:

> Torture for life saving purposes is far removed from many of the instances of the barbaric, punitive forms of torture mentioned by the critics ... There is no relevant evidence that torture cannot work in the circumstances we outline. The 'evidence' to the contrary that is proffered by the critics has been overstated in terms of its relevance to our proposal. (Bagaric and Clarke, 2006, pp. 707–8)

It is not at all clear why evidence of false confessions, inaccurate or delayed disclosure where coercion has been used in other contexts should not be relevant to their proposal (Rumney, 2006). It is not the legal framework in which coercion occurs that determines effectiveness, but human psychology and myriad other factors. If, however, Bagaric and Clarke are correct, it is hardly surprising that there is a lack of evidence, given that they argue that their proposal is 'far removed' from previous uses of torture (Bagaric and Clarke, 2006, p. 707). They also refer to the debate over effectiveness as potentially 'degenerating into a distracting and superficial numbers game' and appear to criticize this author for discussing the 'reasons why torture is supposedly unlikely to work' (Bagaric and Clarke, 2006, pp. 719–20). However, such an analysis has nothing to do with a 'numbers game'. Rather, it should be part of any consideration of problems associated with coercion, as well as potential benefits, surely an essential intellectual process when considering the regulation of coercive interrogation. This is also crucial because Bagaric and Clarke appear to rely on assumptions about human psychology to support their argument that torture has utility. For example, they state: 'we know as a fact that humans dislike pain and will try to avoid it' (Bagaric and Clarke, 2006, p. 720). Yet, the CIA's own interrogation manuals, as well as more recent analysis of these manuals, warn against such simplistic and unscientific reasoning. Indeed, in a recent story in the *New York Times*, specialists with the United States' Intelligence Science Board, described the 'harsh techniques used since the 2001 terrorist attacks [as] outmoded, amateurish and unreliable' (Shane and M. Mazzetti, 2007).

Bagaric and Clarke's analysis of evidence is also open to question, not least because of their failure to consider counter-evidence. In a response to some of their critics, they use an article published in *The Spectator* (Palmer, 2005, p. 40) to provide authority for the claim that torture worked in destroying a terrorist infrastructure in Algeria, while ignoring the work of Rejali who disputes these claims and whose work was cited in an earlier response to their original article (Rumney, 2006, pp. 498–9). Indeed, Rejali's most recent work raises serious doubts that torture was a significant factor in the French victory in the so-called Battle of Algiers (Rejali, 2007). They also cite a misreading of a *Washington Post* story (Brzezinski, 2001) that, again, was highlighted in an earlier response to their work (Rumney, 2006, pp. 487–8). To support their argument on effectiveness, Bagaric and Clarke use the Bush Administration's claims regarding disclosures made by Khaled Sheik Mohammed (KSM), thus:

An aide to United States President George W. Bush recently noted that 'torture light' is an essential tool: 'We're talking about the most successful intelligence gained in the war on terror coming from these programs', he says. Details are hard to come by, but Sen. Kit Bond, a member of the Senate intelligence committee, [said]...that 'enhanced interrogation techniques' worked with at least one high-level Qaeda operative, 9/11 mastermind Khalid Shaikh Mohammed, to thwart a plot. Bond would not say which one, but among foiled plots vaguely described by the White House and linked to 'KSM' was a scheme to attack targets on the West Coast of the United States with hijacked airliners. The planning for such a 'second wave' attack may have been in the early stages. (Bagaric and Clarke, 2006, p. 717)

In judging whether 'enhanced interrogation techniques' worked in the case of KSM a number of issues need to be considered. First, it is worth noting that according to this quote, the most successful information to be gleaned from KSM concerned an attack that 'may have been in the early stages'. Although such disclosures may be useful, it does appear to be of only limited value and certainly does not fall within the 'ticking bomb' hypothetical. The second issue is linked to another point made by Bagaric and Clarke. They refer to the CIA's own interrogation manuals which suggest that physical coercion is often ineffective (Rumney, 2006, pp. 492–7). However, Bagaric and Clarke claim that this cannot be seen as the 'sum experiences or collective attitudes of even the CIA towards torture' (Bagaric and Clarke, 2006, p. 718) and indeed there is further information regarding the effectiveness of torture provided by CIA interrogators in interviews conducted by Ron Suskind (Suskind, 2006). These interviews corroborate the suggestion that the coercion used during KSM's interrogations was largely ineffective. KSM was subjected to various techniques, including sleep deprivation and water boarding. Even his children, who were in US custody, were threatened (Suskind, 2006, pp. 229–30). Suskind's interviews give the clear impression that coercion was not particularly successful. These claims should be taken seriously, since they appear to correspond closely to the Bush Administration's own claims regarding the disclosures KSM made during interrogation. Suskind also refers to the plane plot referred to in the quote used by Bagaric and Clarke (Suskind, 2006, p. 229). Similar problems of ineffectiveness were also in evidence in the interrogation of Ramzi bin al-Shibh (Suskind, 2006, p. 228). In another case involving an al-Qaeda operative detained by the CIA, coercive methods were applied, with decidedly limited results. Abu Zubaydah was subjected to a range of techniques, including threats, beatings and water boarding. He disclosed vague plans about the possible bombing of supermarkets, nuclear plants and apartment buildings (Suskind, 2006, pp. 115–16), but these disclosures could not be 'independently confirmed' (Suskind, 2006, pp. 115–16). The CIA finally obtained verifiable information from Zubaydah when one of his interrogators used passages from the Koran to convince him to cooperate and this led to the capture of an al-Qaeda operative in Pakistan (Suskind, 2006, pp. 116–17). One of Suskind's interviewees notes that when you 'try everything' to get someone to talk 'it's hard to know what worked' (Suskind, 2006, p. 118). While this is a reasonable point, Zubaydah appears not to have disclosed any verifiable information when subjected to coercion, only disclosing verifiable information when the Koran was used to encourage his cooperation. Another interesting aspect of this case was the fact that the Bush Administration appears to have exaggerated the value of the intelligence coming from Zubaydah, as well as the value of the coercive methods used (Froomkin, 2007).

Bagaric and Clarke's comments on the CIA's own interrogation manuals are further undermined by a recent review by members of the United States Intelligence Science Board on Educing Information (Kleinman, 2006). Steven Kleinman analysed the CIA's KUBARK interrogation manual. He refers to the 'paucity of relevant information on effective tactics, techniques, and procedures for the interrogation of adversarial detainees under US control' (Kleinman, 2006, p. 132) and states that KUBARK offers 'unique and exceptional insights into the complex challenges of educing information from a resistant source through non-coercive means'. For those who support a legalized system of coercion, he notes:

> The potential for gain [from coercive interrogation] is arguably problematic since the scientific community has never established that coercive interrogation methods are an effective means of obtaining reliable intelligence information. In essence there seems to be an unsubstantiated assumption that 'compliance' carries the same connotation as 'meaningful cooperation' (i.e. a source induced to provide accurate, relevant information of potential intelligence value). (Kleinman, 2006, pp. 133, 130)

He adds: 'Claims from some members of the operational community as to the alleged effectiveness of coercive methods in educing meaningful information from resistant sources are, at best, anecdotal in nature and would be, in the author's view, unlikely to withstand the rigors of sound scientific inquiry' (Kleinman, 2006, p. 130, n. 91).

Consequently, from a scientific perspective, when examining some of the oft-cited examples of successful coercion, one must question the extent to which it can be argued that coercive interrogation results in accurate *and* timely disclosures often enough to justify its legal regulation. There is undoubtedly evidence that it sometimes works, however one has to consider whether 'sometimes' is good enough to overcome many of the problems associated with its use. In addition, it is evident from this discussion that sources must be read with care so that they are not taken to lend support to positions, which on closer inspection, cannot be sustained.

Conclusion

The UK government has a duty to act within the confines of existing legal prohibitions. However, this does not answer the question of whether or not the absolute prohibition on the use of torture should remain. Indeed, as discussed earlier, the United Kingdom did authorize the use of coercive methods with some success in Northern Ireland. Consequently, the debate surrounding the use of coercive interrogation is not merely of academic significance. The arguments being considered in this debate will undoubtedly continue to influence democracies in their response to terrorist violence. It might be that the ideas put forward by those who support the absolute prohibition are the most convincing in the marketplace of ideas. If that is so, then there is no reason for us to believe that those ideas will not prevail in the current debate. However, as this chapter has demonstrated, some of the arguments used by those who defend the absolute prohibition are weak. In addition, the proponents of a legalized system of coercive interrogation raise a number of questions that the critics need to address. For example, can we continue to prohibit the use of torture to save innocent life, but allow the state to lawfully inflict greater harm in other circumstances? When judging the desirability of coercive interrogation, why are the interests of innocent victims not given equal standing to those of suspected terrorists?

Finally, if legal scholars wish to inform decision making and viewpoints outside of the academy, then it is essential that we be guided by the characteristics of a 'liberal intellectual system' that was discussed earlier. Whatever conclusions are reached, they will have far greater credibility to policymakers, legislators, judges and the wider community if they are produced as a result of detailed, well-informed analysis that takes account of counter-arguments and evidence. While some of those who defend the current absolute prohibition appear fearful of such a debate, the reality is that scholars cannot hope to have influence (or credibility) if they are unwilling to address difficult moral and legal questions.

Part III

Comparative Perspectives

8
Law, Intelligence and Politics in Australia's 'War on Terror'

Christopher Michaelsen

Introduction

While the terrorist attacks against the United States on 11 September 2001 (9/11) shook much of the world to its core, the day's catastrophic events were a world away for many Australians, who felt confident that geographical fortuity insulated them from international turmoil. This ill-fated perception, however, changed thirteen months later when terrorists bombed two night clubs in Kuta, Bali. Among the 202 people killed on 12 October 2002 were 88 Australian tourists. In response to the 9/11 and Bali atrocities and the changed security environment, Canberra took decisive and far-reaching action, both at home and abroad.

At the international level, the Australian government of John Howard was a staunch supporter of the Bush Administration's 'war on terror'. In 2001, parts of Australia's Special Air Services Regiment assisted in the defeat of the Taliban in Afghanistan. In 2003, Australia was one of the few countries contributing ground troops to the invasion of Iraq. Canberra also promoted counterterrorism efforts at the regional level. The Government urged ASEAN's (Association of South East Asian Nations) Regional Forum to focus on increasing counterterrorism cooperation in the region, and signed several counterterrorism agreements with key South-East Asian nations, including Indonesia, Malaysia, Thailand and the Philippines (Department of Foreign Affairs and Trade, 2003). These agreements provided the basis for closer intelligence exchanges and strengthened cooperation between law enforcement agencies.

At the domestic level, counterterrorism and emergency response capabilities were reviewed and upgraded (Ibid.), the Government introduced tighter financial, aviation and border control measures, and a nationwide response mechanism to manage possible terrorism attacks inside Australia was developed. The main focus of Australia's domestic campaign, however, has been on introducing and strengthening federal anti-terrorism laws. Over the last six years, the Commonwealth has enacted no less than forty-one new pieces of legislation on terrorism, or about one new law every seven weeks. Some of the key features of the Australian legal counterterrorism framework shall be subject to a critical examination in this chapter.

9/11 and the 'first wave' of anti-terrorism laws

A first package of anti-terrorism laws, comprising five bills, was introduced into the House of Representatives, the federal parliament, on 12 March 2002. These five bills included the Security Legislation Amendment (Terrorism) Bill 2002, Suppression of the Financing of Terrorism Bill 2002, Criminal Code Amendment (Suppression of Terrorist Bombings) Bill 2002, Border Security Legislation Amendment Bill 2002, and Telecommunications Interception Legislation Amendment Bill 2002. The most important of these was the controversial Security Legislation Amendment (Terrorism) Act 2002 (Cth).[1] The Act drew noticeably on the United Kingdom's Terrorism Act 2000 and passed the House and the Senate (the lower house) only after it had been amended substantially to include recommendations by the Senate Legal and Constitutional Legislation Committee. Another major piece of new anti-terrorism legislation was the Australian Security Intelligence Organisation Legislation Amendment (Terrorism) Act 2003 (Cth) (ASIO Act). Its main purpose was to authorize the detention by ASIO, Australia's domestic intelligence agency, of persons for questioning in relation to terrorism offences, as well as the creation of new offences in respect to withholding of information regarding terrorism.

The Security Legislation Amendment (Terrorism) Act 2002

The Security Legislation Amendment (Terrorism) Act 2002 added a raft of new terrorism offences to the Criminal Code 1995 (Cth). It introduced a definition of 'terrorist act' and criminal sanctions for involvement with a terrorist organization, including for providing support or funding, recruiting members, directing its activities or being a member. According to section 100.1 of the Criminal Code a 'terrorist act' is defined as:

(a) an action [that] falls within subsection (2) and does not fall within subsection (3); and
(b) the action is done or the threat is made with the intention of advancing a political, religious or ideological cause; and
(c) the action is done or the threat is made with the intention of
   (i) coercing, or influencing by intimidation, the government of the Commonwealth or a State, Territory or foreign country, or of part of a State, Territory or foreign country; or
   (ii) intimidating the public or a section of the public.

An action falls within subsection 2 and is classified as a terrorist act (unless it falls within subsection 3) if it:

(a) causes serious harm that is physical harm to a person; or
(b) causes serious damage to property; or
(c) causes a person's death; or
(d) endangers a person's life, other than the life of the person taking the action; or
(e) creates a serious risk to the health or safety of the public or a section of the public; or
(f) seriously interferes with, seriously disrupts, or destroys, an electronic system including, but not limited to:
   (i) an information system; or
   (ii) a telecommunications system; or
   (iii) a financial system; or
   (iv) a system used for the delivery of essential government services; or
   (v) a system used for, or by, an essential public utility; or
   (vii) a system used for, or by, a transport system.

An action falls within subsection 3, and is excluded from the definition of a terrorist act, if it

(a) is advocacy, protest, dissent or industrial action; and
(b) is not intended
   (i) to cause serious harm that is physical harm to a person; or
   (ii) to cause a person's death; or

(iii) to endanger the life of a person, other than the person taking
the action; or
(iv) to create a serious risk to the health and safety of the public or
a section of the public.[2]

This definition of 'terrorist act' is considerably broad and criminalizes
action that goes far beyond the kind of terrorist attacks that motivated
the legislative amendments. While section 100.1(3) explicitly excludes
political protest and industrial action not intended to cause serious
physical harm, etc., the ultimate intent of the act, its political, ideological
or religious motivation, is precisely what distinguishes terrorism from
other forms of criminal violence already covered by existing legislation. Indeed, it is the same intent that lies at the heart of every political
protest and industrial action. As Jenny Hocking has argued persua-
sively, this nexus between 'terrorist act' as defined in section 100.1 and
ordinary political dissent may ultimately criminalize politics (Hocking,
2003, p. 368).

Indeed, the link between 'terrorist act' and ordinary political dissent
is taken further in the Act's introduction of ancillary offences that can
stand even if the terrorist act itself does not occur. These offences include
being connected with a terrorist act; providing or receiving training;
possessing things connected with terrorist acts; collecting or making
documents likely to facilitate terrorist acts, etc.[3] Most of the penalties
for these ancillary offences remain far in excess of those which apply
to comparable criminal acts committed without the critical element of
political, ideological or religious motivation. This not only introduces
a lack of uniformity in penalties for similar offences but also suggests
a disturbing capacity on the part of the prosecution for discretion in
terms of offences to be laid (Ibid.).

The Security Legislation Amendment (Terrorism) Act 2002 also
introduced a definition of 'terrorist organisation'. According to the
new section 102.1(1) of the Criminal Code a 'terrorist organisation' is
(a) an organization that is directly or indirectly engaged in, preparing,
planning, assisting in or fostering the doing of a terrorist act (whether
or not the terrorist act occurs); or (b) an organization that is specified
by the regulations to be a terrorist organization. A person is criminally
liable if he/she directs, recruits for, trains or receives training from,
funds or receives funds from, or provides support or resources for a
terrorist organization as defined in section 102.1(1).

In addition, the Act introduced new powers for the Attorney-General
to outlaw terrorist organizations and organizations threatening the

integrity and security of Australia or another country. It is sufficient for the Attorney-General to be satisfied that the decision is made upon reasonable grounds. For an organization to be specified by regulation (s. 102.1(1)(b)), it originally had to be listed by the UN Security Council. In early March 2004, however, Parliament enacted the Criminal Code Amendment (Terrorist Organisations) Act 2004 (Cth), which removed the requirement for a Security Council decision before an organization can be listed as a terrorist organization for the purpose of domestic law. The Attorney-General may now list organizations as 'terrorist organizations' based on Australia's national interest and security needs and the advice of Australian intelligence agencies. As a consequence, organizations such as Nelson Mandela's African National Congress (ANC), the Free Papua Movement or any other group considered 'terrorist' or 'not conducive to the public good' for reasons of national security may be banned by the government of the day.

The decision by the Attorney-General to outlaw a specific organization is not subject to regular judicial review. Once listed it is almost impossible for an organization to challenge the ban in the courts. Review of proscription decisions is only available under the Administrative Decisions (Judicial Review) Act 1977 (Cth). This means that a listing decision may be reviewed only on questions of law, and not on its merits. What is more, this limited process of judicial review is only available *after* the listing of a terrorist organization by the Attorney-General has occurred. As a consequence, any person seeking to challenge such listing may already be facing prosecution under provisions of the Criminal Code relating to membership in or involvement with a terrorist organization. It is difficult to see how this form of post facto judicial review could be effective as a protection for the organization in question. As Bob Gotterson QC, then President of the Law Council of Australia, has argued, it would have been preferable to incorporate a measure of judicial scrutiny *before* the Attorney-General's decision takes legal effect and potentially criminalizes the conduct of citizens (Gotterson, 2004).

The far-reaching proscription powers of the Attorney-General and the lack of adequate judicial review raise serious concerns in relation to fundamental liberal democratic principles such as the government's duty to respect the rule of law and civil liberties. First, the new proscription provisions and associated offences have significant implications for the right to freedom of association. Second, the new legislation law is open to abuse. It may be argued that the new laws effectively enable the Federal Government to determine who can participate in the political sphere and who cannot (see also, Hocking, 2003, p. 368). Organizations can be outlawed on the dubious grounds of 'security', a term that lacks any specific definition. Indeed, the Attorney-General's prescription powers constitute a worrisome elevation of executive power that resembles Prime Minister Robert Menzies' Communist Party Dissolution Act 1950 in its banning of political organizations by executive decree (see also, Williams, 2003). The Communist Party Dissolution Act, however, was declared invalid by the Australian High Court in 1951.

The Australian Security Intelligence Organisation Legislation Amendment (Terrorism) Act 2003 (Cth) 2003

The second key instrument of the 'first wave' of anti-terrorism laws is the Australian Security Intelligence Organisation Legislation Amendment (Terrorism) Act 2003 (Cth) [hereinafter ASIO Act]. The ASIO Bill was first introduced into Parliament on 21 March 2002 and was subject to heated discussion. While Daryl Williams, the then Attorney-General, was convinced that the new legislation would enable ASIO 'to engage in an appropriate (*sic*) form of interrogation' (Forbes, 2002) to gather relevant information for the prevention of terrorist attacks, critics argued that the Bill was 'rotten to the core' and would establish 'part of the apparatus of a police state' (Williams, 2002). The Senate rejected the legislation on 13 December 2002. After intense negotiations between the Government and the Opposition, however, a revised version of the Bill passed the Senate, coming into force on 26 June 2003.

The revised version of the ASIO Act had been substantially amended in response to reports by the Parliamentary Joint Committee on ASIO, Australian Secret Intelligence Service (ASIS),[4] and Defence Signals Directorate (DSD)[5] and the Senate Legal and Constitutional Committee.[6] The Committees' recommendations tempered many of the most draconian aspects of the original Bill and also led to the introduction of a three-year sunset clause.[7] Nonetheless, the ASIO Act remains highly controversial partly because it vests a domestic intelligence agency with powers of arrest and detention which in Australia are traditionally held by the law enforcement agencies. Indeed, ASIO was specifically created to be separate from the police. Its sole task was to gather information and produce intelligence that enables the agency to warn the government about activities or situations that might endanger Australia's national security.[8]

The new legislation, however, authorizes ASIO to seek a warrant to detain and question people for a maximum time of seven days. In contrast to comparable legislation in the United Kingdom, Canada and the United States, the person detained does not need to be suspected of any offence. People can be taken into custody without charges being laid or even the possibility that they might be laid at a later stage. According to s. 34D(1) of the Act it is sufficient that the 'issuing authority' has 'reasonable grounds for believing that the warrant will substantially assist the collection of intelligence that is important in relation to a terrorism offence'. An 'issuing authority' is defined as a person, appointed by the Minister, who is a federal magistrate or judge, or a member of another class of people nominated in regulations. These arrangements differ significantly from those in other Western liberal democracies such as Canada, where orders for the so-called investigative hearings must be made out by a regular judge who is independent from the executive.

The warrant issued by the 'issuing authority' either requires a person to appear before a 'prescribed authority' to provide information or produce records or things or authorizes a police officer to take the person into custody and bring him or her before a 'prescribed authority' for such purposes. According to s.34B, the 'prescribed authority' may be a retired superior court judge or a President or Deputy President of the Administrative Appeals Tribunal. While a single warrant must not exceed forty-eight hours, it is possible to extend detention by requesting successive warrants. In total, the successive extensions may not result in a continuous period of detention of more than 168 hours (seven days) from the time the person first appeared before any 'prescribed authority' for questioning under an earlier warrant. However, the Act does not contain adequate safeguard provisions in relation to the issuance of the so-called serial warrants (persons are released and detained again shortly afterwards to refresh the detention period). As a consequence, there is the possibility that although a detainee must be released after forty-eight hours or seven days, he/she may be taken into custody again as soon as an hour later. The only criterion to be satisfied is that the new warrant is based on 'materially different' information to any previous warrants.

Equally concerning, the detention decision is not subject to regular judicial review. In fact, the detention is only overseen by a 'prescribed authority'. As indicated, a 'prescribed authority' is either a retired superior court judge or a President or Deputy President of the Administrative Appeals Tribunal. Unlike the Special Immigration Appeals Commission (SIAC) in the United Kingdom, the tribunal is thus not a regular judicial body that is independent from the executive. Its members are the so-called *personae designatae* who are dependent on the favour of the executive if they wish to be reappointed. These provisions raise serious concerns in relation to the fundamental right of habeas corpus. Persons detained under the provisions of the ASIO Act cannot have the detention warrant examined by a court of law. Hence, it may be argued that the detention arrangements under the ASIO Act violate the well-established principle of the prohibition of arbitrary detention because they deny the detainee the essential right to due process.

These arrangements are also incompatible with Australia's obligations under international law, specifically with commitments under the United Nations International Covenant on Civil Political Rights (ICCPR) to which Australia became a party in 1980. Article 9 (1) of the ICCPR specifically provides that 'everyone has the right to liberty and security of person. No one shall be subjected to arbitrary arrest or detention'. Referring to the ICCPR's *travaux préparatoires*, Manfred Nowak has pointed out that the term 'arbitrary' is not to be equated with 'against the law' but includes elements of injustice, unpredictability, unreasonableness, capriciousness and unproportionality (Nowak, 1993, p. 178). Confirming this interpretation, the UN Human Rights Committee (the quasi-judicial monitoring organ established by the ICCPR) has stated in the case of *Van Alphen* v. *The Netherlands* that detention 'must not only be lawful but reasonable in all the circumstances' and 'must be necessary in all the circumstances, for example to prevent flight, interference with evidence, or the recurrence of a crime' (*Van Alphen* v. *The Netherlands*, 1990, para. 5.8). It is difficult to see how the detention of non-suspects for the mere purposes of questioning and intelligence gathering can be regarded as 'necessary and reasonable in all the circumstances' (Michaelsen, 2003, pp. 283–4). Even in circumstances where detention for questioning purposes is considered to be indispensable, there is no clear reason why such detention should not be strictly confined to those reasonably suspected of being terrorists or being involved in terrorist activities.

The ASIO Act also severely limits the right to legal representation. Although the person subjected to a warrant is permitted to contact a lawyer of his/her choice, questioning may commence in the absence of that lawyer if permitted by the 'prescribed authority'. The contact between lawyer and detainee is monitored by a 'person exercising authority'. Also, a lawyer may not intervene in the questioning nor address the 'prescribed authority' during the questioning process. Finally, a lawyer commits an offence if he/she communicates information to an unauthorized third person about the detention or questioning. In essence, these provisions prevent a lawyer from fulfilling his regular professional duties.

The ASIO Act also raises serious concerns in relation to the privilege against self-incrimination, a fundamental principle in any modern legal system. Section 34G of the ASIO Act contains offences (five years imprisonment) for failing to give 'the information, record or thing' requested in accordance with the warrant. 'Strict liability' attaches to this offence and the detainee bears the burden of proof to establish that he/she does not have the information sought.[9] In effect, these provisions remove the fundamental right to silence and reverse the onus of proof. Moreover, while the Act protects the detainee against 'direct' use of answers in criminal proceedings against him/her (except in proceedings for an offence against s. 34G), it does not provide protection from 'derivative' use of any answers in future proceedings. This means, for example, that if the police forces find evidence based on the person's answers during questioning (e.g. by later finding incriminating material at the person's premises), this evidence may be used against the person in criminal proceedings.

Section 34G of the ASIO Act is thus also in violation of international law because it breaches the non-derogable right to be presumed innocent until proved guilty as enshrined in Article 14(2) of the ICCPR and recognized by Article 11 of the Universal Declaration of Human Rights. Article 14(3)(g) of the ICCPR further clarifies that the accused has the right 'not to be compelled to testify against himself or to confess guilt'. One may argue that the detention of persons by ASIO for the purpose of questioning can be regarded as an 'administrative hearing' and is therefore different from 'regular' arrest and detention by law enforcement agencies. Consequently, the limits set by the ICCPR would not apply to non-judicial detention for questioning purposes. In *Saunders v United Kingdom*, however, the European Court of Human Rights expressly stated that it was a violation of the right to a fair trial to admit evidence which had been obtained at an earlier administrative hearing during which the accused had been compelled by statute to answer questions and adduce evidence of a self-incriminatory nature (*Saunders v United Kingdom*, 1996; see also, Michaelsen, 2003, pp. 285–6).

Finally, the ASIO Act permits detention of children between the ages of 16 and 18 and, in certain circumstances, even allows for a strip search. While these powers raise ethical concerns, they also violate essential provisions of the UN Convention on the Rights of the Child (CROC) to which Australia became a party in 1991. In particular, it breaches Article 37 CROC which provides that no child should be deprived of his or her liberty arbitrarily and that any detention should be used only as a 'measure of last resort' and for the 'shortest appropriate period of time'.

Furthermore the detention of children violates Article 40 CROC which states that any child deprived of his or her liberty shall have the right to prompt access to legal and other appropriate assistance and shall be presumed innocent until proven guilty.[10]

The Willie Brigitte Affair, the Jack Roche Case and the 'Second Wave' of Anti-Terrorism Laws

A 'second wave' of anti-terrorism laws was introduced and enacted in late 2003 and throughout 2004, mainly triggered by two incidents – the Willie Brigitte Affair and the Jack Roche Case – which exposed failures in intelligence sharing and communication and had the potential to embarrass the Government in a year of a federal election where 'national security' and 'terrorism' were generally seen as ballot-winning issues. Rather than reviewing the effectiveness of the national security adminis-trative framework, the Government enacted further anti-terrorism laws.

The Willie Brigitte Affair

Willie Brigitte was born on the Caribbean island of Guadeloupe in 1968 and moved to Paris as a teenager in the 1980s. After dropping out of high school and deserting from the Navy he worked in general labouring occupations throughout the 1990s. In 1998, Brigitte converted to Islam, changing his name to Mohammed Abderrahman, or Abderrahman the West Indian. According to Radio Europe 1 correspondent Alain Acco, it was around this time that Brigitte first became known to the Directorate for Territorial Surveillance (DST), the French security and counterin-telligence service.[11] He attended regularly the Omar and Abou Bakr mosques in the poor and immigrant Paris suburb of Couronnes and allegedly associated with people who had links to the Salafist Group For Call and Combat, an Algerian-based extremist group. Subsequently, in 1999 and 2000, Brigitte and 'carloads of bearded Muslims' were observed heading off on several 'strenuous camping trips' in the Fontainebleau Forest just outside Paris. The group, dubbed 'the camper group' by DST, was also seen departing for hiking excursions on remote Normandy beaches (ABC, 2003a).

Two years later, after 9/11, DST reportedly noted that members of the same 'camper group' were reappearing in Afghanistan fighting with the Taliban (Ibid.). Brigitte apparently also headed for Afghanistan in late 2001. However, due to the US-led military campaign, he was unable to cross the Afghanistan–Pakistan border. Instead, he remained in Pakistan where he allegedly spent four months in a Lashkar-e-Taiba training camp in the mountains of the Punjab.[12] According to transcripts of an interrogation conducted by French anti-terrorism magistrate Jean-Louis Bruguiere, Brigitte admitted his presence at the Lashkar-e-Taiba complex near Lahore, Pakistan, in 2001–2002. He then returned to Paris, and, in May 2003, obtained a tourist visa to visit Australia where he arrived on 16 May (Ibid.). Settling in a suburb in Sydney's south-west, Brigitte worked in a halal restaurant in the city. In August 2003, he married 'Sydneysider' Melanie Brown, an Australian Muslim convert. His motives for travelling to Australia, however, remain subject to wild speculation.[13]

Brigitte's trip to Australia and his presence in Sydney were not initially noticed by either the French or the Australian security services. On 16 September 2003, however, DST reportedly confirmed, through a Paris travel agent, that Brigitte had bought a one-way ticket to Australia using his original French name. About six days later, on 22 September, the Australian Embassy in Paris received a letter from DST requesting confirmation that the Frenchman was still in Australia. Although the letter indicated that Brigitte was possibly a member of an Islamist group and that he had received military training in Pakistan, ASIO appears to have treated it as a routine trace request.

Some ten days passed and the French received no reply to their enquiry. Then, on Friday 3 October 2003, the French authorities sent a second message warning that Brigitte could be in Australia in connection with terrorism-related activity and that he was 'possibly dangerous'. This time the information was sent directly to the ASIO headquarters in Canberra. The intelligence communiqué arrived in Canberra at 11pm, a time at which ASIO's communications area was apparently closed for the weekend. Since the following Monday was a public holiday, it was not before Tuesday 7 September – three days later – that ASIO finally received the message. Within two days, the Australian authorities located Brigitte and detained him for breaching his visa conditions. The newly adopted questioning and detention powers of the ASIO Act, however, were not invoked. Brigitte was subsequently deported to France on 17 October 2003.

The glaring failure of intelligence exchange and communication problems between the French and Australian authorities, resulting in a person with suspected links to an Islamic extremist organization being granted a tourist visa, carried significant potential for political damage to the Government, particularly with a federal election a mere eleven months away. The Government thus chose an aggressive response to the Brigitte incident. Rather than reviewing and addressing apparent administrative lapses, however, the Government's political rhetoric focussed heavily on the assertion that Brigitte's presence in Sydney had highlighted the threat of terrorism to mainland Australia, and thus the need for even 'tougher' anti-terrorism legislation.

Attorney-General Philip Ruddock, in particular, sought to capitalize politically on the Brigitte incident. Emphasizing the effectiveness (*sic*) of Australia's co-operative counterterrorism arrangements with France, Ruddock went so far as to claim that the Brigitte case had shown that ASIO's powers were 'clearly inadequate' and that Australia's anti-terrorism legislation ranked only 'third and fourth best' (Banham, 2003). Without even attempting to apply ASIO's new questioning and detention powers to the Brigitte case, the Attorney-General called for further amendments to the ASIO Act. A comparison with French anti-terrorism laws, so Mr Ruddock hinted, required Australia to introduce significant additional arrangements (ABC, 2003b).[14] However, comparing the ASIO Act with the French counterterrorism powers was not only inappropriate for inter-jurisdictional reasons, but also failed to acknowledge the systemic human rights abuses arising from those powers reported by the United Nations human rights treaty bodies, the European Court of Human Rights and Amnesty International (see Carne, 2004).

Seemingly unaffected by such criticisms, the Government moved quickly to expand the legislative counterterrorism framework and introduced into Parliament the ASIO Legislation Amendment Bill 2003 (Cth) on 27 November 2003. The legislation passed the Senate just eight days later. In contrast to the ASIO Act amendments of 2002 (enacted in June 2003), the November 2003 additions were not subject to scrutiny by any parliamentary committee. And although the Greens and Democrats called for the Bill to be referred to the Senate Legal and Constitutional Committee, Labour, fearing to be seen as 'soft' on terrorism, supported the Government's Bill unconditionally.

The Bill doubled the maximum time a person could be questioned under a warrant where an interpreter is needed from twenty-four to forty-eight hours. Despite strong criticism from a number of organizations, including the Australian Broadcasting Corporation and the Australian Press Council, the legislative amendments also tightened secrecy provisions preventing people from discussing information obtained during their interrogation for two years after the warrant has expired. These disclosure offences include unauthorized primary and secondary disclosures of an extensive range of information. The effect of these provisions criminalizes media reporting of material within the broad terms of the prohibitions, including reporting of the fact that a detention and questioning warrant has been issued in relation to a specific matter.

The Government's effort to turn the political negative of Brigitte's presence in Australia into a positive by claiming that recently enhanced ASIO powers were inadequate is remarkable for several reasons. First, it confirmed an unapologetic shift to an overt, professionalized politicisation of counterterrorism issues, juggling partisan political advantage with the security of the nation (Ibid., pp. 597–602). Second, the Attorney-General's call for legislative reform a mere four months after the conclusion of sixteen months of exhaustive debate, and three parliamentary committee reports highly critical of the Government's proposals, was dismissive of the democratic contribution expended in that legislative process. Finally, the legislative response to the Brigitte incident included provisions that encroach upon fundamental freedoms such as the freedom of the press. It is difficult to see, however, how such amendments can constitute an essential tool for effective counterterrorism policy. If anything, they reduce democratic accountability and diminish the vital safeguard of free press reporting, without decreasing the risk of a terrorist attack.

The Jack Roche Case

Jack Roche was born in the United Kingdom in 1953 and moved to Australia in 1978.[15] After working in various general labouring occupations throughout the 1980s, he accepted a job at a Sydney factory which also employed several Indonesian Muslims. Through the contact with his Indonesian workmates, Roche eventually converted to Islam in 1992 and then spent several years in Indonesia learning about Islam and teaching English as a second language. Upon his return to Australia in 1996, Roche came into contact with the Indonesian twin brothers Abdul Rahman and Abdul Rahim Ayub who are believed to have headed the Australian branch of the Indonesian Islamist group Jemaah Islamiah (JI).[16]

In 2000, Roche travelled to Afghanistan, where he allegedly met with al-Qaeda leaders, including Khalid Shaikh Mohammed and Osama Bin Laden (Gibson, 2004). He received training in terrorist techniques and was then instructed to set up a terror cell in Australia and to target Israeli interests, including the Israeli embassy in Canberra. Roche admitted to carrying out surveillance on targets in Australia, but was unsuccessful in bringing in new recruits for the cell. According to Roche, Indonesian Muslim cleric Abu Bakar Bashir, whom Roche named as the head of JI, called him and ordered him to cancel the plan.

Roche's trial commenced on 17 May 2004. During the proceedings he changed his plea and admitted to the charge of conspiring to 'commit an offence contrary to section 8(3C)9a) of the Crimes (Internationally Protected Persons) Act 1976 being to intentionally destroy or damage by means of explosive the official premises of internationally protected persons, namely the Israeli embassy, with intent to endanger the lives of internationally protected persons by that destruction or damage contrary to section 86(1) of the Crimes Act 1914'. On 1 June 2004 he was subsequently sentenced to nine years imprisonment. Since Roche did not have a previous criminal record, he was declared eligible for parole after half of his sentence. According to Justice Healy, Western Australia's most experienced judge, his chances of re-offending were virtually non-existent.

Nonetheless, tabloid front pages and news reports were filled with fury at the Court's treatment of Australia's 'first terrorist'. 'Soft on terror' the Melbourne *Herald Sun* screamed. *The Australian* criticized Justice Healy for failing 'to get with the [anti-terrorism] program'. Media outrage was mirrored by the reaction of the public at large: in an instant internet poll conducted on TV Channel Nine's website http://ninemsn.com.au, over two thirds of respondents thought Roche's sentence 'too lenient'.

This provided another convenient opportunity for the Government to divert attention from the fact that – analogous to the Brigitte affair – the Roche incident had revealed serious administrative failures on the part of ASIO. ASIO's raids on Roche's Perth home in October 2002 and the charges subsequently laid by the police had followed an independent investigation by a newspaper journalist. Further, Roche had attempted to contact the intelligence agency repeatedly over several months in 2000, but the ASIO did not return the calls and he did not spark any further interest from the Government authorities until late 2002.

The Government thus decided to go on the offensive and its response was in many ways similar to the one in the Brigitte affair. Declaring that any inquiry into potential ASIO failures would be 'indulgent' and 'disruptive', the Attorney-General announced that he had instructed the Commonwealth (federal) Director of Public Prosecutions (DPP) to consider appealing against the Roche sentence for being 'too lenient' (Banham, 2004). The next day, however, Ruddock admitted under questioning in Parliament that the federal DPP had sent a letter to Justice Healy at the District Court of Western Australia acknowledging Roche had cooperated with the authorities and therefore deserved a more lenient sentence than the twenty five-year maximum the Crown would ask for in open court (ABC, 2004). (Incidentally, the DPP's appeal was crushed by the Western Australian Court of Criminal Appeal and Roche's sentence upheld on 14 January 2005).

In addition, the Attorney-General announced further changes to federal anti-terrorism laws. In particular, he indicated that the Government was looking at immediately introducing new legislation that would set a non-parole period for persons convicted of 'terrorist' offences. Subsequently, on June 30, 2004, Parliament passed the Anti-Terrorism Act 2004 (Cth), which provided for minimum non-parole periods for persons convicted of, and sentenced for committing terrorism offences and certain other offences 'that are relevant to terrorist activity'.

The Anti-Terrorism Act 2004 also amended the Proceeds of Crime Act 2002 (Cth). Under the new arrangements the Commonwealth is entitled to seek a restraining order 'if there are reasonable grounds to suspect (*sic*) that a person has committed an indictable offence or a foreign indictable offence, and that the person has derived literary proceeds in relation to the offence'. In effect, this provision enables the Government to prevent persons from making money by selling books or memoirs about training and contact with banned organizations. As the amendment operates retrospectively, it potentially applies not only to the Roche case but also to the two former Australian Guantánamo Bay detainees, David Hicks and Mamdouh Habib.[17]

The Jack Roche case was another remarkable example of the Howard Government's ability to instrumentalize public sentiment to divert attention from serious administrative inadequacies in handling public line calls on the part of ASIO. These inadequacies could have embarrassed the Government in the later federal elections, especially as the Coalition had heavily invested in its election campaign on 'national security' that included the establishment of a 'national security hot-line', guidance on 'how to spot a terrorist' and freely dispatched (to every household) fridge-magnets advising Australians to be 'alert but not alarmed' (Walsh, 2003). The Government thus chose an aggressive response to the Roche case that appears to have been primarily moti-vated by a desire to maintain an image of being 'tough on terrorism'. In effect, however, the measures introduced constituted a disturbing inter-ference in the administration of justice and the courts' discretion to set parole. Furthermore, they unduly encroached upon the freedom of speech in an apparent attempt to silence 'alleged terrorists' from telling their part of the story. Again it is difficult to see how such legislative measures may contribute to decreasing the risk of terrorist attacks.

The latest catalogue of legislative amendments entered into force on 16 August 2004 when the Anti-Terrorism Acts (No. 2) and (No. 3) 2004 received royal assent. Schedule 3 of the Anti-Terrorism Act (No. 2) is particularly problematic as it amended the Criminal Code (Cth) to create the offence of 'associating with terrorist organisations'. According to the new section 102.8 it is an offence to intentionally associate with a person who is member or who 'promotes or directs' the activities of a listed terrorist organization and that association provides support that would help the terrorist organization to continue to exist or to expand. The term 'associate' is defined in subsection 102.1(1) of the Criminal Code as 'meeting or communicating with the other person'. The definition of 'associating with terrorist organisations' is thus again very broad and criminalizes action that goes far beyond the kind of terrorist attacks that motivated the legislative amendments.

The London 7/7 Bombings and the 'Third Wave' of Anti-Terrorism Laws

The London tube bombings of 7 July 2005(7/7) and the controversial debate about the adequacy of existing anti-terrorism legislation in the United Kingdom throughout 2005 were closely observed by the Australian Government in Canberra. It was felt that in Australia, too, there was a need to further strengthen and expand the already comprehensive legal counterterrorism framework. Attorney-General Ruddock argued that in light of the London bombings, it was of the utmost importance to 'undertake a thorough review of all of the measures that have been implemented abroad and to see whether any of them were measures that we could usefully add to our armoury here (...)' (ABC, 2005). Neither the Attorney-General nor any other Government representative explained how exactly the bombings in London had changed the level of threat of terrorism in Australia, or whether there was any evidence to suggest that the security situation in Australia was comparable to that of the United Kingdom's.

Nonetheless, less than four months after the London bombing, Canberra had put together a comprehensive package of measures largely copying those contained in the United Kingdom's Prevention of Terrorism Act (2005). Interestingly, the Government initially planned to introduce the new laws on Tuesday, 2 November 2005. The first Tuesday of November is marked in the Australian calendar as the day on which the country's richest horse race, the Melbourne Cup, is run. The significance of the Cup to national life is summed up in the cliché that it is 'the race that stops the nation'. The occasion is a public holiday in Melbourne and, for a variety of reasons, might fairly be said to account for a heightened level of distraction throughout the Australian community. The planned date of introduction of the new laws was leaked to the media, and following much public outcry, the Government postponed the tabling in Parliament for exactly one day.

Subsequently, the Anti-Terrorism Bill 2005 was introduced and passed by the House of Representatives on 2 November 2005 and by the Senate on 3 November. The Anti-Terrorism Act 2005 commenced operation on 4 November 2005. It clarifies that, in the prosecution of a terrorism-related offence, it is not necessary to identify a particular terrorist act. Instead it will be enough for the prosecution to prove that the particular conduct was related to 'a' terrorist act (Lynch, 2006). In effect, the Anti-Terrorism Act 2005 further broadened the scope and application of the already exceptionally broad provisions enacted by Security Legislation Amendment (Terrorism) Act 2002 which had added a raft of new terrorism offences to the Criminal Code 1995.

One day later, on 3 November 2005, a second piece of legislation, the Anti-Terrorism Bill (No. 2) 2005, was introduced into Parliament and referred to the Senate Legal and Constitutional Legislation Committee for inquiry and report by 28 November 2005. Given that the legislative changes extended to about 170 pages, a three-week enquiry was fairly problematic. Nonetheless, following public hearings on 14, 17 and 18 November, the Senate Committee tabled a report containing a number of recommendations, including a number of amendments. The Government considered those recommendations, and following brief consultation with States and Territories due to constitutional requirements, introduced only very minor changes. The Bill, as amended, was passed on 7 December, receiving royal assent on 14 December 2005.

The measures that commenced on 15 December 2005 included provisions extending the criteria for listing terrorist organizations to cover those that advocate terrorism. They also strengthened financing terrorism offences and introduced new powers authorizing the Australian Federal Police (AFP) to stop, question and search people in Commonwealth places. Perhaps most controversial, the legislative changes added divisions 104 and 105 to Part 5.3 of the Criminal Code and introduced a control order and preventative detention regime, briefly discussed below.

While both control orders and preventative detention orders are expressly designed to protect the public from a terrorist act, they differ in an important way. Preventative detention orders are relatively short term, and are aimed at either preventing an imminent terrorist attack or preserving evidence relating to a terrorist act that has recently taken place. Control orders, on the other hand, while still ultimately aimed at prevention, are not predicated on the existence of an imminent risk of terrorist attack. They may also last much longer – up to a year, with the possibility of renewal.

Control orders impose a variety of obligations and restrictions on a person for the purpose of protecting the public from a terrorist act. The potential scope of a control order ranges from a very minimal intrusion on an individual's freedom to an extreme deprivation of a person's liberty. The order can include prohibitions and restrictions on the individual being at specified areas or places, leaving Australia, communicating or associating with certain people, accessing or using certain forms of telecommunication or technology (including the Internet), possessing or using certain things or substances, and carrying out specific activities (including activities related to the person's work or occupation). The order can also include the requirement that the person remain at a specified place between certain times each day, wear a tracking device, and report to specified people at specified times and places. A person who contravenes the terms of a control order commits an offence with a maximum penalty of five years imprisonment.

Only senior members of the AFP may seek control orders. They must first obtain written consent of the Attorney-General to request an interim order from an issuing court (the Federal Court, the Family Court or the Federal Magistrates Court). Before seeking consent, the competent AFP officer must have 'reasonable grounds' for either believing that:

- making the order would substantially assist in preventing a terrorist act, or
- that the person subject to the order has provided training to, or received training from, a listed terrorist organization.

In determining whether or not to grant permission to employ a control order, the competent court applies the test of 'balance of probabilities'. The 'balance of possibilities' test is merely a civil, not criminal ('beyond reasonable doubt') standard of proof. Given the serious consequences that an order may have for an individual's freedom, it is highly questionable whether the civil standard of proof is appropriate.

The Anti-Terrorism Act (No. 2) 2005 also created a new regime for preventative detention orders. The new Division 105 of the Criminal Code provides for a preventative detention regime that allows the AFP to take a person into custody and detain them to prevent a terrorist attack occurring, or preserve evidence of a recent terrorist attack. Where a preventative detention order is sought to prevent a terrorist act, the AFP must establish that detaining the person is reasonably necessary for the purpose of substantially assisting in preventing a terrorist act. It must also be shown that:

- there are reasonable grounds to suspect that either the person will engage in a terrorist act, the person possesses a thing connected with the preparation for or engagement in a terrorist act, or the person has done an act in preparation for or planning a terrorist attack, and a terrorist act is imminent, or
- a terrorist act has occurred in the last twenty-eight days and detaining the person is necessary to preserve evidence of or relating to a terrorist act.

Where a preventative detention order is sought to preserve evidence, the AFP must establish that a terrorist attack has occurred within the last twenty-eight days, and that the order is necessary to preserve evidence relating to the act, and detaining the person is reasonably necessary. The maximum period of detention under the preventative detention regime is forty-eight hours. Subject to the existence of a prohibited contact order, the person detained may only contact a number of people while in detention, including a lawyer, a family member, their employer and another person at the discretion of the police officer. A prohibited contact order can be made where it is reasonably necessary to preserve evidence of, or relating to, a terrorist act. Other than verifying the person's identity, members of the AFP (or ASIO) are not allowed to question him/her. However, the order may be used to take potentially dangerous people off the streets for a day or two while the AFP considers laying charges or ASIO prepares an application for questioning.

The control order and preventative detention order regime has no precedent in Australia and raises several concerns. First, the new measures give the Government a 'second chance' to deprive someone of their liberty even after they have been acquitted in a fair trial or had any convictions quashed on appeal. Second, the control order and preventative detention regime poses a challenge to the traditional purpose of legal regulation and is highly problematic in relation to the fundamental rights to liberty and to a fair trial, respectively. Persons on whom orders are served do not have to be found guilty of, or even be suspected of committing, a crime. As Andrew Lynch and George Williams have pointed out, 'this is more than a breach of the old "innocent until proven guilty" maxim: it ignores the notion of guilt altogether' (Lynch and Williams, 2006, p. 42). As such, the new provisions are also likely to breach several of Australia's obligations under the ICCPR. Finally, the control order and preventative detention regime also raises several constitutional concerns (Lynch and Reilly, 2007).

Defending the new measures, the Australian Government has frequently suggested that they were comparable to, and inspired by, the measures enacted in the United Kingdom. However, first, the security situation in the United Kingdom was distinctively different from the situation in Australia. To this date, there is little evidence to suggest that Australia is a target for a major terrorist attack. Indeed, for several reasons outlined elsewhere, the risk of a terrorist attack occurring in Australia continues to be considerably lower than in the United Kingdom (Michaelsen, 2005b).

Second, even if one accepts that the threat of terrorism required such drastic measures, the political context in Australia was still very different from that of the United Kingdom. In the United Kingdom the legislative changes were introduced only after the House of Lords, in the *Belmarsh detainees* case, had declared the previous detention regime (established by part 4 of the Anti-Terrorism, Crime and Security Act 2001) unlawful. Also, the introduction of the control order regime in the United Kingdom led to a constitutional crisis, a Labour back-bench rebellion and much debate in Parliament, the public and the media. In Australia, on the other hand, the legislative changes were rushed through Parliament with comparatively little scrutiny and debate. With the Government winning control of the Senate in 2005, the brief enquiry held by the Senate Legal and Constitutional Committee into the Anti-Terrorism Bill (No. 2) 2005 was more a political formality than effective parliamentary scrutiny.

Third, the British scheme of preventative detention is different from the one in place in Australia. In the United Kingdom, the police may detain a person who is reasonably believed to be a terrorist for up to forty-eight hours for a number of purposes, but the prevention of an 'imminent' terrorist act is not one of them. Any extensions of the detention period can only be authorized if there are 'reasonable grounds for believing that the further detention (...) is necessary to obtain relevant evidence', whether by questioning or by preservation. The British system thus has a strong investigatory purpose, designed to facilitate the laying of charges. The Australian scheme does not have a similar focus. As indicated earlier, the AFP may not even question a person subjected to a preventative detention order.

Finally, the United Kingdom's system contains significant safeguards, which are lacking in Australia. All British law must be read against the Human Rights Act (HRA) 1998. The United Kingdom is also subject to the European Convention on Human Rights (ECHR). Both instruments ensure that the British anti-terrorism legislation does not undermine the rule of law or the values one is seeking to protect (see also, Williams and MacDonald, 2006). In addition, an independent reviewer (Lord Carlile) and the Parliament's Joint Committee on Human Rights play important roles in supervising the operation of the laws (see Walker, this volume). Australia, on the other hand, neither has a constitutional bill of rights (like the United States or Germany), nor does it have any special act of parliament protecting the citizens' basic rights and freedoms (like the United Kingdom and New Zealand). Although Australia has been a party to the ICCPR since 1980, it has failed so far to give domestic effect to its international obligations (again in contrast to the United Kingdom).[18] In addition, Australia is lacking an independent monitoring body or committee comparable to the United Kingdom institutions (see also, Michaelsen, 2005c).

Conclusion

Australia's legislative response to the threat of terrorism can be divided into three different phases. Responding to the 9/11 attacks, Canberra enacted a wide range of anti-terrorism laws that added a raft of new terrorism offences to the Criminal Code and also introduced a definition of a 'terrorist act'. In this first phase, ASIO was also given unprecedented powers that enable the domestic intelligence agency to detain persons not suspected of any offence for up to seven days without charge or trial. The second phase saw the Government extending the legislative framework in response to incidents involving individuals suspected of being involved in terrorism activity. Rather than demonstrating a coherent approach to legislative reform, the Brigitte and Roche cases were distinctive for the Government's overt political approach in shifting responsibility for, and in seeking remedy of a national security administrative and policy failure through the expansion of the legislative counterterrorism framework. In the third phase, the Government invoked the tragic events of the London 7/7 bombings to introduce a further extension of the legislative framework. This included adopting a comprehensive regime of control and preventative detention orders that was largely modelled on the British Prevention of Terrorism Act 2005.

What all legislative changes have in common is that they have eroded fundamental rule of law principles such as accountability and scrutiny of authority, due process, separation of powers, and coherent justification for the introduction of intrusive measures. This erosion is reflected in the attitudes of the legislative proponents and apparent in the legislative amendments themselves. At no point did the Government demonstrate adequately that the changes in law were necessary, let alone effective in the fight against terrorism. Importantly, the legislative changes were adopted without essential safeguards. Unlike their British, Canadian or German counterparts, Australian judges have little if any power to subject the unprecedented anti-terrorism laws to judicial scrutiny. And in the very limited circumstances where judicial scrutiny of such laws is possible, Australian courts cannot examine their compatibility with any human rights instrument. The reason for this lack of human rights protection is simple: Australia does neither have a constitutional bill of rights nor does it have any special act of parliament protecting the citizens' basic rights and freedoms or incorporating international human rights obligations.

In the absence of any domestic human rights instrument and in light of limited judicial review, it is clear that effective parliamentary review of the anti-terrorism laws is all the more important. Indeed, it was the Senate committee process that successfully toned down many of the worst parts of the anti-terrorism legislation introduced by the Howard government in 2002–2004. However, with both Houses of Parliament under Government control, the process of reviewing legislation *before* it is enacted is unlikely to continue to provide effective and adequate safeguards. As far as parliamentary review of *existing* anti-terrorism legislation is concerned, the possibilities for meaningful oversight are very limited as well. In contrast to the United Kingdom, Australia's anti-terrorism legislation does not generally empower any parliamentary committee or independent body to oversee or review the operation, effectiveness and implications of the respective laws *per se*. These are significant shortcomings that the Australian Government needs to address urgently if it wants to combat terrorism successfully and in a way that does not sacrifice the very principles and standards that define the Australian way of life in the first place.

Notes

1. For the Act and other key pieces of Australia's national security legislation see http://www.nationalsecurity.gov.au.

2. Under s.101.1, a person is liable for life imprisonment if he/she commits a terrorist act. Under s.101.1(2), the person is liable under Australian law even if the terrorist conduct and its results occur wholly overseas.
3. See Division 101 – Terrorism, Security Legislation (Terrorism) Amendment Act 2002.
4. ASIS is Australia's overseas intelligence collection agency, see http://www.asis.gov.au.
5. DSD is Australia's national authority for signals intelligence and information security, see http://www.dsd.gov.au.
6. See the respective committee's websites: http://www.aph.gov.au/house/committee/pjcaad/ and http://www.aph.gov.au/senate/committee/legcon_ctte/.
7. The original Bill had allowed the detention of children as young as 12 years of age (now 16). It did not grant detainees access to a lawyer of their choice (access to a lawyer of choice now can be only limited where the lawyer poses a security risk).
8. The ASIO Act defines 'security' as the protection of Australia and its people from espionage, sabotage, politically motivated violence, the promotion of communal violence, attacks on Australia's defence system, and acts of foreign interference.
9. For 'strict liability', see section 6.1 of the Australian *Criminal Code* (Cth).
10. In addition, the ASIO Act may be in breach of Articles 2(2), 3(1) and 19(1) CROC. Article 2(2) provides that a child must not be discriminated against on the basis of the expressed opinions of their parents. Article 3(1) provides that in all actions concerning children the best interests of the child shall be a primary consideration. Article 19(1) provides that the State must take all appropriate measures to protect the child from all forms of injury or abuse.
11. Alain Acco's report was derived from what Brigitte is alleged to have told DST under interrogation. His account depended entirely on information supplied by an unnamed 'senior member of the French police' and an anonymous 'Parisian anti-terrorist magistrate'. Acco's report was virtually the sole basis of the subsequent wave of sensational and embroidered media reports in Australia.
12. Lashkar-e-Taiba, or LET, is a Pakistani group formed to fight for the liberation of Kashmir from India.
13. Brigitte's lawyers claimed that their client 'was off to Australia to start a new life'. Ibid. According to (then) ASIO Director-General, Dennis Richardson, 'Brigitte was almost certainly involved in activities with the intention of doing harm in Australia' (Wroe, 2003). However, when ABC TV correspondent Tony Jones directly asked the Attorney-General whether he believed that Brigitte 'was plotting some kind of terrorist action', Mr Ruddock's reply was 'No' (ABC, 2003a).
14. This comparison has also been used to explain the deportation of Brigitte on the grounds of the supposed inadequacy of the ASIO detention and questioning regime.
15. Unless referenced otherwise, the information on Roche provided in this chapter is based on the sentencing remarks by Justice Healy, District Court of Western Australia; Sentencing Remarks – IND 03/0622 – (The

Queen v. J Roche), http://www.districtcourt.wa.gov.au/content/files/binaryFiles/Roche_sentence.pdf

16. Abdul Rahman is a militant cleric and veteran of the 'Islamic holy war in Afghanistan' and a graduate of the infamous Ngruki School founded by radical Muslim cleric and alleged JI spiritual leader Abu Bakar Bashir. ABC, Transcript TV Program, *Four Corners – The Australian Connections*, http://www.abc.net.au/4corners/content/2003/transcripts/s878332.htm. Abdul Rahman applied for refugee status but lost his case in the Refugee Review Tribunal and was deported in 1999. Abdul Rahim left Australia for Indonesia in September 2002. Indonesia's national intelligence agency, BIN, located Abdul Rahim Ayub in West Java in early 2004. However, according to Indonesian officials neither Abdul Rahim, nor his twin brother Abdul Rahman, have been linked to any terrorist act in Indonesia or raised the interest of Indonesian counterterrorism police. See Chulov (2004).

17. Indeed, when Mamdouh Habib returned to Australia from Guantánamo Bay in late January 2005 (without conviction or charge), Attorney-General Ruddock initially indicated that he was looking into trying to prevent Habib from selling his story to Australian television. However, no application for a restraining order was made (Michaelsen, 2005a).

18. Leading to commentators such as Williams (2004) calling for an Australian Bill of Rights.

9
Counterterrorism in the Netherlands after 9/11: The 'Dutch Approach'

Beatrice A. de Graaf and Bob G.J. de Graaff

Introduction

November 2, 2004 was a turning point in Dutch political history. In the early morning of that day, Mohammed Bouyeri, the son of Moroccan immigrants, shot the controversial Dutch filmmaker Theo van Gogh, great-grandnephew of the painter Vincent van Gogh, from his bicycle and slaughtered him to death with a curved machete. With a smaller knife, he pinned a letter to Van Gogh's chest, in which he announced more death verdicts against famous Dutch politicians, notably Somali-born Ayaan Hirsi Ali (Buruma, 2006). The murder sent shockwaves throughout the country and across the world. Home-grown terrorism had emerged even in relatively complacent, laid-back Holland. The ensuing turmoil and mass hysteria continued for many months, and had a huge impact on the – until that time – moderate terrorism debate. Radical counterterrorism measures were demanded and implemented, Finance Minister Gerrit Zalm even declared that 'we' were 'at war' with terrorists (*Algemeen Dagblad*, 2004).

This chapter analyses the development of the Dutch approach to countering Jihadi terrorism. The discussion did not start in November 2004, however. The Dutch National Security Service (*Binnenlandse Veiligheidsdienst*, BVD) had pointed to the danger of Islamist radicalism as far back as 1992, although the public had not paid much heed to these warnings. The so-called broad approach that had characterized Dutch counterterrorism since the 1970s, was invoked again, and brandished as the answer to radicalism and terrorism. Here, both the terrorist threat towards the Netherlands, the ensuing counter terrorism (CT) measures and the re-enactment of the 'Dutch approach' will be the object of our interest.

The Dutch approach

In the Netherlands the prevailing CT measures are, from time to time, considered to comprise a 'Dutch approach', a comprehensive approach towards terrorism in which the Dutch authorities cooperate to 'tackle the dangers of radicalisation and terrorism as a coherent whole'. This approach 'includes repressive measures against terrorists, but puts an equal emphasis on prevention', according to the Dutch Deputy Coordinator for Counterterrorism, Lidewij Ongering in a session before the Senate Committee on Homeland Security and Governmental Affairs in June 2007 (Ongering, 2007, p. 6).

With this emphasis on both prevention and repression, CT instruments can vary from political, financial, judicial and intelligence measures to social, cultural and economic instruments; but they have to be put into practice in a combined manner. From this comprehensive point of view even the furthering of apprentice and work opportunities, better housing and education for minorities, combating social exclusion and discrimination, as well as the implementation of quality standards for Imams can be part of a counterterrorism strategy.

In a historical perspective, government officials tend to contrast this approach with, for example, the West German approach to combating left-wing terrorism in the 1970s, where the so-called Berufsverbote were implemented, extremist political attitudes could serve as grounds for persecution and computer-engineered data mining was introduced (Peters, 2004). In contrast to this, the Dutch authorities adopted a totally different policy, which critics sometimes dismissed as 'soft'. According to an official of the agency of the Dutch National Coordinator for Counterterrorism (*Nationaal Coördinator Terrorismebestrijding*, NCTb), this historical approach 'was characterized by a search for nonviolent solutions, as long as there was any space for them'. The emphasis was not on persecution and prosecution, but on the integration of radical political protest within the Dutch democratic system, even if these protests were pursued by violent means (Abels, 2007, p. 123).

In reality, this 'Dutch approach' was not so much a premeditated policy or strategy, adopted by a left-wing government that did not want to copy the German 'hard line', and more a reactive and tactical answer to the activities of South Moluccan radicals and other terrorist groups in the 1970s.

Historical background

In August 1970, thirty-three South Moluccan radicals raided the Indonesian embassy, killing a police officer and taking all the employees hostage. Their aim was to coerce the Dutch government into advocating the creation of an independent South Moluccan Republic in Indonesia. After one day, they surrendered. Imported terrorism caused problems as well: the Palestinian organization Black September – a militant Palestinian group, founded in 1970, and a split off from the Al-Fatah-movement, the armed branch of Yasser Arafat's Palestine Liberation Organisation (Cooley, 1973) – tried to blow up oil and gas installations in April 1972; in September 1974 the pro-Palestinian Japanese Red Army took the French Ambassador and some of his staff hostage, and in September 1975 the BVD foiled a plot by four members of the Syrian Saiqa-organization to hijack the Moscow-Warsaw-Hoek van Holland railway-express (that was said to arrive with Russian Jewish immigrants on board) (Engelen, 2002, pp. 61–75; Eikelenboom, 2007, pp. 88–109).

Against this background, but heavily influenced by the September 1972 Munich tragedy, the Dutch authorities announced and implemented new CT instruments. In the first place, the police improved their information position by establishing a Special Cases Agency (BZC) at the Central Criminal Investigation Intelligence (CRI) in The Hague to collect terrorist-related intelligence on behalf of the police forces. At the same time, the regular Security Service intensified its use of the so-called Regional Intelligence Units, placed under the local police forces. Second, special sniper units, close combat forces and a National Support Team Counterterrorism (LBT) were created to assist local police forces with terrorist investigations and actions. Third, an Interdepartmental Steering Committee Terrorist Actions (ASTA) was formed at the ministerial level, and a Public Prosecutor for Counterterrorism was appointed, to help ensure better coordination and control on the political and judicial levels (Fijnaut, 1989, p. 504; Klerks, 1989; Eikelenboom, 2007, pp. 194–216).

Notwithstanding all these new police instruments, the Dutch social-democratic Prime Minister in the 1973–1977 centre-left cabinet, Joop den Uyl, was hesitant about conducting an openly repressive counter-terrorism campaign, and tried to solve the hostage situations involving Japanese Red Army terrorists (see above) and South Moluccan terrorists in 1970, 1975 and 1977 by negotiation. In the case of the Moluccans, the government especially tried to address the political, social and economic grievances of the distressed Moluccan minority, thereby introducing the comprehensive 'Dutch approach'. It negotiated travels for Moluccan youths to Indonesia and initiated a dialogue. The government was indeed successful in co-opting respected representatives from the Moluccan community. Religious and political spokesmen and women complied with the request and bargained a compromise with the terrorists. This resulted in the surrender in 1970 and 1975 of the Moluccan train hijackers (Bootsma, 2000).

This 'pacification approach', however, reached its limits on 11 June 1977, when Moluccan radicals hijacked a train for the second time. Negotiations lasted for almost three weeks(!), while passengers suffered in the cramped passenger carriages, before the stalemate was finally broken and the recently established Dutch special forces intervened and stormed the train. This resulted in the deaths of six hijackers and two passengers – thus demonstrating that the 'Dutch approach' could be harsh as well, if need be (Eikelenboom, 2007, pp. 131–5). Nevertheless, governmental measures aimed at improving the social and economic integration of the South Moluccan minority into Dutch society remained an important, if not central, part of the CT package. In the end, this succeeded in appeasing the larger part of the community and draining the recruitment basin. After 1978, the Moluccan terrorist threat ceased to pose any real danger (Bootsma, 2000).

Effective CT measures were also affected by the decentralized Dutch security infrastructure. The police were (and still are) compartmentalized in a national force that covers the countryside and in some fifteen urban forces that strictly protected their respective autonomy. This explains why special forces were not even contacted when police officers detected fugitive German terrorists, belonging to the Red Army Faction (RAF), carrying out logistical operations in the Netherlands in 1977 and 1978. In Utrecht, one police officer lost his life in the ensuing shoot out, and in Den Haag and Amsterdam two others were heavily wounded. In 1978, two customs officials lost their lives after they tried to arrest another RAF couple (Eikelenboom, 2007, pp. 179–84, 191–2).

In this context, the BVD remained the most effective and central agency within the Dutch CT infrastructure. Its 'disruptive' approach achieved some remarkable results. The BVD prevented the kidnapping of Queen Juliana by ten Moluccan youths and the already mentioned attack on the express train from Moscow by four Syrians. The BVD also contributed to the withering away of the Red Assistance/Red Youth by downplaying the threat they posed and not granting them the status of political enemy, by 'disruptive measures' (ostentatiously following, visiting, etc.) and by a de-escalative approach. The BVD did not stigmatize their members as terrorists. Instead, the activities of these suspected terrorist groups were defined as 'political radical violence' (as long as they were not aimed at killing people) and prosecuted like criminal offences (Hoekstra, 2004, pp. 67–76; Verbij, 2005).[1]

In the 1980s, preventing international terrorists (mainly the Provisional IRA and *Euskadi Ta Askatasuna* (ETA)) from importing their political conflicts into the Netherlands or turning the country into a safe haven, became the main task of the BVD.[2] Disruption of potentially violent groups – not only international terrorist organizations, but 'homegrown' groups with an anti-racist signature, or right-wing extremism and white nationalism as well – still constituted the main targets for Dutch CT in this period. This was a logical consequence of the central starting points of the Dutch counterterrorism approach: the authorities favoured a moderate discourse, avoided special anti-terrorism legislation, tried to keep the military in their barracks, differed between 'political violent activism' (sabotage, material damage) and terrorism (aimed at taking human lives) and, on the whole, applied a differentiated and proportional CT strategy within the existing security framework (Fijnaut, 1989, pp. 501–5; Abels, 2007, pp. 121–5; Hoekstra, 2004, pp. 67, 121).

It should be stressed though, that this liberal climate pertaining to political violence was also possible thanks to the absence of intense and prolonged 'home-grown' terrorist violence on the one hand, and a lack of collective anxiety regarding the attacks that did take place on the other. The groups mentioned above represented relatively isolated single-issue networks or imported elements. The 'home-grown' Dutch 'Revolutionary Youth' (*Rode Jeugd*) and anti-racist RaRa organization (*Revolutionaire Anti-Racistische Actie*) occupied themselves with incidental acts of sabotage, and never committed attacks against people (Muller, 1994, pp. 370–6). Compared to revolutionary groups in Germany and Italy, their 'mental distance' from the rest of Dutch society was never unbridgeable. These groups were therefore never perceived as a homogeneous threat to Dutch national security (de Graaf, 2007). Only the Moluccan hijackings in 1975 and 1977 induced people to avoid taking the train on specific routes. But on the whole an amorphous terrorist threat and climate of fear, which would have injected CT politics with its own dynamic, did not emerge, and the state of law was not affected until after 11 September 2001 (9/11).

'The multicultural drama'

Interestingly enough, the current debate on terrorism in the Netherlands is intrinsically connected to the immigration and integration debate and dominated by a so-called pedagogical discourse, that is, inter-preting radicalization as a socio-economic and/or educational prob-lem (Sunier, 2006). Whereas in the United States and, to a somewhat lesser extent in the United Kingdom, the political agenda on counter-terrorism is set by an ideologically charged global 'war on terror' (Thachuk, 2006, p. 2), for the Netherlands, a war will do little to resolve criminal and social problems. Since the terrorist threat in the Netherlands emanates in the first place from 'home-grown' Islamic radicals with Dutch nationality, the authorities believe that the best methods for halting the spread of terrorism require enhanced judicial and intelligence cooperation and attention to the conditions of social exclusion and deprivation that give rise to violent expressions of indignation and powerlessness (Letters of the Ministers of the Interior and Justice, 2006).

Therefore, the discussion in the Netherlands centres around the phenomenon of radicalization as a social-psychological process. Radicalization should be understood, as explained by government officials, politicians and academics, as integration and social affiliation of certain immigrants and their descendants gone awry (van Gemert, 1998; Kleijwegt, 2005; Ministry of Justice, 2005; Werdmölder , 2005; Buys et al., 2006). It is argued that there is a relationship between derailed social, economic and political integration and growing alienation amongst a small minority of second-generation immigrants on the one hand and the development of 'home-grown' terrorist cells on the other. In this context, terrorism is not in the first place defined as a rational political choice in opposition to the existing system. It is viewed as a behavioural disorder, resulting from a 'clash of cultures' and an 'integration paradox' – that is, the phenomenon that young Moroccans are at the same time more involved in Dutch society compared to their parents, but are also more often confronted with experiences of exclusion and discrimination – which can ignite a process of radicalization (Buys et al., pp. 201–36).

This discussion was informed by the debate on the side-effects of integration and multiculturalism that started in the 1990s. One of the first government agencies to break the taboo on the downside of a liberal integration policy was the Dutch secret service, the BVD. In its first threat analysis, published in February 1992, the BVD took many threats into consideration. Organized crime, espionage, political inter-ventions originating or supported from Dutch territory, proliferation, several types of terrorism (right wing and other), extremism and political violence were all covered. But the sting was buried in the paragraph on international terrorism. The BVD reported religious isolationist and anti-integrative tendencies within immigrant circles, especially amongst young, dissatisfied Muslims of Moroccan origin, that undermined social cohesion and democratic order – in international perspective a remarkable 'early warning' (BVD, 1992, p. 25; Abels and Willemse, 2004, p. 91).

In May 1998 the BVD published a report on *Political Islam in the Netherlands* (BVD, 1998), and in 1999 announced in its annual report that it had started collecting information on possible Saoudian, Libyan and other Arabic recruiting activities among Dutch Muslims (BVD, 1999/2000, pp. 1516). The perceived terrorist threat to the Netherlands associated with radical Islamism was specified in a report on *Terrorism at the Beginning of the 21st Century: Threat perception and positioning of the BVD*, published in April 2001. Religiously inspired terrorism by Osama bin Laden's network, sheltered by rogue states such as Afghanistan and Sudan, was viewed as the main terrorist threat to the Western world.

Home-grown terrorism did not present a danger to Dutch society (yet), nor did the BVD assess terrorist attacks on Western targets with weapons of mass destruction or other non-conventional arms as being very likely in the short term. Nevertheless, the BVD did not advocate a policy of sit and wait, but was committed to following international security risks back to their origins. It signalled an approach of 'offensive prevention' and participation in international counterterrorism efforts (BVD, 2001).

At the same time the BVD explicitly stressed the importance of a 'narrow' definition of terrorism and a traditionally broad, but reluctant counterterrorism approach. This was inspired by the above-mentioned experiences in the Federal Republic of Germany. Terrorism was still defined as 'committing or threatening to commit violence directed at human life, in order to bring about social change or to influence the political decision-making process'. This definition did not include political radicalism or non-lethal political violence, the threshold being the deliberate threat to human lives (Ibid., pp. 7–9). Nor did it lead to special legislation. Terrorist or extremist activities were still prosecuted according to existing criminal law.

Nevertheless, the BVD's revelations that developments in Islamic fundamentalism in the Middle East and Mediterranean countries might lead to conflict between the majority of the population and ethnic minorities in the Netherlands caused some indignation. Many politicians and political commentators accused the BVD of 'demagoguery' and needlessly attacking the Muslim community and Islam. They also reproached the Service for desperately looking for a new enemy, now that the communist threat had withered away (see, for example, *NRC Handelsblad*, 1992; Schmidt, 1998; van Boxtel, 2000; Schans, Wil van der, E. Timmerman and W. Wagenaar, 2003).

The BVD's revelations were flanked, however, by a mounting protest against immigration policies, voiced by right-wing and conservative politicians belonging to the oppositional factions in Parliament. During the second social-liberal cabinet headed by Prime Minister Wim Kok (1998–2002), tensions arose relating to economic recession, immigration politics and national security that produced a political climate in which the conservative and confessional opposition thrived. As a consequence, this time the BVD issued a warning about the growing number of racist crimes carried out by youngsters (Trouw, 2000).

The turning point in the discussion on radicalism as a side-effect of terrorism was the publication of an article on the 'multicultural drama' by a famous Dutch publicist, Paul Scheffer. His attack (not from 'the right', but from the social-democratic 'left') on official ignorance of the dangers of economic and social alienation and radicalization broke the taboo in liberal circles on addressing the flipside of immigration politics (Scheffer, 2000). This politicized atmosphere was ignited by two major events in the Autumn of 2001: the 9/11 attacks and the sudden emergence of a new charismatic and right-wing politician on the Dutch national stage. They completely altered the Dutch counterterrorism landscape.

The impact of '9/11' and '5/6'

The al-Qaeda attacks on the twin towers of the World Trade Center catapulted international terrorism onto the Dutch political agenda. The Dutch government was nevertheless hesitant in responding to this new challenge. In the Netherlands, counterterrorism policy was framed in relation to immigration and asylum politics, but the ruling social-democratic and liberal parties were divided over the issue. Their constituencies had gone adrift. Ideological and confessional ties between parties and their constituencies had been severed, partly because of the growing unrest pertaining to multiculturalism and immigration politics.

This became clear when in November 2001 a complete outsider named Pim Fortuyn – a former Marxist turned right-wing populist entertainer who openly celebrated a dandy life – stepped into the limelight of political theatre and undermined the established parties.

With his stated mission to get rid of the 'ruins of the purple coalition', that is, the liberal-left coalition, and to close Dutch borders to new asylum seekers, he hit a nerve with large parts of the no longer traditionally bounded constituency and was expected to drive a wedge into the political establishment via the elections of 15 May 2002. On 6 May, however, he was murdered by Volkert van der Graaf, an animal rights activist, whose motives were never fully clarified (BVD, 1999/2000, p. 44).

Although Fortuyn was killed by a 'white' animal rights activist, his anti-Islamic propaganda and fulminations against 'false' asylum seekers had exposed an until then more or less mute and politically hardly articulated, but deep-rooted dissatisfaction with 'alien cultures' permeating Dutch society. Fortuyn had channelled these grievances, made 'political correctness' and multiculturalism dirty words and gave voice to the many 'common' and frustrated citizens that felt the traditional political parties had not taken them seriously enough before. Fortuyn's murder did not deflate this popular unrest, which was manipulated and channelled by new (would-be) political entrepreneurs. In the election, his party, *Lijst Pim Fortuyn* (LPF), gained 17.5% of the votes, at the expense of the ruling parties. The new populist representatives now embarked on introducing CT proposals in Parliament as a successful means of getting attention and votes.

Against this polarized background an incident occurred that proved that jihadist terrorism was not just an international problem when, in January 2002, two young Dutch Muslims were killed in Kashmir, where they had undertaken an attack on a heavily armed Indian patrol. The two boys had been recruited for jihad by Salafist militants in their hometown, Eindhoven, and had travelled to India to die as martyrs. AIVD-director[3] Van Hulst announced that 'several tens' of mostly Moroccan youths were involved in recruiting in the Netherlands – although they were still choosing their battlegrounds abroad, at notorious theatres of global jihad such as Kashmir, Chechnya and the Middle East (AIVD, 2002, 2003, p. 9; Ellian, 2002). This announcement was met with disbelief among the Muslim community, but the trip by two young Amsterdam Muslims to the Ukraine in January of the following year, to support the Chechen rebels there, supported Van Hulst's point (AIVD, 2004a, p. 17).

The AIVD concluded that the threat Islamic terrorism posed for the Netherlands was primarily a derivative of the international threat. No attempted Islamic terrorist attacks had yet been observed in the Netherlands, but the above incidents showed that recruitment and support activities of a financial, material or logistical nature were taking place at home. To improve intelligence gathering and investigation activities, and based on the Action Plan for Counterterrorism and Security drawn up in 2001, information exchange with the police, notably with the National Police Agency's (KLPD) Counterterrorism and Special Tasks Unit, was increased. In this way, the AIVD and the KLPD could make a more effective and efficient use of each other's records relating to radicalization and terrorism. This was a highly necessary step considering that, apart from the central KLPD, twenty-five regional police forces[4] were active in the field of counterterrorism and that, in spite of the measures undertaken in the 1970s, police intelligence was still rather fragmented (Ibid., p. 60).

Consequently, in 2002 and 2003 the police were able to arrest several dozen people based on AIVD-evidence, among them a group that had formed around a leader affiliated to the Algerian terrorist group GSPC (*Groupe Salafiste pour la Prédication et le Combat*); and another group that was linked to the LIFG (Libyan Islamic Fighting Group) (AIVD, 2002, 2003, pp. 16–19). However, twelve other suspects arrested for involvement in recruitment for and support of violent jihad in Spring 2003 were acquitted in June of that year. This was a consequence of the fact that evidence produced by the Public Prosecutor was mainly supplied by the AIVD – evidence that the judges could not verify and therefore rejected (AIVD, 2004a, p. 17). Hence, new legislation was proposed to remove this obstacle to counterterrorism.

This was embedded within an already announced integrated vision on counterterrorism, *Terrorism and the Protection of Society*, presented by the Ministers of the Interior and Justice in June 2003. From this point on, the Minister of Justice became the coordinating minister for counterterrorism and a new administrative taskforce was appointed (Minister of Justice, 2003). However, notwithstanding these initiatives, political and administrative attention towards terrorism abated subsequently. It would take another international disaster to instil a sense of urgency again (Bekke and de Vries, 2007, p. 7).

Meanwhile, the AIVD made good use of the new Law on the Intelligence and Security Services, enacted in February 2002. This law coincided with the new terrorist threat, but had already been under consideration since 1998 and had been announced in March 2001. The 9/11 attacks of course informed the implementation, especially the creation of a brand new Foreign Intelligence Directorate (*Directie Inlichtingen Buitenland*, DIB) within the AIVD. The initial DIB staff base was 70, growing to over 100 in the following years.

International counterterrorism cooperation was stimulated within the so-called second pillar of the EU (common foreign and security policy). The AIVD participates in the Clearing House, the Situation Centre (the Civil Intelligence Capability) and the Committee on Terrorism (COTER). Within the 'third pillar' (police and judicial cooperation in criminal matters) the Dutch delegation is informed by the AIVD as well. At the AIVD's request, the EU Council on Justice and Home Affairs founded a Counter Terrorist Group (CTG) on 19 September 2001, that provides a forum for cooperation between the European heads of intelligence and security services (Commissie Bestuurlijke Evaluatie AIVD, 2004, pp. 115–17). Since the Netherlands ostensibly served as a transit country or temporary quarters for jihadist fighters and other members of Islamic terrorist networks with international branches, international information exchange was seen as being of paramount importance (AIVD, 2003, p. 21).

The Netherlands also ratified the UN Convention for the Suppression of the Financing of Terrorism (December 1999) on 1 January 2002 via an amendment to the Dutch Sanctions Act. This enabled the Dutch authorities to confiscate the proceeds of crime, and prosecute financing of terrorism and laundering of money to commit or prepare a terrorist offence. These measures ensured that the 'international terrorists' mentioned on the EU and UN lists would have their assets frozen. Investigation in the Netherlands mainly focussed on two Islamic NGOs that were suspected of financing terrorism: the Benevolence International Foundation (BIF) and Al Aqsa, a Dutch-Palestinian charitable organization that allegedly financed Hamas-affiliated groups (AIVD, 2002, p. 18; Eikelenboom, 2007, pp. 245–52).

These CT measures did not attract much public attention. Terrorism was mainly associated with attacks abroad, whereas the main Dutch debate was focussed on the broader issue of radicalization at home. However, the Madrid attacks in 2004 provided the connection between the two phenomena and infused the Dutch discourse with a new sense of urgency.

The impact of the Madrid train attacks ('3/11')

The Madrid train attacks on 11 March 2004, when ten bombs exploded on four packed early morning commuter trains, killing 191 people and leaving at least 1800 injured, convinced the Dutch government of the necessity of embedding Dutch activities more deeply within the broader framework of the international counterterrorism community.

To coordinate and direct the CT efforts of the AIVD, the Immigration and Naturalisation Service, the police forces, the MIVD, the Federal Prosecutor and other parties involved, the government decided to create a National Coordinator for Counter Terrorism (*Nationale Coördinator voor Terrorismebestrijding*, NCTb) in 2004, overseen by both the Ministers of Justice and Internal Affairs (AIVD, 2005, p. 10).

Another direct consequence of Madrid was the so-called Counterterrorism-Infobox. To communicate another political signal to the public as well as improving the information flow beyond bureaucratic boundaries, the government set up this information exchange system within the AIVD. Since the AIVD had pointed out that between 100 and 200 people were involved in terrorism-related activities, timely information sharing seemed paramount. The 'CT-Infobox' was designed to concentrate information pertaining to possible terrorist threats in one place, thereby enabling the organizations involved to combine their snippets of information and eliminate the risk that an attack might not be detected in advance because of compartmentalization. Moreover, this exchange also served to initiate judicial or administrative measures (AIVD, 2006a). Extra funds for rising material costs and for more manpower to combat Islamist terrorism were envisaged: €15 million in 2005, growing to €46 million in 2009 (the total budget in 2004, when AIVD staff grew by more than 100 new employees, amounted to €87.5 million; in 2005 it amounted to €111.7 million, with 150 new employees) (AIVD, 2005, p. 69; AIVD, 2006b, pp. 106–7).

On 10 August 2004 the Dutch government followed the EU Framework Decision on Combating Terrorism of 13 June 2002 by announcing a Crimes of Terrorism Act. From now on, the existence of terrorist intent when committing a punishable offence was defined as a crime of terrorism and made liable to a heavier penalty; jurisdiction over terrorist offences was expanded, membership of terrorist organizations, conspiracy to commit terrorist offences and recruiting someone for jihad were made criminal offences (Parliamentary Paper 28, p. 463).

The new CT infrastructure marked a break from the traditional Dutch CT approach in the sense that it visibly raised the stakes in laying the ground work for a new organizational as well as a legal framework to combat terrorism. AIVD and NCTb still professed a 'broad approach', aimed at prevention, deradicalization and empowerment of society against terrorist threats rather than repression (Ministry of Justice/ Directie Algemene Justitiële Strategie, 2005). But demands for a tough stand against terrorism from right-wing politicians, and their constituency, as well as peer pressure from foreign services inspired the conservative government to propose new laws for preventive arrests and indictment.

The murder of Theo van Gogh ('2/11')

Meanwhile, at home, the debate on the relationship between radicalization and terrorism became more heated. The balance had now been tipped towards the other extreme: if AIVD warnings had been shrugged off before, now people overreacted by blaming the Muslim community for all sorts of wrongs. This new climate placed restraints on the AIVD as it tried to differentiate between Jihadi terrorists, radical and orthodox Muslims and to continue the moderate discourse on activism and terrorism that had provided results in the past.

In November 2003 Labour MP Ella Kalsbeek asked Home Secretary Remkes to submit a profile of persons in the Netherlands who were going through a process of recruitment for violent jihad. The AIVD replied with a memorandum, in which it described potential circumstances that could influence this process. Among other factors, the AIVD stated: 'It can be concluded that a growing number of Muslims feel treated disrespectfully by opinion-makers and opinion-leaders in social intercourse' (AIVD, 2004b).

This cautious remark was perceived by some as a warning to publicists to refrain from offending the Muslim community and thereby contributing to polarization in society. It caused considerable irritation in media and Parliament. MP Joost Eerdmans [*List Pim Fortuyn* (LPF)] accused the AIVD of infringing free speech. The parliamentary leader of the Conservative Liberals (the VVD), Jozias van Aartsen, asked the AIVD to refrain from commenting on the quality of public discussion (Schulte, 2004). The AIVD, however, had highlighted a real risk.

On 2 November 2004, the film director and notorious publicist Theo van Gogh, whose work was perceived as scabrous and insulting by religious minorities, was murdered by Mohammed Bouyeri. The self-proclaimed Moroccan Jihadist had intended to be killed by the police afterwards, but in the event was wounded and captured alive. This murder drove home the reality that young Dutch Muslims could indeed be recruited, and that they did not only choose far away war theatres to become martyrs, but could turn against their own society and strike at domestic targets as well. Mohammed B., as the Dutch media constantly referred to him, belonged to a circle of young jihadists who had fallen under the sway of a Salafist from Syria. The AIVD had already detected their meetings, and had dubbed the participants the 'Hofstad group'. Although close tabs were kept on the members, the security service had not recognized that Mohammed B. had been planning an attack on his own on a single individual.

The impact of 9/11 and 5/6 on the Dutch national intelligence culture and structure was probably superseded by the tectonic waves generated by the latter attack. The brutal character of the murder (Bouyeri shot Van Gogh to death, slit his throat, and stabbed a note on his chest in which he announced that more politicians would follow) appalled the public and led to a verdict in which the judge explicitly took into account the societal disruption Bouyeri had wanted to cause and sentenced him to life imprisonment. The political murder was convicted as a terrorist act, signalling that 'home-grown' terrorism had sprouted in the Netherlands. (Bouyeri was born in the Netherlands, went to school and worked here and held Dutch nationality.) In December 2004 the AIVD characterized the development of the terrorist threat as involving decentralization, radicalization, virtualization and being 'bottom up' – that is, not recruited by foreign veterans, but 'self-incendiary' (AIVD, 2004c). Between September 2004 and August 2005 fear of terrorist attacks rose to affect 50% of Dutch society (an increase of 14%), while 55% thought an attack likely to happen (an increase of 25%) (Frerichs and Schildmeijer, 2005, p. 3).

The legislative proposal by the Minister of Justice to allow the use of AIVD information as evidence in criminal proceedings was now taken into consideration by the two chambers of Parliament. Security was tightened around a number of buildings and sites, as well as in relation to government officials.[5] Several people were arrested because they were suspected of mapping potential targets for attack. Vigilance was also stepped up regarding the travel and immigration movements of those suspected of playing a role within international terrorist networks, such as veterans, facilitators and, of course, recruits (AIVD, 2005, pp. 15, 21). The AIVD published a report on radicalization, *From Dawa to Jihad*, in December 2004, to increase public awareness of the issue (AIVD, 2004c). At the same time, the authorities started large-scale research programmes into the roots of radicalization – attempts to link to the 'broad' and preventive approach of the past.

The link with integration was once again stressed: among the series of new bills the Cabinet sent to the Second Chamber of Parliament eight days after the murder of Van Gogh was a proposal to counter the possession of dual citizenship. This was inspired by the fact that right-wing MPs had demanded the withdrawal of Dutch citizenship from radical imams, and that Mohammed Bouyeri had held two passports (de Hart, 2005, pp. 4, 224–38). Minister of Justice P.H. Donner defended the proposal against left-wing critics by arguing that restriction of dual nationality for immigrants could advance integration and remove a breeding ground for radicalization.[6] This showed once again that the ruling elites might indeed favour an approach directed at pacification and prevention of conflicts, but that they did not recoil from using the same instruments in a rather repressive way if they thought it necessary.

Recent developments and (pending) legislation (2007/8)

Viewed as a whole, the current Dutch CT approach is aimed, first of all, at stopping people from becoming susceptible to radical ideas. The set of measures designed to achieve this is meant to give people a greater stake in Dutch society and increase social cohesion. The measures constitute three pillars. First, in order to prevent radicalization and the ensuing recruitment of radical Muslims by Salafist jihadis, efforts were intensified to integrate Muslims into Dutch society. More attention was paid to identity issues, to combating discrimination in schools, in the labour market and in the hospitality industry and to encouraging Muslims to participate in society and politics. The authorities even supported Dutch imam training programmes, to allow clerics to become better informed about life in the West.

Second, social resistance to radicalization and terrorism, especially within the Muslim community, was supported. A programme was developed in dialogue with minorities and Muslim organizations aimed at counteracting radicalization by strengthening social ties and civil society. The third pillar pertained to the prevention of radicalization by identifying, isolating and containing the processes of radicalization. In major Dutch cities systems have been developed 'to funnel reports of suspected radicalisation to a central information point at a local level, where they can be assessed and used to develop a customised approach'. In this context special attention is paid to the so-called hotbeds of radicalization, that is, a small number of locations in the Netherlands, such as some Salafist centres and mosques, that have been identified as potential gateways to radical milieux (Ongering, 2007, pp. 8–10). These malignant expressions of radicalism can be combated through the criminal law, although the effectiveness of using criminal law against radicalism depends to a great extent on mastering the grey area between behaviour that would constitute a criminal offence and behaviour that is merely deemed to be socially unacceptable.

Recently, the third category measures have been strengthened by means of new CT projects and instruments. Early in 2007 the NCTb identified the global dissemination of violent jihadist ideology as one of the central factors contributing to the development of radicalism and terrorism in the Netherlands. The agency therefore started an investigation and monitoring project of radical Islamist sites that spread al-Qaeda propaganda all over the world and succeed in mobilizing individual Muslims in the West to participate in jihad (NCTb, 2006).

Already in 2006, in a development analogous to measures taken in the United Kingdom, the Minister of the Interior and Kingdom Relations and the Minister of Justice submitted a bill on 'administrative measures [concerning] national security', that would impose restrictions on the freedom of people suspected of (supporting) terrorist activities (NCTb/ Directie Beleid en Strategie, 2006, p. 19).[7] In March 2007, this bill passed through the Second Chamber of Parliament and at the time of writing is under consideration in the First Chamber.

In the meantime, the March 2006 acquittal by the Court of Rotterdam of five out of the fourteen defendants charged with membership of a terrorist organization in the so-called Hofstad-case, demonstrated the independence of the judicial system – although critics interpreted these acquittals as leniency or as a result of lapses in the legal framework (*NRC Handelsblad*, 2006). To forestall acquittals like this, on 1 January 2006 an Act amending the Code of Criminal Procedure to regulate powers to demand data had already been implemented. Furthermore, a bill to expand the scope for investigating and prosecuting terrorist crimes was passed in November 2006 and enacted in February 2007. And in September 2006 a bill that would allow courts to investigate information in the hands of the AIVD by cross-examining protected witnesses was enacted (Committee of Experts on Terrorism, 2006).

Other proposals currently under consideration are a bill aimed at extending the possibilities of banning NGOs with terrorist affiliations; a proposal, submitted in 2005, that defined glorification, trivialization or negation of serious crimes a punishable offence – the so-called apology-ban; a proposal to make participation in a terrorist training camp a crime; and a bill to expand the possibilities of removing someone from office who is involved in recruiting activities or inciting hate (Eikelenboom, 2007, pp. 233, 253).

On a more long-term basis, the authorities aimed to increase resistance in society (the so-called second pillar of the CT approach) by conducting a media campaign calling on the public, civic bodies, and the business community to stay alert and report any suspicious circumstances. They are also supporting initiatives in Muslim circles to discuss and resist radicalization, through programmes and discussion evenings in mosques, or in FORUM – a Dutch NGO aimed at promoting multiculturalism in society. Crucial to the building of resilience is the availability of information on moderate Islam. Therefore, on the one hand, the NCTb set out to take the most radical sites offline by initiating a 'notice and take down' procedure with the providers. On the other hand, institutions that voice moderate views and pass on factual information about religion are supported (e.g. with more funding) (Benschop, 2006; NCTb, 2006).

Dilemmas and possible effects of the 'comprehensive approach'

So far, CT measures have led to many successes. Several terrorist networks have been dismantled and disrupted, including the Hofstad group. Many jihadists have been arrested, convicted and given prison sentences. Recruitment has also been tackled. Taken together, these results even prompted the NCTb to lower the general threat level for the Netherlands in June 2007 from 'substantial' to 'limited'. This lower threat level however 'is no reason to be less stringent in any of the measures we have taken, [...]' it 'encourage[s] us to push ahead with the course we have been following', as deputy National Coordinator Lidewij Ongering stated in June 2007 (Ongering, 2007, p. 7).

In short, the result of this 'comprehensive approach' can be summarized as the dissection, isolation and neutralization of 'real terrorists' from their direct environment; a policy that is generally supported by the academic literature on historical experiences with counterterrorism (O'Neill, 2005, pp. 172, 179). In this context, CT strategy has to include the battle for the 'hearts and minds' of the potential recruits. Notwithstanding the results obtained, this broad approach raises some questions.

In the first place, the new bills and measures mentioned above can cut both ways. The Ministers of Justice and the Interior and a majority in the Second Chamber view them as necessary amendments to the Criminal Law, given the character of the new terrorist threats, but argue that they still fit in with the comprehensive Dutch CT approach. Legal experts, however, are more sceptical. They fear, in the first place, a blurring of police and intelligence competences, since the police can now already start collecting data or conduct body searches based on indications of a crime rather than only on the basis of reasonable suspicion. Second, proportionality seems endangered when people can be kept in custody based on very light suspicions and information can be withheld from them. Third, AIVD information used in court is very hard to control, even for the judges. Taken together, fears have arisen that these measures could contribute to a stigmatization and isolation of parts of the immigrant population (de Roos, 2006). An 'apology-ban' could even hinder public debate, deepen mistrust in society and turn offenders into martyrs (Council of State, 2005).

On the other hand, some argue, expanding police competences prevents the *'Vernachrichtendienstlichung'* of the Criminal Procedure, that is, the growing reliance on the intelligence services. It does not blur the boundaries between police and intelligence activities; on the contrary, it enables the intelligence services to follow their long-term strategy instead of compelling them to act as camouflaged investigation services. This also gives them more leeway to communicate and exchange information with foreign services, who might otherwise be reluctant to provide information that might be used in court, thereby revealing their sources. Thus, from this perspective, the extension of suitable preventive instruments minimizes violence and enables a flexible response, embedded in the 'broad CT approach' (Fijnaut, 2007).

A contrary view suggests that preventive and disruptive interventions might be the very reason for further radicalization and stigmatization. There is some evidence for this assertion. Although prevention might seem 'soft' compared to straightforward repression, it cuts a lot deeper into society. A repressive approach addresses relatively small groups of perpetrators, whereas the preventive strategy can involve a much broader context. In other words, this approach interferes with a lot more, mainly innocent people, maybe even creating new grounds for radicalization and resentment in its wake. In the United States, for example, enhanced attention to potential radicals after 9/11 led to more thorough control of immigrants, which in turn caused enormous delays in handling visa requests. This can induce frustration and create a heightened security risk due to the fact that the more malicious remain in the country pending the decision (Birt, 2006, p. 9; Briggs et al., 2006, pp. 28–30, 41).

Second, the comprehensive approach and the dialogue programmes towards the Muslim community compel a secular government to interfere in the religious attitudes of its citizens. Authorities are forced to differentiate between moderate and radical Islam, but how should they define the boundary between moderate and extremist Muslims? Should authorities maintain relations with moderate Salafists (Buys and

Demant, n.d., p. 20; Buys et al., 2006)? How can they be certain who the real moderates are (Eikelenboom, 2007, p. 240)?

Third, in addressing religious groups and differentiating between Muslim and non-Muslim citizens, polarization in society can be increased instead of being neutralized. Each form of positive intervention on behalf of a specific group, or making concessions to causes espoused by terrorists, can arouse hostility from those who believe that terrorism is 'being rewarded' (Pitchford, 2003). Deradicalization of one group (e.g. specific Muslim groups) can therefore contribute to radicalization of another (e.g. extreme right wing groups).

Fourth, we still lack evidence on the relation between immigration, integration and terrorism. CT strategy is aimed at facilitating integration. But do we know for certain that integration itself can't be a 'root cause' of radicalization and terrorism? Van Gogh's murderer, Mohammed Bouyeri, was a fully integrated Dutch citizen, active in community projects who held a higher education degree. In this, he was fully consistent with the profile of many terrorists who started as social activists and, driven by a strong sense of urgency, decided to embark on a course of violence (Twemlow and Sacco, 2002). The 'integration paradox' of Buys et al. (see above) has still not been solved.

Fifth, the CT strategy of building resilience and public resistance to terrorism can itself pose a danger to social cohesion. Authorities are asking teachers, social workers, police officers and regular citizens to act as informers and spy on each other.[8] This strategy informs a 'culture of prevention' that hardly puts limits to intelligence gathering, and where 'caution about dissent becomes an accepted social custom' (Heymann, 2003, pp. 135–9). In this context, non-conformism and diversity, according to the president of the Council of State of the Netherlands, Herman Tjeenk Willink, 'a characteristic of democracy and the secret of its resilience', become endangered virtues (Willink, 2007).

Finally, we don't yet know whether prevention really works. Preventive instruments require synchronization between the various policymakers and authorities, something that is usually lacking in a democracy. Each agency involved tends to hold its own view regarding the terrorist danger (Clutterbuck, 2004, p. 145; Cronin, 2004, p. 285). Even if there is enough goodwill, the response will dwindle after the immediate crisis is overcome (Matthew and Shambaugh, 2005). Finally, the effectiveness of a preventive approach is very difficult to measure and academic literature hardly comes forward with examined instruments (Art and Richardson, 2007, pp. 574, 577). Therefore, the core element of the 'Dutch approach', the role of persuasion in the struggle against terrorism, remains to be tested.

Notes

1. The BVD also conducted disruptions and tried to frame radical activists, according to OBIV (OBIV, 1998, pp. 29–30).
2. The BVD even conducted espionage operations against the IRA on British soil (Lagas and Sierksma, 1993).
3. In 2002 the BVD was renamed the General Intelligence and Security Service (*Algemene Inlichtingen- en Veiligheidsdienst*, AIVD), integrating both national security tasks and foreign intelligence activities.
4. The separate national and urban police forces were now integrated, thereby creating a more unified police apparatus compared to that which existed in the 1970s and 1980s, although it was still structured into twenty-five regional divisions.
5. A bill on a new system for safety and security was submitted to the Second Chamber in 2005. Parliamentary reports II 2002/03, 28974, no 2. The bill was already drafted in 2002.
6. Handelingen Tweede Kamer (Parliamentary records) 2004–2005, 11 November 2005. 29854, pp. 22–1329.
7. Administrative measures can include a territorial ban, or a ban on going near certain persons.
8. 'Terrorismebestrijding', answer to parliamentary questions by the Minister of the Interior, 5 October 2006. TK, 2006–2007, 29754, Nr. 83, p. 10.

10
The Spanish Experience of Countering Terrorism: From ETA to al-Qaeda

Rogelio Alonso

Introduction

Spain and the United Kingdom have been two of the liberal democracies most deeply concerned with a persistent challenge from terrorism. Since the late 1960s ETA (*Euskadi Ta Askatasuna*) the Basque terrorist group, as part of what Professor David Rapoport has termed the third wave of modern terrorism (Rapoport 1994, pp. 46–73), has espoused an ethno-nationalist ideology on the basis of which it has justified an intense campaign of killings.

ETA has been responsible for the killing of 854 people from the beginning of its campaign up to December 2007, when the killing paused again for a few months. Although this chapter will focus on ETA and al-Qaeda, which are the terrorist groups responsible for the highest levels of violence in Spain, the country has also seen violence perpetrated by other groups. In the second-half of the 1970s after the death of General Franco, right-wing extremists related to reactionary members of the State security agencies killed ten people in France and twenty-three others inside Spain, victims presumably being chosen because of their alleged relationship with ETA. The other main terrorist group active in Spain until the 1990s has been the left-wing Antifascist Group of Resistance First of October (GRAPO, *Grupo de Resistencia Antifascista Primero de Octubre*) (Alonso 2005, pp. 113–50).

After suffering a protracted campaign of violence from ETA, Spain witnessed a decrease in the activities of this group. Just as the levels of ETA's violence were decreasing, Spain witnessed the emergence of a new terrorist threat in the form of jihadist terrorism with quite distinctive characteristics, such as its religious inspiration, global objectives, high levels of lethality, and indiscrimination. The terrorist attacks on Madrid of 11 March 2004, when Muslim extremists killed 191 and injured hundreds more after ten bombs went off on commuter trains during the morning rush hour, showed that the jihadist threat had reached Spain. Subsequent detentions and foiled attacks confirmed the seriousness of the threat facing the country.

Although the threat of international terrorism inspired by Islamic fundamentalism differs from the one posed for so long by ETA, important similarities emerge when analysing these terrorist phenomena (Alonso, 2008). Therefore, the lessons learned throughout the years of dealing with ETA should not be ignored when attempting to understand the current terrorist challenge. In fact, to a great extent the experience of countering ETA's protracted terrorist campaign has informed the Spanish response to the terrorist threat now posed by al-Qaeda. Accordingly this chapter will provide a historical overview of the evolution of the Spanish strategy for dealing with terrorism. This analysis will reveal how the key pillars on which previous counterterrorist campaigns were built are still maintained to confront the current threat posed by international terrorism. Thus, intelligence gathering and coordination between the main agencies involved in counterterrorism remain two of the most important tools in the Spanish counterterrorist repertoire.

ETA's terrorism: the challenge and the response

ETA's current and recent levels of violence are clearly a long way from the dramatic escalation that took place during the period of transition from dictatorship to democracy. ETA was formed in 1959 by young nationalists, mostly students, who belonged to the Basque middle class. They became involved in violence in defiance of the State and as an attempt to impose a nationalist and Marxist agenda on the region (Elorza, 2006). This violence emerged in the late 1960s, coinciding with the later stages of General Franco's regime. The death of the dictator in 1975 and the process of democratization that followed did not deter ETA, which in fact perpetrated the vast majority of its killings once democracy had stabilized. Despite ETA's violence having declined in frequency throughout the 1980s, the 1990s and particularly during the first years of the twenty-first century, it has remained a major source of concern for Spanish citizens as a whole and for the residents of the Basque Country in particular. Nonetheless, a comprehensive set of initiatives managed to contain ETA's violence to the point where the group ceased to be a major threat to democratic stability.

Political, police, social and
judicial counterterrorist measures

ETA's containment and decline over the years was achieved through a comprehensive set of measures that can be summarized as follows: various political initiatives linked to the democratization of the country's political system (this functioned as an efficient anti-terrorist instrument that progressively deprived the terrorist group of wide support); law enforcement efforts characterized by a gradual increase in international cooperation and the improvement of intelligence capabilities, together with the professionalization and enhancement of efficiency of the main counterterrorist agencies; judicial and legislative responses that included the introduction of new terrorist offences and the proscription of political and social organizations linked to the terrorist group; and finally social reinsertion and penitentiary provisions (Reinares & Alonso, 2007).

In significant part, the decline of ETA's terrorist campaign was a result of the process of democratization initiated in the wake of the dictatorship. This structural dynamic created a crisis of legitimacy for ETA, since certain social sectors may have supported terrorism had the State not reformed the context in which violence emerged and existed. However, the 'democratic deficit' gradually disappeared in the aftermath of the dictatorship as new political institutions and a legal framework were put into place following the end of Franco's regime. In 1978 a new Spanish Constitution was endorsed by the electorate, opening the door for the decentralization of the State and the 1979 Statute of Autonomy for the Basque Country that was also approved in a referendum. The Statute, upon which Basque institutions of territorial self-government were created, has the rank of constitutional law and provides extensive powers for the autonomous authorities. Moreover, between 1975 and 1977 nearly 900 members and collaborators of ETA exiled or imprisoned under the dictatorship were freed. In 1977 the Spanish National Court was set up, constituting a fundamental jurisdictional change since from that moment onwards terrorist crimes would be dealt with by judges instead of military courts. Finally, from 1982 social reinsertion measures based on individual pardons were also applied to individuals prepared to distance themselves from the terrorist organization (Escrivá, 2006).

This political consolidation was aided by the gradual professionalization and modernization of security agencies that had earlier been viewed with distrust by society because of their association with the previous authoritarian regime. In the early years of the transition the two main law enforcement agencies, the National Police (*Policía*

Nacional) and the Civil Guard (*Guardia Civil*), remained highly militarized, as well as poorly trained and equipped to confront terrorism, and lacking in any kind of coordination that would facilitate an effective performance against ETA (Jaime, 2002). This situation gradually changed and levels of police efficiency in the late 1990s and at the turn of the century were markedly improved. Whereas in the early years of the battle against ETA the lack of good intelligence led to a large number of detentions that were not followed by prosecutions, this pattern was progressively reversed. This also had a political effect, since it reduced the alienation that less selective policing had generated in certain communities and that had facilitated ETA's recruitment of supporters and sympathizers (Domínguez, 1998a, pp. 201–21). This improvement in police efficiency was greatly assisted by the strengthening of cooperation between Spain and France (Morán, 1997). The neighbouring country was seen for many years as a refuge for ETA's leadership, but France's increasing political, police and judicial cooperation benefited Spanish counterterrorist efforts. This was particularly the case from the 1990s when French authorities allowed Spanish police to operate across the border, with the percentage of detentions in France soon growing as a result. ETA's leadership was twice dismantled in France after close cooperation between French and Spanish police forces resulted in very successful operations in 1992 and 2004 (Domínguez, 2006a and b). These setbacks suffered by the terrorist group seriously affected ETA's structural organization and activities (Domínguez, 1998b).

The law enforcement response also benefited from the setting up of the Basque autonomous police force, the *Ertzaintza*, composed of over 7000 members. The Basque autonomous police engaged in counterterrorism from 1986, and as their activity increased, ETA responded, killing four autonomous police officials during the 1990s.

Despite the existence of a significant section of society that still empathized with terrorist groups or those who represented them politically, this combination of political and security factors limited the terrorist phenomenon in Spain. The rejection of ETA among Basque citizens gradually increased throughout the years in parallel with the democratization process, a trend evidenced in regular social surveys. Significantly, support and justification for violence decreased to a low level among the constituency of ETA's political wing, *Batasuna* (Euskobarómetro, 2007).

In May 2006, total support for ETA was only expressed by 0.9% of those polled by the *Euskobarómetro*, with only 7% of voters of a party supportive of ETA showing some kind of endorsement of the terrorist group. In 1978 nearly half of Basque adults perceived ETA members as either patriots or idealists, whereas only 7% of those interviewed in public opinion surveys would call them plain criminals. However, in 1989 less than one-quarter of Basque citizens referred to them in more or less favourable terms, those who portrayed members of ETA simply as criminals having more than doubled in comparison with figures from the previous decade.

Batasuna performed poorly in general elections, confirming the decreasing support for violent nationalism among the Basque people (Unzueta & Barbería, 2003, pp. 306–15). Another indicator of decreasing support for ETA's terrorism can be located in the growing dissociation of important sections of Basque society from the group (Uriarte, 2003), as evidenced by an increasing mobilization of citizens against violence, a phenomenon articulated in a number of associations that regularly held public demonstrations with strong turn outs demanding an end to terrorism (Funes, 1998, pp. 493–510). The lack of wide support for ETA's violence made it possible for the Spanish State to ban *Batasuna* on the basis that the party was a component part of a complex network of organizations ultimately led by ETA (Mata, 1993).

This initiative was initially widely criticized by nationalist politicians in the Basque Country, who claimed that it would trigger more violence, deepening the delegitimization of the State. However, the outcome of such a controversial measure was quite positive in democratic terms. First of all, lethal terrorist actions as well as urban terrorism decreased, with ETA being unable to regain the popular support lost over the years. Second, the banning of *Batasuna* had significant material consequences since the measure deprived the political party of the public funding that represented a highly valuable source of income for ETA (Buesa, 2006). In addition, since the proscription of *Batasuna* resulted in the expulsion of the party from the institutions of municipal and local government throughout the Basque Country, the organization's ability to exert a considerable social and political control over the population was negatively affected. These material gains were complemented by another positive outcome. By proscribing *Batasuna* the State was seen to be confronting terrorism through legal means rather than the illegal ones opted for in the early 1980s when members of the Spanish Interior Ministry were linked to the terrorist actions of the so-called Liberation Anti-Terrorist Groups (*Grupos Antiterroristas de Liberación*, GAL).

Between 1983 and 1987 GAL carried out a campaign of terrorist activity against suspected members and supporters of ETA, resulting in the killing of twenty-seven individuals (Woodworth, 2001). This illegal group was secretly coordinated by police officials who recruited mercenary assassins among organized criminals in France and Portugal. GAL benefited from the passivity and allegiance of some prominent politicians. They targeted ETA members and sympathizers living across the border in the south of France, though around half the people killed had no links whatsoever with the Basque terrorist organization. Spain proved to be a functioning democratic regime after the rule of law was finally applied to policemen, gangsters, and some politicians belonging to the Socialist, all of whom received severe sentences for their illegal activities as part of GAL. From 1988 police counterterrorist operations became much more discriminate and selective, and no single episode of illegal violence in the State's response to ETA has been reported since that time.

The effectiveness of counterterrorism and its reversal

Hence, the 2002 proscription of *Batasuna* and the dismantling of its satellite structures which, under the disguise of cultural and social organizations, lent their support to ETA, together with the increase of formal sanctions on violent activism, actually accelerated the decline of the terrorist organization and reduced levels of social control imposed by the criminal network. These draconian measures were made possible after the two major parties in Spain signed a broad anti-terrorist agreement in 2000 denying the terrorist group any expectation of success, while committing themselves to the defeat of terrorism (Elorza, 2003, pp. 149–284). The strong consensus enshrined in the Agreement for Liberties and Against Terrorism (*Pacto por las Libertades y Contra el Terrorismo*) enabled the State to simultaneously apply pressure on ETA at the political, police, social, and judicial levels. This combined action seriously damaged ETA's ability to operate, also reducing popular support and the group's capacity to mobilize supporters and activists. ETA's internal documentation of the time reveals how damaging the government's strategy was, since it privately acknowledged the effectiveness of the State's policies (Alonso, 2007a).

This view was reinforced by a letter written in the summer of 2004 by six leading members of ETA who were serving prison sentences, including the man who was at the top of the organization during the 1990s. These prominent activists acknowledged that ETA had been defeated by the Spanish State's strategies and demanded that the organization give up its terrorist campaign. The leadership of ETA subsequently expelled these dissidents in an attempt to exert tight control over the group's strategy. Nonetheless, such an unambiguous acknowledgement by activists who years ago were themselves responsible for repressing voices who had called for an end to ETA's violence, demonstrated the success of the Spanish State in countering terrorism. Contrary to those who argued that terrorism could only end in exchange for concessions, the criticism voiced by such prominent activists demonstrated that it was both possible and realistic to expect the conclusion of the group's campaign of violence without granting political concessions in return. In fact such a move came only years after a new political party, *Aralar*, was formed in 2002 by disillusioned members of *Batasuna* who left the party as a result of the continuation of ETA's violence despite widespread criticism within Basque society, including by radical nationalist voters.

Hence, in combating ETA Spanish counterterrorism had achieved a considerable degree of effectiveness, providing a very successful model based on the combined implementation of initiatives such as the ones previously described, among them, the democratization of the political system, the professionalization of the security forces, penitentiary and judicial measures, as well as political responses aimed at strengthening the consensus of those who were fighting ETA, thus increasing the isolation of the terrorist group. While previous counterterrorist strategies had put special emphasis on certain fronts, the policy applied between 2000 and 2004 brought together all these various dimensions, also benefiting from the maturation of previous initiatives that were finally producing positive results. It should be stressed that certain counterterrorist tools do need time to show their full potential, as revealed by the effectiveness of some of them in the medium term in the Spanish context.

ETA's March 2006 'ceasefire' declaration generated hopes that the terrorist group was willing to end its violent campaign. However, sceptics proved to be right since the terrorist group, despite the effectiveness of the anti-terrorist tactics described above, was still reluctant to disappear. (Europol, 2007). In fact, it can be argued that ETA found considerable relief in the significant policy shift which came after the Socialist Party won the country's general election on 14 March 2004 (Alonso, 2007, pp. 145–74). In contravention of the anti-terrorist pact signed by the two main political parties, representatives of the Socialist Party had maintained contacts with the terrorist group since at least 2002. Government representatives negotiated a truce with ETA in exchange for political concessions, conveying the message to the terrorist group that the threat of violence could 'pay off'.

The authorities' response was destined to weaken those within the terrorist organization arguing for the abandonment of violence, given the high cost of such a tactic. Furthermore, negotiations with ETA took place as the State considerably reduced the pressure on the terrorist group that had been applied in the previous years, an attitude strongly criticized by Spanish and French counterterrorist officials. As senior counterterrorist experts put it, the policy implemented by the Spanish Socialist government had provided ETA with oxygen at a time when the group had been on the brink of being asphyxiated (Alonso and Reinares, 2008, p. 113).

In June 2007 ETA issued a public statement ending their 'cessation' of violence, and declaring that the terrorist organization had opened again 'all fronts' against the Spanish State. ETA's terrorist activities had not ceased during the truce (Buesa, 2006). Nonetheless, the Spanish government authorized negotiations with the terrorist group to carry on, thus contravening the parliamentary resolution approved in May 2005 by which 'dialogue with those willing to put an end to violence' could only begin if ETA demonstrated 'clearly' and 'unequivocally' its willingness to cease terrorism (Congress Resolution, 2005). The fact that ETA showed no signs of willingness to put an end to violence did not deter the Spanish President, José Luis Rodríguez Zapatero, who authorized negotiations with the terrorist group before and after the resolution. This significant shift in the government's policy strengthened ETA's stance since, from its perspective, the Spanish government had gone against Parliament's mandate, despite the threat of violence having been maintained.

ETA's coercion had been underestimated by the Spanish government, to some extent due to the emergence of the new terrorist threat represented by the attacks perpetrated in Madrid on 11 March 2004. The lethality and level of indiscrimination involved in these attacks to an extent overshadowed the threat still posed by ETA. In fact, ETA benefited from the comparison with a new, more lethal and indiscriminate, type of terrorism, since it seemed that ETA could damage the political and social system without engaging in the same kind of violence as Muslim extremists. For example ETA's activities of extortion and intimidation were considered more 'acceptable'. One of the most damaging consequences of such an approach occurred in June 2006, when a police operation against ETA's network in charge of raising money through extortion was about to be aborted because of a 'tip off'. ETA's suspects were alerted to the police operation in a development that effectively amounted to collaboration with a terrorist organization, or at least the misuse of policing. It seemed that the lessons of years of counterterrorism had not been properly learned by some.

From ETA to al-Qaeda:
the counterterrorist transition

The lessons learned during the protracted fight against ETA meant that Spain was well equipped to counter this new terrorism. However, the framework in place to counter violence perpetrated by Muslim extremists at the time of the 11 March 2004 terrorist attacks was not well developed. The origins of the jihadist threat to Spain can be traced back to the previous decade when the first networks, mainly composed of Algerian and Syrian individuals, started to settle in Spain. Although police surveillance led to important successes at the turn of the century, efforts directed at countering Islamic terrorism were restricted by the limited amount of human and material resources available. The emergence and development of the threat since the 1990s raised concerns among the main security agencies, that is, National Police (*Policía Nacional*), Civil Guard (*Guardia Civil*), and the National Centre of Intelligence (*Centro Nacional de Inteligencia, CNI*). Nonetheless, the commitment to confront Islamic terrorism became stronger as a result of the 9/11 terrorist attacks and, in particular, after the atrocity perpetrated in Madrid in 2004.

In fact, the 9/11 attacks in the United States led to a slight increase in police personnel followed by another small boost after the 2003 Casablanca terrorist attacks in neighbouring Morocco. During this period, the Spanish National Police increased its capacity by 25%, forming up to seventy specialists on Islamic terrorism and doubling those who concentrated on the Maghreb region, regarded as the main area of threat (Commission of Enquiry, 2004). At the same time the Civil Guard also increased its specialists on the subject, although the sixty experts available before 11 March 2004 were still regarded as insufficient. Despite these efforts it was still felt that levels of police and intelligence personnel, including translators, required strengthening, and initiatives aimed at preventing the radicalization and recruitment of radicals with the potential to perpetrate terrorist attacks remained scarce. It was only after Spain had suffered a major setback on 11 March and the loss of almost 200 people that a broader counterterrorist framework was put into place. In fact, the inertia associated with a protracted campaign against ETA's terrorism led the Spanish authorities to initially blame the Basque terrorist group for the 11 March atrocity, in spite of the fact that jihadist terrorism had clearly emerged as a very serious threat over the previous years.

In the aftermath of the terrorist attacks different measures were announced by the newly elected Spanish government. The scope of these initiatives coincided with the objectives set out by the European Union's strategy for combating terrorism and the radicalization and recruitment of individuals: disrupt the activities of the networks and individuals who draw people into terrorism, ensure that voices of mainstream opinion prevail over those of extremism, and promote yet more vigorously security, justice, democracy, and opportunity for all (Council of the European Union, 2005). The measures implemented by the Spanish authorities to fulfil these objectives have included: a significant increase in intelligence capabilities; the improvement and enhancement of coordination and cooperation between security agencies and governments; a few legislative reforms; the implementation of a programme designed to enhance the protection of targets and the responses to terrorist attacks; and, finally, measures aimed at the prevention of radicalization and recruitment (Alonso, 2006, pp. 17–23).

Increase in intelligence capabilities

The Spanish institutional counterterrorist framework that evolved in relation to ETA benefited from the input of several ministries, with the Ministry of the Interior being in charge of directing police efforts throughout the years. The State law enforcement agencies have been under the direction and coordination of the Minister of the Interior and the Secretary of State for Security. As mentioned above, the two main police forces in charge of counterterrorism in the country are the National Police and the Civil Guard. Within these forces there are two bodies that integrate specialized units with competence in terrorist matters, both of them reporting directly to the Secretary of State for Security: the General Office for Information, which is part of the Directorate General of Police, and the Office of the Chief for Information and Judicial Police, which is part of the Directorate General of the Civil Guard. Both directorates were brought together in September 2006 in an attempt to improve coordination between the two main Spanish police forces. Police forces in autonomous communities such as Catalonia and the Basque Country have also developed responsibilities vis-à-vis counter-terrorism, and have improved levels of coordination.

Complementing the efforts of the police, the CNI, under the Ministry of Defence, has also provided information and analysis with the aim of preventing terrorism. From its creation in 1977 until 2002 the Centre was known as the Higher Defence Intelligence Centre (*Centro Superior de Información de la Defensa*, CESID). The evolution of the intelligence services marked a significant professionalization of the institution that turned into a fully civilian agency after having been mostly operated by the military in the past (Díaz, 2005). The activities of the CNI have been coordinated with law enforcement agencies such as the National Police and the Civil Guard through the Government Commission for Intelligence Affairs. As will be seen below, in the aftermath of the 11 March 2004 terrorist attacks a new body was set up with the aim of improving coordination and cooperation between the National Police, the Civil Guard, and the Intelligence Service. The creation of the National Centre for the Coordination of Antiterrorism (*Centro Nacional de Coordinación Antiterrorista*, CNCA) was intended to overcome serious flaws around the process of intelligence gathering and the exploitation of this valuable resource.

Serious intelligence shortcomings were revealed by the fact that prior to the massacre perpetrated in Madrid, many of the terrorist suspects involved in the 11 March attacks had already been under scrutiny in the course of investigations into Islamist terrorism and other crimes. By 2002 Spain had already become an important 'sanctuary' for Muslim extremists (Valenzuela 2002, p. 64), although police successes against networks of activists led the United States to describe Spain as the 'champion' in the fight against Islamist terrorism (Alonso, 2007c, p. 209). Spain was also regarded by Italian judicial authorities as 'the main base of al-Qaeda' (Alonso, 2007c, p. 203). Despite various warnings (Europol, 2003, p. 37), terrorists struck in March 2004 revealing the inefficiency of police structures as regards Islamist terrorism (Irujo, 2005, p. 207). Overall, the security forces had still been oriented towards confronting ETA's terrorism, a fact that inhibited investigations into Islamist terrorism.

The limited human and material resources available seriously constrained the work that the security agencies could do. Therefore, it was necessary to significantly increase resources, something that was announced immediately after the attacks. This response was also influenced by an awareness of how fast jihadist terrorists may progress from the preparatory stages of their attacks to the actual execution of indiscriminate and lethal violent actions. Considerable effort was required to apply efficient preventive intelligence methods that would allow for the prevention of terrorist plots through anticipation and disruption. An increase in the number of translators and interpreters was particularly important in the aftermath of the atrocity, given the surprisingly small number of professionals devoted to such an important part of the investigation process, as was the presence of police and agents capable of working within the communities in question. The vast number of dialects and unfamiliar cultural and social codes constituted important barriers to a better understanding of the current terrorist phenomenon and the activities of individuals under investigation, and the complexities of access to what are very closed clusters constitute a daunting task that will require a coherent policy for the penetration of terrorist cells.

Between 2004 and 2007, 600 new policemen were recruited to fight Islamist terrorism. Three hundred more were being trained, the intention being to have over a thousand specialists. As well as more informers, undercover and infiltrated agents, this approach also requires better technical means to intercept communications and carry out surveillance and scientific investigations. Therefore it was not enough for the two main police bodies in the country to simply increase their numbers. New agents had to be filtered and properly selected before recruitment. Later on they had to be trained, a slow process that would require existing members to devote some of their time and energy to the newcomers, thus stretching already limited resources until the new agents were fully operational. The limited presence of police and intelligence personnel abroad was also a problem that the authorities started to address. As a result, police representatives were sent to key areas such as Pakistan, Syria, Libya, Algeria, Jordan, Indonesia, the Philippines, and Saudi Arabia. However, this should not obscure the fact that in terms of resources, only 10% of Spanish intelligence was deployed abroad.

Improvements in coordination

Coordination among different security agencies involved in counterterrorism remains an important challenge. In an attempt to improve this matter, a National Centre for the Coordination of Antiterrorism was created in May 2004. The Centre's main aim is to receive, process, and assess strategic information available from various sources and agencies, thus integrating information from the main security forces and the CNI. The Centre brings together representatives of the two main police forces and the intelligence service, and one of its main objectives is to enable a proper exchange of information to take place through the correct management of databases. Although progress has been made, important challenges still lie ahead. Thus, threat assessment has become a key activity for the Centre, which produces reports that have very little impact on the operational level. As police officers themselves acknowledged in interviews with the author, this limitation stems from the nature of the information handled, which usually lacks a strong operational component, and prevents joint investigations from becoming more frequent and effective.

Traditionally, the main agencies have been very reluctant to share information and this has led to mistakes that on occasion have seriously endangered the lives of members of these bodies and anti-terrorist operations. So far the Centre has been unable to overcome this legacy, even with the addition of another institution created after the 11 March bombings with the aim of improving coordination, namely the Unified Command Executive Committee (*Comité Ejecutivo para el Mando Unificado,* CEMU), whose main task is to guarantee that the two main Spanish police forces, the National Police and the Civil Guard, perform in an efficient and coordinated manner.

Improved cooperation between police agencies, both internally and externally, must be complemented by effective coordination at a political and judicial level. To this extent, the reluctance to share sensitive information creates important obstacles that are not only limited to the domestic level but are also common internationally. At the same time the seriousness of the problem is not perceived in the same way by all EU member states, different experiences of Islamist terrorism having shaped each state's understanding, degree of concern and reaction to the phenomenon. This has led a group of five European partners – Spain, the United Kingdom, France, Germany and Italy – to convene periodically with a view to seeking ways of overcoming the obstacles that prevent more effective cooperation and coordination. The initiatives being considered by the group initially known as the G5, but now referred to as the G6 after the addition of Poland in 2006, include the preparation of a list of terrorist suspects that could be shared by the different country members. The complexity surrounding these issues is even more evident when efforts are directed towards improving the coordination and cooperation between European and Arab countries, a necessary objective that is of particular relevance to Spain, given its geo-strategic situation, and one which has led the authorities to increase various initiatives in that direction.

Legislative reforms

Spain's protracted fight against terrorism during the last thirty years has provided it with a legal framework dating back to 1977, when the National Court (*Audiencia Nacional*) was set up in Madrid to deal with serious organized crime and terrorist offences. Various reforms of the Criminal Code over the years introduced new terrorist offences in advance of the March 2004 terrorist attacks in Madrid. As a result of this gradual upgrading political and judicial authorities considered that, in essence, the legal framework already existed and did not require further amendments to properly confront Islamist terrorism. The effectiveness of the system is demonstrated by its capacity to consistently sentence individuals who have been related to this type of terrorist activity. For example, in September 2005 a total of eighteen men were found guilty of membership and collaboration with al-Qaeda. Furthermore, twenty people were convicted in 2007 for their involvement in the March 11, 2004 terrorist attacks. This approach contrasts sharply with that of the UK and Australia, detailed elsewhere in this volume.

Other legislative amendments aimed at strengthening the control of private sector activities have been considered over the last few years but have failed to materialize so far. Among these new legal provisions, there is particular concern about the need to develop legislation on telecommunications with the intention of achieving better cooperation from operators and the identification of pre-pay cards for use with mobile phones to properly identify callers. The importance of mobile phones and phone conversations in police and judicial investigations related to Islamist terrorism has to be stressed since the tracking of suspects has been greatly aided by the ability to locate their calls.

Given the importance of the Internet in the radicalization and recruitment of individuals susceptible to involvement in terrorist activities, amendments to the 1999 Data Protection Law have also been considered to require Internet providers to retain data on users for a year. At the same time, pre-existing legislation has also been reinforced and extended to include stricter mechanisms of control aimed at preventing financial institutions from carrying out operations that may help to finance terrorist activities or organized crime.

Protection of targets and response

Since 11 March 2004 a response plan (*Plan Operativo de Lucha contra el Terrorismo*) has been designed contemplating the participation of the Spanish Army should it be required for the protection of strategic installations, including communication networks and nuclear power stations. The protection of important events and the monitoring of bus and train stations, ports, and airports, is of particular importance once the programme is activated as a result of a terrorist threat. This was the case during the Christmas season and in the aftermath of the London terrorist attacks on 7 July 2005. However this programme was not put in place during the Christmas season in 2006, when, on 30 December, ETA's terrorist attack on Madrid's international airport killed two people and caused extensive material damage.

Complementing the response programme the Army and the Civil Guard have also increased their capabilities and preparedness to deal with a non-conventional terrorist attack. Thus, stocks of several vaccines have been considerably increased and the Civil Guard has designed a special plan for the prevention of and the reaction to threats and attacks with nuclear, radiological, bacteriological, and/or chemical components. Spain has also introduced rules requiring air companies to hand in to the authorities passengers' lists for international flights (Rodríguez, 2006). Moreover, a new information system is being developed with the intention of improving the quality and the amount of data about people who wish to enter the country. This is nonetheless a difficult task, given the open nature of borders within the Schengen area. Spain's geographical location, which provides a bridge between Europe and North Africa, where radical Islamism is particularly strong, as well as the constant flux of immigrants from this underdeveloped region, has demonstrated the complexity of border control. Revealingly a very high percentage of prison inmates incarcerated in Spanish jails for their involvement in crimes related to jihadist terrorism originated from the Maghreb.

Confronting radicalization

Spain's specific initiatives in relation to radicalization and recruitment can be defined as multifaceted, thus requiring the participation of different ministries in their design and implementation (Council of the European Union, 2004). The main measures implemented in this area have been coordinated by the Ministry of Justice and the Ministry of the Interior. They share the common objective of improving the relationship between the authorities and the Muslim community in Spain and its main representatives. Although the Spanish State and the Islamic Commission of Spain did sign a cooperation agreement in 1992 in which important aspects of the relationship between Muslims and the authorities were set out, many of the issues covered by such a text were not fully developed. The Office of Religious Affairs of the Ministry of Justice, as the body in charge of the preparation, coordination, and implementation of the government's policy on religious matters, including relations with Islamic communities, has been responsible for the assessment and development of the 1992 agreement.

Social and cultural initiatives have been funded through the Foundation for Plurality and Life Together (*Fundación Pluralismo y Convivencia*). This institution, which was created at the end of 2004 by the Ministry of Justice, and falls under the supervision of the Office of

Religious Affairs, aims to enable local communities to engage in the formation and education of their members. Given that youngsters are particularly vulnerable and susceptible to radicalization, these projects are seen as a practical alternative since they allow young individuals to get involved in activities that may keep them away from radicals. It is believed that the influence exerted over youngsters by radicals may be neutralized by their involvement in cultural, educational, and sports activities similar to the ones currently funded by this Foundation. New members of the community who arrive from abroad very often knowing little about the country of arrival, sometimes lacking an important support network of relatives and friends, can also benefit from such an initiative given their propensity to being lured into radical groups.

The prevention and detection of radicalization requires ample cooperation from representatives and members of the communities where radicals are most likely to attempt to attract youngsters. It is at this level that early indicators can be more easily identified, providing the opportunity to disrupt the radicalization process. Such an acknowledgement has led the Spanish authorities to increase contacts with Islamic communities, also involving the police in this process of improving relations with those who are seen as key players in the detection process. One of the most successful initiatives in this area to date has involved the introduction of an online alert system that allows the police to highlight those issues that may be of concern for Islamic communities and which have the potential to turn into controversial grievances if they are not properly addressed.

To defuse sensitive issues that could be conveniently manipulated by radicals, Spanish police have increased contacts with local communities via the deployment of liaison officers. Officers who fulfil this role are not assigned investigative tasks so as to enhance their position as a kind of social mediator between the authorities and the community. This system has been used to warn about xenophobic attitudes towards certain Muslim communities at an early stage. Various concerns about security forces' activities have also been aired through these means, for example, when police raids have taken place coinciding with major Muslim festivals or when detentions have not been followed by prosecutions. The negative impact on the Muslim community of police investigation comes from the use of usually reliable intelligence and disruption in the absence of sufficient evidence to guarantee a prosecution, a process also evident in the United Kingdom.

The role of communities is particularly relevant when confronting violence perpetrated by individuals who espouse a radical and fundamentalist interpretation of Islam. Experience demonstrates that condemnation of violence by the majority and its consequent delegitimization will prevent terrorists from increasing their social support (Schmid, 1993, pp. 14–25). Therefore, counterterrorism also needs to include measures that encourage such condemnation and delegitimization. This is particularly effective when coming from political or religious leaders who are respected in the community, and thus able to exert a positive influence on other members of that particular section of the population. Thus the 'battle for hearts and minds' is seen as being a key part of the counterterrorist framework against Muslim extremists, just as it has in the Netherlands and, particularly under Gordon Brown's premiership, in the United Kingdom.

As a result, contacts with the Arab media and governments in the Arab world have also been intensified. The Spanish government has engaged in a type of public diplomacy aimed at better explaining to a wide Arab audience its foreign policy, the country's realities and its policies relating to issues such as immigration as well as other areas with the potential to become mobilization factors for certain individuals. In this regard, of particular significance remains the role played by certain Arab media, among them *al Jazeera*, whose coverage and interpretation of current affairs contributes to strengthening the bonds of solidarity between Muslims throughout the world by the portrayal of a global Muslim community at times portrayed as victimized and humiliated by Western forces.

By way of example, the September 2003 detention of Taysir Alouny, *al Jazeera*'s correspondent in Spain and the man who interviewed Osama bin Laden shortly after 9/11, was portrayed by the television station as an attack which would have consequences for a country whose image was going to deteriorate in certain parts of the Arab world. Violence polarises and forces audiences to take part by choosing one side, either that of the victims or that of the terrorist. Therefore, the media provide 'identification machines' since 'the terrorist's invitation to identification is brought home to us by the public and the private media' (Schmid, 1989, p. 545). So far it has proved extremely difficult to confront this dimension as well as the increasing influence that the Internet exerts on individuals who can easily access sites where violence in the name of Islam is not only justified but actively encouraged.

The Spanish government has also introduced measures aimed at preventing the radicalisation and recruitment of incarcerated individuals. In November 2004 the dismantling of a terrorist cell inside a prison, and evidence of other cases where radicalisation of prisoners has occurred, led the authorities to opt for the dispersal of those inmates who were linked to jihadist terrorism, allocating them to thirty different centres across the country. Dispersal of prisoners constitutes an important policy adopted in the mid-1980s to confront ETA's terrorism, which has been maintained since then given its efficiency in preventing the association of members of the same ideology that could strengthen the group's pressure over the individual. This pressure hampers hypothetical processes of disengagement from the terrorist organization, also increasing the chances of posing various challenges to the prison authorities. With such a background the dispersal of prisoners associated with jihadist terrorism was also seen as a positive initiative although the outcome could vary as a result of the key differences between these types of terrorism. The dispersal of individuals linked to jihadist terrorism may actually enable them to contact other inmates, creating the risk of further radicalisation and recruitment, a possibility that has led the prison authorities to apply strict control of communications to this type of inmate. Whereas the nationalist ideology espoused by ETA activists was unlikely to be an effective tool for the indoctrination of other prison inmates with no connection with the terrorist organisation given the sheer rejection of ETA's objectives by the majority of the Spanish prison population, the same could not be said of Islamism. The search for new recruits by jihadist terrorists has often extended to marginal groups and criminal circles where individuals are prone to accept ideological doctrines convenient for their criminal acts to be seen in a different light. In other words, a radical interpretation of Islam may become a useful instrument to justify previous and further transgressions shielding the individual from the self-questioning and criticism which usually follows from decisions that generate negative consequences.

Conclusions

The threat posed by international terrorism has evolved, adopting a more indiscriminate form characterized by suicide attacks without warning. Nonetheless, the current threat also retains some of the patterns previously seen in ETA's terrorist campaign, and this legacy influences Spain's response to al-Qaeda. Intelligence gathering and coordination between the main agencies involved in counterterrorism, as well as cooperation between states, still remain some of the most important tools in the counterterrorist repertoire applied by Spain. At the same time the strict adherence to democracy represents a key element of the nation's counterterrorist strategy. The protracted experience of confronting ETA's terrorism has also informed the Spanish state's current response to international terrorism – successful enforcement of law and order may contain violence without fully eradicating it. Nevertheless, counterterrorist strategy obviously aims to keep to a minimum the supportive social environment for terrorism thus preventing widespread legitimization of such a course of action. Similarly, disproportionate responses by the State or its agents must be avoided, since in the past over-reactions and illegal actions have seriously damaged democracy and the fight against terrorism.

At the same time the marked intensity of violence that characterizes the new threat should not lead policymakers to underestimate the challenges that an older terrorist group such as ETA still poses to the democratic governance of Spain, despite the decrease in its activities. Some official surveys reveal that ETA is seen as the main threat by Spanish citizens despite the considerable decrease in the level of killings of the last couple of years. For example, in a February 2007 survey conducted by the Centre for Sociological Research, ETA's terrorism was described by 42.5% of the population as their 'main problem', followed by unemployment, which was regarded as such by 40.5% of those polled. Other polls demonstrate that a high percentage of those surveyed see ETA and al-Qaeda as equally threatening. Despite these differences, these studies confirm that Spain doesn't face a single terrorist threat but a double one, an acknowledgement that must also be reflected in the State's response to terrorism. Indeed, although much attention is rightly focussed on Muslim terrorist cells inside Spain, it is the Basque Country that is probably the only region in Western Europe where citizens are deprived of their civil rights and liberties by the coercion of a terrorist group. Although elections are regularly held, a significant section of the population is unable to freely exercise their democratic rights, since a fundamental right such as the right to life is still under threat. The seriousness of the situation was demonstrated by events in June 2007, when some elected representatives at the local elections in the Basque Country refused to take office as a result of the pressure and threats exerted by ETA's terrorist network, and exemplifying these points, the murder of the Socialist politician Isaias Carrasco by ETA may have played a role in increasing PSOE (Partido Socialista Obrero Español) support in certain Basque areas in Spain's general election of 2008.

Conclusion: Future Directions in the 'War on Terror'

Jon Moran and Mark Phythian

Given their countries' historical experiences in dealing with ETA and the Provisional IRA, politicians in Spain and the United Kingdom were well placed to understand that the 'war on terror' was likely to be generational in scope. Hence, in the United Kingdom politicians have prepared the public for a long haul. Indeed, in 2006 Home Secretary John Reid explained that the conflict would continue for, 'longer than a generation', explaining: 'When it came to the struggle against republican terrorism in Ireland and in the mainland here, that lasted 30 years, and there is no indication to me that this is going to be resolved any quicker than that' (Woodward, 2006).

Nevertheless, the Brown government has made a concerted effort to navigate its way out of the 'war on terror' quagmire it inherited from its predecessor, although Brown himself of course contributed to this inheritance by virtue of his contributions and silences in the Blair Cabinet during discussions on Iraq (Dunne, 2008).

Perhaps the most persistent feature of the post-9/11 legislative climate in the United Kingdom has been the continued effort by both the Blair and Brown governments to extend the period of pre-charge detention. Efforts to pass legislation that would allow for ninety-day pre-charge detention, condemned by critics as internment by another name but deemed necessary by the government because of the complexities of gathering evidence in terrorism cases, were defeated due to backbench rebellion in November 2005, and despite the mobilization by the Blair government of senior police officers in support of their case. While the Terrorism Act 2006 did provide for a compromise of twenty-eight-day period of pre-charge detention, Gordon Brown soon made clear his determination to legislate to increase the period to fifty-six days. It is difficult to understand the Labour governments' dogged commitment

Conclusion 223

to this cause, one that is not deemed necessary elsewhere by countries facing an Islamist terrorist threat. This difficulty leads to the suspicion that the primary purpose of such a tough stance is that it would allow the government to reject any blame for any future terrorist attack where it is otherwise vulnerable to blame because of the motivating impact of the Iraq intervention and subsequent events there.

The commitment to an extended period of pre-charge detention clashes with the acknowledged need to develop a 'hearts and minds' approach to defeating the Islamist terrorist threat, since within the Muslim community in the United Kingdom such legislation is seen as being aimed primarily at Muslims, risking further alienation. This could have two consequences. First, as the experience of Northern Ireland demonstrates, extreme reactions by the state to terrorist activity aimed at the community from which the terrorists are drawn can act as a radicalizing factor, since what is viewed as state repression further pushes individuals towards terrorist networks. As Lord Dear, a former Chief Constable of West Midlands Police and HM Inspector of Constabulary pointed out:

> Make no mistake, extending pre-charge detention would most certainly be a propaganda coup for al-Qaida. When I was an undergraduate reading law at university in the 1960s, every self-respecting student had a poster on their wall of Ché Guevara and knew something of the writings of Marcuse. Both of those terrorist luminaries said repeatedly that the best course for a terrorist was to provoke a government to overreact to a threat by eroding civil liberties, increasing executive powers and diminishing due process by the denial of justice. That allows the terrorist to point to those actions and cite them as proof that the government is repressive. The immediate danger if we travel down this road is that we will lose the battle for hearts and minds abroad, and particularly in the minority groups in this country, whose long-term support is vital if we are to counter and remove the threat of terrorism. (Dear, 2008)

While Dear may have been thinking more about Brazilian theorist of urban guerrilla warfare (as it was then termed) Carlos Marighela (1971, pp. 45–51) than Herbert Marcuse, his point is nevertheless well made. As the experience of Northern Ireland also shows, there are varying degrees and means of supporting terrorist groups within communities that regard themselves as embattled. These can range from, at the upper end of the scale, involvement in preparations for terrorist attacks to, at the lower end, simply protecting individuals who they know or suspect of terrorist activity by, for example, providing safe havens or simply declining to pass on information to the authorities. This leads us to the second possible consequence of the government's commitment to extended periods of pre-charge detention; its likely impact on the flow of intelligence from the Muslim community. Increasing this flow has been a post-7/7 priority for the security services, but one that has yielded only limited results thus far. A January 2008 Home Office consultation paper confirmed fears that extended pre-charge detention might well undermine this already problematic aim (Travis, 2008a). For the Labour government, this alienation is doubly damaging, as it affects what have long been regarded as core Labour Party supporters, potentially undermining the Party's electoral prospects in constituencies with large Muslim populations.

Winning hearts and minds is also hindered by 'intermestic' factors relating to the activities of the United States. The detention without charge of British nationals by the United States at Guantánamo Bay in Cuba is one, and recognition of this may have underpinned the belated distancing by government ministers from this distinctively US approach to counterterrorism. A second is the British government's role in the US practice of extraordinary rendition. This was defined by the ISC as the, 'extra-judicial transfer of persons from one jurisdiction or State to another, for the purpose of detention and interrogation outside the normal legal system, where there is a real risk of torture or cruel, inhuman or degrading treatment' (ISC, 2007, para. 7). The significance of the practice, and the Guantánamo detentions, needs to be seen in the context of US approaches to interrogation, which Conservative MP Andrew Tyrie, who established the All-Party Parliamentary Group on Extraordinary Rendition, has described thus:

> the US uses a lower standard of 'acceptable treatment'. Detainees may be subject to interrogation methods which the UK, and almost all other Western countries, would consider to constitute torture, or inhuman or degrading treatment. These are believed to include extended sleep deprivation, 'waterboarding', hypothermia and sensory deprivation. Such treatment is widely held to be widespread in a number of extra-territorial US bases. (Tyrie, 2006)

In late 2002 two UK residents, Bisher al-Rawi and Jamil el-Banna were rendered from Gambia by the United States to Guantánamo Bay, possibly via Afghanistan, where they were held without charge for several years, on the basis of information supplied by MI5. However, in passing information about the travel arrangements of the two to US intelligence, MI5 had made it clear that this information should not be used as a basis to detain them. As the ISC concluded:

> This case shows a lack of regard, on the part of the US, for UK concerns. Despite the Security Service [MI5] prohibiting any action being taken as a result of its intelligence, the US nonetheless planned to render the men to Guantánamo Bay. They then ignored the subsequent protests of both the Security Service and the Government. This has serious implications for the working relationship between the US and UK intelligence agencies. (ISC, 2007, para. V)

The actions of both MI5 and the United States in this case also have domestic 'war on terror' implications, and serve as a disincentive for the Muslim community to co-operate with the security agencies. Al-Rawi was finally released in 2007 after almost five years' detention, and el-Banna followed at the end of that year. However, the damage had been done. Their cases had become a cause célèbre as knowledge of the conditions under which detainees were held became more widespread (Stafford-Smith, 2007), joining those of other British citizens and residents who had been detained at Guantánamo such as Moazzam Begg (Begg and Brittain, 2006) and Martin Mubanga, both of whom had had contact or links with British security and intelligence agencies, and the latter of whom also claimed they had played a role in his rendition from Zambia.

Hence, there is a very real sense in which governmental involvement at the fringes of rendition and the failure of the government to condemn the US practice openly and promptly have made the United Kingdom less rather than more secure, a concern behind Andrew Tyrie's suggestion to the ISC that:

> If you conclude that extraordinary rendition is helping make Britain more secure, the Committee should consider advising the Government to amend the law to enable it to conduct renditions of its own. Indeed, if that was your view it would be remiss of the Committee not to advise the Government to do so. The only alternative logical position would be to argue that although this information may benefit the UK, it would be morally unacceptable to obtain it in this way. In that event, it is incumbent on the Government to condemn rendition, just as belatedly it has started to condemn Guantánamo. (Tyrie, 2006)

The question of the full extent of its knowledge of US use of British airspace, airports and overseas territories for extraordinary rendition has continued to dog the Brown government (Doward, 2008). At the same time, however, there have been more positive developments. The Brown government recognized the importance of a shift of tone and emphasis in its characterization of the threat facing the United Kingdom. Just months after Blair's Director of Public Prosecutions, Sir Ken Macdonald, had denied that Britain was after all engaged in a 'war on terror', reflecting the fact that it would be difficult to declare victory in such a war because no one could say for sure what victory would look like, and insisted that it was, instead, dealing with criminality (Dyer, 2007), Brown's government dropped the Blair government's confrontational and polarizing 'war on terror' rhetoric to instead emphasize the criminal nature of terrorist attacks and planning (Wintour, 2007). A new counter-terrorist phrase book was drawn up advising civil servants on the language to use in framing the terrorist threat, so as to 'avoid implying that specific communities are to blame' (Travis, 2008b).

After some delay, in March 2008 the Brown government also published its first national security strategy, *Security in an Interdependent World*, which in a number of respects represented a welcome advance. The strategy adopted a broad view of the nature of the security challenges facing the United Kingdom, embracing climate change, competition for natural resources, fragile and failed states, nuclear proliferation, and global pandemics alongside the terrorist threat. It recognized the need for a more integrated governmental approach as, 'the distinction between "domestic" and "foreign" policy is unhelpful in a world where globalisation can exacerbate domestic security challenges' (Cabinet Office, 2008, para. 2.6). However, the primary focus remained on the terrorist threat. Without reflecting on why the United Kingdom faced such a threat, but reflecting the new approach to the use of language in depicting the threat, the Strategy explained that the country:

> faces a serious and sustained threat from violent extremists claiming to act in the name of Islam. Although they have very little support among communities in this country, and their claims to religious justification are widely regarded as false, the threat is greater in scale and ambition than terrorist threats we have faced in the past. (Cabinet Office, 2008, para. 3.2)

It went on to outline how:

> At any one time the police and the security and intelligence agencies are contending with around 30 plots, 200 groups or networks, and 2,000 individuals who are judged to pose a terrorist threat. ... While terrorism represents a threat to all our communities, and an attack on our values and our way of life, it does not at present amount to a strategic threat. But it is qualitatively and quantitatively more serious than the terrorist threats we have faced in the past, and it is likely to persist for many years. (Ibid., paras 3.4; 3.9)

This fact was reinforced by the contemporaneous trial of eight British Muslims charged with attempting to blow up seven trans-Atlantic aircraft in mid-air, following their August 2006 arrest. The extensive preparation for the case had involved analysis of some 200 mobile phones, 400 computers, 8000 CDs, DVDs and disks containing 6000 gigabytes of data, searches of almost 70 premises, and enquiries across three continents. The case demonstrated both the impact of the example of the 7/7 bombers on the airline conspirators and the ongoing relevance of the wars in Iraq and Afghanistan through the 'martyrdom videos' the would-be suicide bombers had prepared in which they explained the motivations underpinning their intended actions.

In doing this, there is a sense in which the trial also exposed the contradiction at the heart of the government's National Security Strategy. Within this, CONTEST with its four objectives – Pursue, Protect, Prepare, Prevent – remained the government's counter-terrorism strategy. The Strategy spoke of the role of intelligence and police work, the need to strengthen the legislative framework and the importance of international co-operation (Pursue); the importance of working with private and local government partners to improve protection of critical infrastructure (Protect); the importance of co-operation between government, police and emergency services on the one hand and the private sector and local government on the other in preparing for and mitigating the consequences of any terrorist attack (Prepare); before explaining that the Prevent dimension recognized the need to:

> work to challenge the ideology behind violent extremism and to support the voices of the peaceful majority; action to disrupt those who promote violent extremism and to support communities and institutions (for example, mosques, colleges, universities, and prisons)

in developing strategies to resist it; giving advice and support to young people and their families to resist recruitment to violent extremism; and addressing grievances exploited by those who promote terrorism, for example highlighting our positive work overseas, including support for the Middle East peace process, to challenge the violent extremist narrative. (Ibid., para. 4.8)

However, this leads us, inexorably, to the wider problem. Iraq is not quite the elephant in the room here, it is addressed, if obliquely. However, the Iraq situation is clearly counter-productive in terms of the CONTEST aims. There is a much reduced chance of an early resolution of the domestic UK 'war on terror', while the interventionist foreign policy that acted as a spur to Islamist terror plots is maintained. In this respect, the government's counter-terrorist strategy is hobbled by an apparent refusal to act on the logic of the 'intermestic' nature of the threat that it recognizes as facing the United Kingdom. There are other blind spots in the Strategy linked to this – the section on the United Kingdom's role in opposing challenges to the rules-based international system (Ibid., paras 3.30–3.33) will doubtless amuse those, particularly in France, who followed the Blair government's construction and selling of the case for war with Iraq outside the UN framework. The 'hearts and minds' approach remains constrained unless it recognizes the significant contribution made by the foreign policy choices of the Blair government in shaping the contemporary security environment in the United Kingdom.

However, the British government has little room for manoeuvre here, as it is through its military involvement in Iraq and Afghanistan that it has sought to demonstrate to the United States the continuing benefits of a 'special relationship'. The wisdom of the UK military presence in Iraq and Afghanistan and the alliance with the United States are, of course, taken as givens in the National Security Strategy. Moreover, in the context of the general reluctance of NATO member states to commit troops to the 'forever war' that is Afghanistan, any withdrawal of British troops would serve to undermine the whole alliance. Indeed, the trend in Afghanistan is towards the commitment of greater numbers of British troops to help compensate for this reluctance in other NATO capitals. Hence, from the perspective of 2008, one thing that can be safely said is that the 'war on terror' will be a feature of British politics for the foreseeable future, as the British government is unwilling, because of wider alliance considerations, to eliminate the conditions that provided the tipping point for the small numbers of alienated young British Muslims who have engaged in terrorist plots targeting the United Kingdom.

Is an end to the terrorist threat to the United Kingdom in sight? As government ministers continue to warn, the threat is at least medium-term in nature. It is in this context that former Blair chief of staff Jonathan Powell has advocated replicating the experience that produced an end to the conflict in Northern Ireland by maintaining the capacity and willingness to talk to terrorist groups to seek common ground and a resolution. In the case of Northern Ireland, Powell revealed, ongoing covert contact was maintained with the Provisional IRA. Moreover, towards the end of that conflict, Tony Blair was so committed to avoiding the collapse of the peace process that he sought repeatedly to meet with the IRA's Army Council to ensure their agreement (Watt, 2008). On the basis of this experience, Powell argued that: 'There's nothing to say to al-Qaida and they've got nothing to say to us at the moment but at some stage you're going to have to come to a political solution as well as a security solution. And that means you need the ability to talk' (Katz, 2008). Is it possible to talk to an organization that lacks the clearly hierarchic structure of the Provisional IRA, and where a voluntarist ethic drives much of the terrorist activity? Alternatively, does Powell's intervention point to the need to listen to and act on the grievances of the community from where the post-9/11 UK terrorists are essentially drawn, rather than simply 'sell' UK military interventions overseas to them, the implication underpinning the National Security Strategy? The Brown government has recognized the centrality of the 'hearts and minds' dimension to overcoming the threat from Islamist terrorism, and the 'intermestic' nature of the threat. Accelerated withdrawal from Iraq should be the next logical step in the process.

Bibliography

ABC (Australian Broadcasting Corporation). 2003a. Transcript TV Program, *Four Corners – Willie Brigitte*, http://www.abc.net.au/4corners/content/2003/ transcripts/s1040952.htm

ABC. 2003b. Transcript TV Program *'Lateline' – Intelligence delay has Ruddock asking questions*, 27 Oct. 2003, http://www.abc.net.au/lateline/content/2003/ s976417.htm

ABC. 2004. Transcript AM Radio Program, *DPP appeals against the sentence of Jack Roche*. 28 May. http://www.abc.net.au/am/content/2004/s1130575.htm

ABC. 2005. Transcript TV Program, *Insiders – Counter-terrorism laws a balancing exercise: Ruddock*. 11 September. http://www.abc.net.au/insiders/content/2005/ s1457695.htm

Abels, P. 2007. '"Je wilt niet geloven dat zoiets in Nederland kan." Het Nederlandse contraterrorisme beleid sinds 1973', in Duyvesteyn, I. and de Graaf, B. (eds.), *Terroristen en hun bestrijders, vroeger en nu*. (Uitgeverij Boom: Amsterdam), pp. 12–18.

Abels P.H.A.M. and R. Willemse. 2004. 'Veiligheidsdienst in verandering. De BVD-AIVD sinds het einde van de Koude Oorlog', *Justitiële Verkenningen*, 30 (3), 83–98.

Acuerdo de Cooperación del Estado Español con la Comisión Islámica de España, approved by Law 26/1992, of 10 November 1992, *Boletín Oficial del Estado de 12 de noviembre de 1999*, http://www.mju.es/asuntos_religiosos/ar_n08_e.htm

Ackerman, B. 2004. 'The Emergency Constitution', *Yale Law Journal*, 113 (5), 1029–91.

Ackerman, B. 2006. *Before the Next Attack: Preserving civil liberties in an age of terrorism*. (Yale University Press: Yale).

Adam, D. and P. Wintour. 2006. 'Most Britons willing to pay green taxes to save the environment', *Guardian*, 22 February. http://politics.guardian.co.uk/polls/ story/0,,1717302,00.html

Ahdar, R. and Leigh, I. 2005. *Religious Freedom in the Liberal State*. (Oxford University Press: Oxford).

AIVD. 2002. *Recruitment for the Jihad in the Netherlands: From incident to trend*. (The Hague).

AIVD. 2003. *Annual Report 2002 General Intelligence and Security Service*. (Leidschendam).

AIVD. 2004a. *Annual Report 2003*. (The Hague).

AIVD. 2004b. 'Background of Jihad Recruits in the Netherlands'. Letter to Parliament. 10 March. https://www.aivd.nl/actueel_publicaties/parlementaire/ algemeen/background_of_jihad.

AIVD. 2004c. *From Dawa to Jihad: The various threats from radical Islam to the democratic legal order*. (The Hague).

AIVD. 2005. *Annual Report 2004*. (The Hague).

AIVD. 2006a. *Violent Jihad in the Netherlands*. (The Hague).

AIVD. 2006b. *Jaarverslag 2005*. (The Hague).

Algemeen Dagblad 2004. 'Zalm: we zijn in oorlog!' 6 November.

Alldridge, P. 2003. *Money Laundering Law*. (Hart: Oxford/Portland).

Alleg, H. 1958/2006. *The Question*. (Bison Books: University of Nebraska).

Alonso, R. 2004. 'Pathways out of Terrorism in Northern Ireland and the Basque Country: the misrepresentation of the Irish model'. *Terrorism and Political Violence*, 16 (4), 695–713.

Alonso, R. 2005. 'El nuevo terrorismo: factores de cambio y permanencia', in Blanco, A., del Águila, R. and Sabucedo, José Manuel (eds.), *Madrid 11-M. Un análisis del mal y sus consecuencias*. (Editorial Trotta: Madrid), pp. 113–50.

Alonso, R. 2006. 'El fenómeno terrorista en España: principales amenazas y respuestas gubernamentales'. *Revista Iberoamericana de Análisis Político*, no. 4/5, 14–33.

Alonso, R. 2007a. 'Politicos Antiterroristas y "procesos de paz": Qué papel y qué consecuencias para las víctimas del terrorismo?', in Cuesta, C. and Alonso, R. (eds.), *Las víctimas del terrorismo en el discurso político*. (Dilex: Madrid), pp. 147–83.

Alonso, R. 2007b. 'La política antiterrorista frente a ETA entre 2004 y 2006: del consenso al *proceso de paz*', in González, J. (ed.), *Fuerzas Armadas y Seguridad Pública: Consideraciones en torno al terrorismo y la inmigración*, Publicaciones de la Universitat Jaume I, Colección 'Estudios Jurídicos', no. 14, Castellón de la Plana, pp. 145–74.

Alonso, R. 2007c. 'The Madrid attacks on March 11: an analysis of the jihadist threat in Spain and main counterterrorist measures', in Forest, J. (ed.), *Countering Terrorism in the 21st century: International Perspectives*. (Praeger Security International: Westport), pp. 202–21.

Alonso, R. 2008. 'The evolution of the terrorist threat in Spain and the United Kingdom: from ethnonationalist terrorism to jihadist terrorism', in Bowden, B. and Davis, M. (eds.), *Terror from Tyrannicide to Terrorism in Europe: 1605-Future*. (Routledge: London/New York).

Alonso, R. and Reinares, F. 2005. 'Terrorism, Human Rights and Law Enforcement in Spain'. *Terrorism and Political Violence*, 17 (1–2), 265–78.

Alonso, R. and Reinares, F. 2008. 'L'Espagne face aux terrorismes', *Pouvoirs*, 124, 107–21.

Amnesty International. 2006a. *Below the Radar: Secret flights to torture and 'disappearance'*. (Amnesty: London) (51/051/2006).

Amnesty International. 2006b. *Human Rights: A broken promise*. (Amnesty: London) (EUR 45/004/2006).

Amoore, L. and De Goede, M. 2005. 'Governance, Risk and Dataveillance in the War on Terror', *Crime, Law & Social Change*, 43 (2–3), 149–73.

Art, R.J. and L. Richardson. 2007. 'Conclusion', in Art, R.J. and Richardson, L. (eds.), *Democracy and Counterterrorism: Lessons from the Past*. (USIP: Washington, D.C.).

Ashworth, A. 2004. 'Social control and Anti-Social Behaviour Order: The subversion of human rights?', *Law Quarterly Review*, 120 (April), 263–91.

Atkins, C., S. Bee and F. Button. 2007. *Taking Liberties Since 1997*. (Revolver: London).

Bagaric, M. and J. Clarke. 2005. 'Not enough official torture in the world? The circumstances in which torture is morally justifiable', *University of San Francisco Law Review*, (39), 581–616.

Bagaric, M. and J. Clarke. 2006. 'Tortured responses (A reply to our critics): Physically persuading suspects is morally preferable to allowing the innocent to be murdered', *University of San Francisco Law Review*, (40), 703–37.

Bagaric, M. 2007. 'Time to face the truth – he's guilty', *The Age*, 8 April http://www.theage.com.au/news/national/time-to-face-the-truth--hes-guilty/2007/04/07/1175366538309.html

Banham, C. 2003. 'ASIO laws inferior insists Ruddock', *Sydney Morning Herald*, 4 November.

Banham, C. 2004. 'Courts too "lenient" on terrorists', *Sydney Morning Herald*, 3 June.

Barnett, A. 2007. 'MI5 Braced for Fresh 7/7 Disclosures', *The Observer*, 14 January.

Barómetro del Real Instituto Elcano, *Decimocuarta oleada*, March 2007, http://www.realinstitutoelcano.org/wps/portal

BBC News. 2001. 'Blair statement in full', 7 October. http://news.bbc.co.uk/1/hi/uk_politics/1585238.stm

BBC News. 2003a, 'Cleric preached racist views', 24 February. http://news.bbc.co.uk/1/hi/uk/2784591.stm

BBC News. 2003b. 'Terror-link pair jailed'. 1 April. http://news.bbc.co.uk/2/hi/uk_news/england/2907427.stm

BBC News. 2004a. 'Abu Hamza and the Mosque', 28 May. http://news.bbc.co.uk/1/hi/uk/3756675.stm

BBC News. 2004b. 'Hamza followers disrupt prayers', 6 August. http://news.bbc.co.uk/1/hi/england/london/3542564.stm

BBC News. 2005a. 'New start for extremist Mosque', 11 February. http://news.bbc.co.uk/1/hi/uk/4258891.stm

BBC News. 2005b. 'Mystery still surrounds killer', 13 April. http://news.bbc.co.uk/1/hi/uk/4440953.stm

BBC News. 2005c. 'Q & A: Hizb ut –Tahrir', 6 August. http://news.bbc.co.uk/1/hi/uk/4127688.stm

BBC News. 2005d. 'Treason terror charge considered', 8 August. http://news.bbc.co.uk/1/hi/uk_politics/4130454.stm#

BBC News. 2005e. 'Police stop and search "rising"', 23 October. http://news.bbc.co.uk/1/hi/uk/4368524.stm

BBC News. 2005f. 'Uzbek crisis poses dilemma for US', 16 May. http://news.bbc.co.uk/1/hi/world/asia-pacific/4552463.stm

BBC News. 2005g. 'US targets Sahara "terrorist haven"', 8 August. http://news.bbc.co.uk/1/hi/world/africa/4749357.stm

BBC News. 2006a. 'Abu Hamza jailed for 7 years', 7 February. http://news.bbc.co.uk/1/hi/uk/4690224.stm

BBC News. 2006b. 'Profile: Zacarias Moussaoui', 25 April. http://news.bbc.co.uk/1/hi/world/americas/4471245.stm

BBC News. 2006c. 'Groups banned by new terror law', 17 July. http://news.bbc.co.uk/1/hi/uk_politics/5188136.stm

BBC News. 2006d. 'Extremist students are sentenced', 26 July. http://news.bbc.co.uk/1/hi/uk/6917288.stm

BBC News. 2006e. 'In quotes: Jack Straw on the veil', 6 October. http://news.bbc.co.uk/1/hi/uk_politics/5413470.stm

BBC News. 2006f. '"Rendition flights" landed in NI', 17 March 2006. http://news.bbc.co.uk/1/hi/northern_ireland/4818256.stm

BBC News. 2006g. 'One third support "some torture"', 19 October. http://news.bbc.co.uk/1/hi/world/6063386.stm

BBC News. 2006h. 'Bush praises Pakistan terror role', 4 March. http://news.bbc.
co.uk/1/hi/world/south_asia/4772134.stm
BBC News. 2006i. '7/7 bomber linked to Israel pair', 9 July. http://news.bbc.co.
uk/1/hi/uk/5161390.stm
BBC News. 2007a. 'Pair cleared of air base damage', 22 May. http://news.bbc.co.
uk/1/hi/england/gloucestershire/6681639.stm
BBC News. 2007b. 'Blair speech on Islam', 4 June. http://news.bbc.co.uk/1/hi/
uk_politics/6719153.stm
BBC News. 2007c. 'UK Al Qaeda cell members jailed', 15 June. http://news.bbc.
co.uk/1/hi/uk/6755797.stm
BBC News. 2007d. 'UK Unity will defeat Terrorists', 2 July. http://news.bbc.co.
uk/1/hi/uk_politics/6260252.stm
BBC News. 2007e. 'Pair guilty over break in at base'. 6 July. http://news.bbc.
co.uk/1/hi/england/gloucestershire/6277954.stm
BBC News. 2007f. 'Africa's year of terror tactics', 2 January 2007. http://news.bbc.
co.uk/1/hi/world/africa/6217895
BBC News. 2007g. 'Call for kidnap plot "anonymity"', 4 February. http://news.
bbc.co.uk/1/hi/uk/6328689.stm
BBC News. 2007h. 'Kidnap plot charge man in court'. 9 February. http://news.
bbc.co.uk/1/hi/uk/6346991.stm
BBC News. 2007i. 'Teabags in 21/7 bomb – jury told'. 9 March. http://news.bbc.
co.uk/1/hi/uk/6435195.stm
BBC News. 2007j. 'Benn criticizes "war on terror"', 16 April. http://news.bbc.
co.uk/1/hi/uk_politics/6558569.stm
BBC News. 2007k. 'MI5 watch 2,000 terror suspects', 1 May. http://news.bbc.
co.uk/2/hi/uk_news/6613963.stm
BBC News. 2007l. 'UK to get "unified" border force', 25 July. http://news.bbc.
co.uk/1/hi/uk_politics/6914834.stm
BBC News. 2007m. 'Terror fight "may take 15 years"', 8 July. http://news.bbc.
co.uk/1/hi/uk/6281388.stm
BBC News. 2008. 'No CPS appeal over terror ruling', 20 February. http://news.
bbc.co.uk/1/hi/uk7255050.stm
BBC Radio 4. 2005. *The World at One*, 9 August.
Begg, M. and V. Brittain. 2006. *Enemy Combatant. A British Muslim's journey to Guantanamo and back*. (Free Press: London).
Bekke, A.J.G.M. and J. de Vries. 2007. *U bent herkend. Aantreden en optreden van de Nationaal Coördinator Terrorismebestrijding NCTb*. (Apeldoorn: Leiden).
Beland. 2005. 'Insecurity, citizenship and globalization: the multiple faces of state protection', *Sociological Theory*, 23 (1), 25–41.
Bell, J. 2005. *One Thousand Shades of Gray: The effectiveness of torture*. Indiana University School of Law-Bloomington Legal Studies Research Paper Series, 37.
Bennett Committee. 1979. *Report of the Committee of Inquiry into the Police Interrogation Procedures in Northern Ireland*. Cmnd 7497. (HMSO: London).
Bennetto, J. 2005. 'British Muslim admits plot to blow up airliner', *The Independent*, 1 March.
Benschop, A. 2006. 'Virtuele jihad en de cultuur van de grote bekken', in Harchaoui, S. (ed.), *Hedendaags radicalisme*. (Het Spinhuis: Amsterdam), pp. 140–79.
Beresford, D. 1987. *Ten Men Dead*. (Grafton: London).

Bichard Inquiry. 2004. *Report*. 2003–04 HC 653. (HMSO: London).

Bichard Inquiry. 2005. *Final Report*. (HMSO: London).

Birt, Y. 2006. 'Islamic citizenship in Britain after 7/7: Tackling extremism and preserving freedoms', in Malik, A.A. (ed.), *The State We Are In: Identity, terror and the Law of Jihad*. (Amal Press: Bristol).

Blair, T. 2005a. 'Full text: Blair speech on terror', *BBC News*, 16 July. http://news.bbc.co.uk/1/hi/uk/4689363.stm

Blair, T. 2005b. *Press Conference*. 5 August. http://www.number10.gov.uk/output/Page8041.asp

Blick, A., Choudhury, T. and Weir, S. 2006. *The Rules of the Game*. (Joseph Rowntree Reform Trust: York).

Bottoms, A. and R. Brownsword. 1983. 'Dangerousness and rights', in Hinton, J.W. (ed.), *Dangerousness*. (Allen & Unwin: London), pp. 9–22.

Branigan, T. 2007a. 'Blair rules out new investigation into bomb links', *The Guardian*, 3 May.

Branigan, T. 2007b. '42 day detention plan attacked as constitutionally illiterate', *The Guardian*, 8 December.

Brecher, B. 2007. *Torture and the Ticking Bomb*. (Blackwell: Oxford).

Briggs, R, C. Freschi and H. Lownsbrough. 2006. *Bringing It Home: Community based approaches to counter-terrorism*. (Demos: London).

Bright, M. 2004. 'Guantanamo has "Failed to Prevent Terror Attacks"', *The Observer*, 3 October. http://www.guardian.co.uk/guantanamo/story/0,13743,1318702,00.html

Bright, M. 2005. 'Leak shows Blair told of Iraq war terror link', *The Observer*, 28 August.

Brodeur, J-P. 1983. 'High policing and low policing', *Social Problems*, 30 (5), 507–20.

Brown, C. 2007. 'We will not be intimidated. Terror will not undermine our way of life', *The Independent*, 2 July.

Brown, G. 2006a. 'Securing Our Future' Speech at the Royal United Services Institute. 13 February. http://www.hm-treasury.gov.uk/newsroom_and_speeches/speeches/chancellorexchequer/speech_chex_130206.cfm

Brown, G. 2006b. 'Meeting the terrorist challenge' Speech at Chatham House. 10 October. http://www.hm-treasury.gov.uk/newsroom_and_speeches/press/2006/press_72_06.cfm

M. Brzezinski, M. 2001. 'Bust or Boom', *Washington Post*, 30 December, W09.

Buesa, M. 2006. *ETA en 'alto el fuego': nueve meses de actividad terrorista. Quinto informe de verificación de la violencia terrorista*, 3, Documentos Foro de Ermua, http://www.foroermua.com/html/descargas/5Informe_verificacion061231.pdf

Buesa, M. 2006. *Consecuencias económicas del terrorismo nacionalista en el País Vasco*, Universidad Complutense, Instituto de Análisis Industrial y Financiero, Working Paper, no. 53, Madrid, www.ucm.es/bucm/cee/iaif

Burke, J. 2004. *Al Qaeda*. (Penguin: London).

Burke, J. 2006. 'Britain stops talk of "war on terror"', *The Observer*, 10 December. http://observer.guardian.co.uk/politics/story/0,,1968668,00.html

Burke, J. 2007. *On the Road to Kandahar*. (Penguin: London).

Burke, J. 2008. 'The Britons who became bombers', *The Observer Magazine*, 20 January.

Buruma, I. 2006. *Murder in Amsterdam*. (Penguin: New York).

Butler, Lord Robin. 2004. *Review of Intelligence on Weapons of Mass Destruction: Report of a Committee of Privy Counsellors*. (The Stationery Office: London), HC898. July.

Butt, R. and V. Dodd. 2006. 'Anti-terror laws alienate Muslims, says top policeman', *The Guardian*, 7 August.

Buys, F. and F. Demant. 2007. 'Die Reaktion der Niederlande auf dem Mord an Theo van Gogh', in Brenner, Th. and S. Flechtner (eds.), *Demokratien und Terrorismus. Erfahrungen mit der Bewältigung und Bekämpfung von Terroranschlägen*. (Friedrich Ebert Stiftung: Bonn), pp. 15–19.

Buys, F.J., F. Demant and A. Hamdy. (2006). *Strijders van eigen bodem. Radicale en democratische moslims in Nederland*. (Amsterdam University Press: Amsterdam).

BVD. 1992. *Ontwikkelingen op het gebied van de binnenlandse veiligheid. Taakstelling en werkwijze van de BVD*. (The Hague).

BVD. 1998. *De politieke Islam in Nederland*. (The Hague).

BVD. 1999/2000. *Annual Report 1999*. (The Hague).

BVD. 2001. *Terrorisme aan het begin van de 21e eeuw. Dreigingsbeeld en positionering BVD*. (Leidschendam).

Cabinet Office. 2008. *The National Security Strategy of the United Kingdom: Security in an Interdependent World*. (HMSO: London), Cm.7291, March.

Campbell, C. 2005. ' "War on terrorism" and vicarious hegemons', *International & Comparative Law Quarterly*, 54 (April), 321–56.

Campbell C. and I. Connolly. 2007. 'A deadly complexity: Law, social movements and political violence,' *Minnesota Journal of International Law*, 16, 265310.

Campbell, D. 2006. 'Plot to blow up airlines "Sanctioned by al-Qaida Chief" ', *The Guardian*, 18 August.

Card, R. 2000. *Public Order Law*. (Jordan's: Bristol).

Carne, G. 2004. 'Brigitte and the French Connection: Security Carte Blanche or a la Carte?', *Deakin Law Review*, 9 (2), 604–10.

Centro de Análisis y Prospectiva de la Guardia Civil, *Escenarios sobre la inmigración*, Madrid, 2 July 2002.

Charity Commission. 2003. *North Central London Mosque Trust*. Charity Commission.

Chulov, M. 2004. 'Indonesian agents track down JI's Australian "leader" ', *The Australian*, 16 July.

CIS. 2007. *Centro de Investigaciones Sociológicas, Barómetro de Febrero, Avance de resultados, Estudio no. 2677*, February. http://www.cis.es/cis/export/sites/default/-Archivos/Marginales/2660_2679/2677/Es2677mar_A.pdf

Clarke, P. 2007. 'Learning from experience – counter terrorism in the UK since 9/11', *Colin Cramphorn Memorial Lecture*, 24 April. (Policy Exchange: London).

Clunan, A.L. 2005. 'U.S. and international responses to terrorist financing strategic insights', IV (1). http://www.ccc.nps.navy.mil/si/2005/Jan/clunanJan05.asp

Clutterbuck, L. 2004. 'Law enforcement', in Cronin, A.K. and Ludes, J.M. (eds.), *Attacking Terrorism: Elements of a grand strategy*. (Georgetown University Press: Washington, D.C.), pp. 140–62.

Cobain, I., David Hencke and Richard Norton-Taylor. 2007. 'MI5 Told MPs on eve of 7/7: No imminent terror threat', *The Guardian*, 9 January.

Cobain, I. and R. Norton-Taylor. 2007. 'The phone call that asked: How do you make a bomb?', *The Guardian*, 1 May.

Cobain, I., R. Norton-Taylor and J. Vasagar. 2007. 'How MI5 missed the links to the July 7 suicide bombers', *The Guardian*, 1 May.

Commissie Bestuurlijke Evaluatie AIVD. 2004. *De AIVD in verandering*. (Baarn).

Commission of Inquiry. 1987. *Into the Methods of Investigation of the General Security Service Regarding Possible Terrorist Activity* (Government of Israel).

Commission of Enquiry. 2004. Testimony by Jesús de la Morena, senior police officer responsible for counter terrorism, given before the Commission of Enquiry set up by the Spanish Parliament to investigate the March 11 attacks. Cortes Generales. *Diario de Sesiones del Congreso de los Diputados. Comisiones de Investigación, Año 2004, VIII Legislatura Núm. 3, Sesión núm. 7*, 7 July.

Commission of the European Communities. 2005. 'Communication from the Commission to the European Parliament and the Council concerning terrorist recruitment: Addressing the factors contributing to violent radicalisation', Brussels, 21.9.2005, COM (2005) 313 final.

Commission of the European Communities. 2006. 'Commission Decision of 19 April 2006 setting up a group of experts to provide policy advice to the Commission on fighting violent radicalisation' (2006/299/EC), *Official Journal of the European Union*, 25.4.2006, L 111/9.

Committee of Experts on Terrorism (CODEXTER) of the Council of Europe. 2006. 'Profiles on counter-terrorist capacity: Netherlands', June http://www.coe.int.gmt

Committee of Privy Counsellors. 2004. *Review of Intelligence on Weapons of Mass Destruction*. (The Stationery Office: London), 2003–04 HC 898.

Committee on International Human Rights of the Association of the Bar of the City of New York and Center for Human Rights and Global Justice. 2004. *Torture by Proxy: International and Domestic Law Applicable to 'Extraordinary Renditions'*. (ABCNY & NYU School of Law: New York).

Compton Committee. 1971. *Report of the enquiry into allegations against the Security Forces of physical brutality in Northern Ireland arising out of events on the 9th August, 1971* Cmnd 4823. (Her Majesty's Stationery Office: London).

Cook, R. 2003. *The Point of Departure*. (Simon & Schuster: London).

Cooley, J.K. 1973. *Black September Green March: The Story of the Palestinian Arabs*. (Frank Cass: London).

Cope, N. 2004. 'Intelligence led policing or policing led intelligence?', *British Journal of Criminology*, 44 (2), 188–203.

Cottee, S.R. 2006. 'Excusing terror', *Journal of Human Rights*, 5 (2), 149–62.

Council of State (Netherlands). 2005. *Letter to the Minister of Justice*. 15 September. http://www.rechtspraak.nl/NR/rdonlyres/8B263F4A-D0F9-43E9-9F4F-BC9E6 D2900BC/0/7245Adviesinzakeverheerlijknigetc3.pdf

Council of the European Union. 2004. 14894/04 (Presse 332), *Press Release*, Council Meeting, Justice and Home Affairs, Brussels, 2 December.

Council of the European Union. 2005. 'The European Union strategy for combating radicalisation and recruitment to terrorism', Brussels 24 November, 14781/1/05 REV 1, JAI 452 ENFOPOL 164, COTER 81.

Crenshaw, M. 2003. 'The causes of terrorism', in Kegley, C. (ed.), *The New Global Terrorism. Characteristics, causes, controls*. (Prentice Hall: New Jersey), pp. 93–105.

Crenshaw, M. 2006. 'Have motivations for terrorism changed?', in Jeff Victoroff (ed.), *Tangled Roots: Social and psychological factors in the genesis of terrorism*. (IOS Press: Amsterdam), pp. 51–7.
Cronin, A.K. 2004. 'Toward an effective Grand Strategy', in Cronin, A.K. and Ludes, J.M. (eds.), *Attacking Terrorism: Elements of a Grand Strategy*. (Georgetown University Press: Washington, D.C.), pp. 285–300.
Cuéllar, M. 2004. 'The mismatch between state power and state capacity in transnational law enforcement', *Berkeley Journal of International Law*, 22, 15–58.
Davenport, A. 2005. 'Court of Appeal – Stop and search: Lawfulness of extended powers', *Journal of Criminal Law*, 69 (1), 25–8.
Davenport, A. 2007. 'Apprehended breach of the peace: Lawfulness and proportionality of preventative action', *Journal of Criminal Law*, 71 (3), 211–14.
Dear, G. 2008. 'A propaganda coup for al-Qaida', *The Guardian*, 31 March.
Defence Select Committee. 2002. *The Threat from Terrorism*. 2001–02: HC 348-I.
Denbeaux, M.P. and J. Denbeaux. 2006. *Report on Guantánamo Detainees: A profile of 517 detainees through analysis of department of Defense data*. (The Stationery Office: London).
Denbeaux, M.P. and J. Denbeaux. 2006a. *Second Report on the Guantánamo Detainees: Inter- and intra-departmental disagreements about who is our enemy*. (Seton Hall University School of Law).
Department for Constitutional Affairs. 2006. *Review of the Implementation of the Human Rights Act*. (DCA: London).
Department of Foreign Affairs & Trade (Australia). 2003. *White Paper on Foreign Affairs and Trade: Advancing the National Interest*, Canberra.
Dershowitz, A.M. 2002. *Why Terrorism Works: Understanding the threat, responding to the challenge*. (Yale University Press: Yale).
Díaz, A. 2005. *Los servicios de inteligencia españoles. Desde la guerra civil hasta el 11-M. Historia de una transición*. (Alianza Editorial: Madrid).
Dickson, B. 2006. 'The House of Lords and the Northern Ireland conflict – a sequel'. *Modern Law Review*, 69 (3), 383–417.
Dodd, V. 2005. 'Special Branch to track Muslims across UK', *The Guardian*, 20 July.
Dodd, V. 2007a. 'Extremists used Internet to urge Muslims to follow Bin Laden and join Holy War, court told', *The Guardian*, 24 April.
Dodd, V. 2007b. 'Al-Qaida Thriving Despite War on Terror – Yard Chief', *The Guardian*, 25 April.
Dodd, V. 2007c. 'Met chief is mauled by watchdog over de Menezes killing', *Guardian*, 7 September.
Dodd, V. 2008. 'Life sentence for the extremist who plotted to murder soldier', *The Guardian*, 19 February.
Dodd, V., I. Cobain and H. Carter. 2007. 'Leader was watched months before 7/7', *The Guardian*, 3 May.
Dodge, T. 2006. 'Iraq: The contradictions of exogenous state building in comparative perspective', *Third World Quarterly*, 27 (1), 187–200.
Doig, A. and M. Phythian. 2005. 'The national interest and the politics of threat exaggeration: the Blair Government's case for the war against Iraq', *The Political Quarterly*, 368–76.
Domínguez, F. 2005. 'ETA, las políticas antiterroristas', in *Cuadernos de Alzate*, no. 33, 153–67.
Domínguez, F. 1998a. *De la Negociación a la Tregua: el Final de ETA?*. (Taurus: Madrid).

238   *Bibliography*

Domínguez, F. 1998b. *ETA: Estrategia Organizativa y Actuaciones. 1978–1992.* (Servicio Editorial de la Universidad del País Vasco: Bilbao).

Domínguez, F. 2006a. *Josu Ternera. Una vida en ETA.* (La esfera de los libros: Madrid).

Domínguez, F. 2006b. 'El enfrentamiento de ETA con la democracia', in Antonio Elorza (ed.), *La Historia de ETA.* (Temas de Hoy: Madrid), pp. 273–435.

Donahue, L. 2006. 'Anti-terrorism finance in the United Kingdom and the United States', *Michigan Journal of International Law*, 27 (Winter), 303–435.

Doward, J. 2008. 'UN Rejects British denial on rendition', *The Observer*, 2 March.

Doward, J. and M. Townsend. 2006. 'US pushed MI5 into airport terror swoop', *The Observer*, 1 October.

Dratel, J. 2005. 'A curious debate,' in Karen J. Greenberg (ed.), *The Torture Debate in America.* (Cambridge University Press: Cambridge).

Duffy, H. 2005. *The 'War on Terror' and the Framework of International Law.* (Cambridge University Press: New York).

Dunne, T. 2008. 'What did you do in the Iraq War, Gordon?', *Times Higher Education*, 27 March. http://www.timeshighereducation.co.uk/story.asp?sectioncode=26&storycode=401243&c=1

Dyer, C. 2007. 'There is no war on terror', *The Guardian*, 24 January.

The Economist. 2002. 'The Needle in the Haystack', 12 December, p. 226.

The Economist. 2005. 'Financing Terrorism: Looking in the Wrong Places', 20 October.

The Economist. 2007a. 'Waiting for al-Qaeda's next bomb', 5 May, p. 25.

The Economist. 2007b. 'A world wide web of terror', 14 July, pp. 28–30.

Eikelenboom, S. 2007. *Niet bang om te sterven. Dertig jaar terrorisme in Nederland* (New Amsterdam: Amsterdam).

Ellian, A. 2002. 'Politieke Islam zal ook Europa ontwrichten', *NRC Handelsbad*, 29 May.

Elorza, A. 2003. *La hora de Euzkadi. Disidencias I. Artículos y Ensayos.* (Galaxia Gutenberg: Barcelona).

Elorza, A. 2006. (ed.), *La Historia de ETA.* (Temas de Hoy: Madrid).

Engelen, D. 2002. *Per undas adversas. Een institutioneel onderzoek naar het handelen van de Binnenlandse Veiligheidsdienst en zijn voorgangers, 1945–2002.* (Rijksarchiefdienst/PIVOT: 'sGravenhage), pp. 61–75.

Escrivá, A. 2006, *ETA. El camino de vuelta.* (Seix Barral: Barcelona).

Europol. 2003. *Terrorist Activity in the European Union: Situation and trends report* (TE-SAT), October 2002–15 October 2003.

Europol. 2007. *TE-SAT 2007. EU terrorism situation and trend report 2007,* Corporate Communications, The Hague.

Euskobarómetro, Department of Political Science and Public Administration at the University of the Basque Country, http://www.ehu.es/cpvweb/paginas/euskobarometro.html

Evans, C. 2001. *Freedom of Religion under the European Convention on Human Rights.* (Oxford University Press: Oxford).

Evans, M.D. 2006. 'Torture', *European Human Rights Law Review*, 2 (2006), 101.

Farson, S. 1992. 'Security intelligence v. Criminal intelligence', *Policing & Society*, 2, 65–87.

Fenwick, H. 2002. *Civil Liberties and Human Rights,* 3rd ed. (Routledge: London).

Ferrari, S. 2004. 'Individual religious freedom and national security in Europe after September 11', *Brigham Young University Law Review*, 2004 (2), 357–83.
Fijnaut, C. 1989. 'Politiek geweld en de politiële bestrijding hiervan in Nederland', *Tijdschrift voor de Politie*, 51 (11), 501–5.
Fijnaut, C. 2007. 'Islamitische terreur vergt uitzonderlijke maatregelen', *Socialisme & Democratie*, 64 (6), 39–47.
Fish, S. 2001. *The Trouble with Principle*. (Harvard University Press: Cambridge, MA).
Florence, J. 2006. 'Making the no fly list fly: A due process model for terrorist watchlists', *Yale Law Journal*, 115 (8), 2418–81.
Forbes, M. 2002. 'Deadlock on ASIO Bill', *The Age* (Melbourne), 13 December.
Ford, R. 2007. 'Terror controls full of holes, says Reid'. *The Times*, 25 January.
Foreign Affairs Committee. 2005. *Human Rights Annual Report 2005*. First Report, Session 2005–06.
Foreign and Commonwealth Office (n.d.), *Counter-Terrorism Legislation and Practice: A survey of selected countries* http://www.fco.gov.uk/Files/kfile/QS%20Draft%2010%20FINAL.1.pdf
Foster K.R. and P.W. Huber. 1997. *Judging Science*. (MIT Press: Cambridge, MA).
Frerichs, R. and R. Schildmeijer. 2005. *Verkennend onderzoek terrorisme: Bestemd voor NCTb*. TNS NIPO-report, ISO 9001. (Amsterdam).
Froomkin, D. 2007. 'Bush's Exhibit A for torture', Washingstonpost.com Tuesday 18 December http://www.washingtonpost.com/wp-dyn/content/blog/2007/12/18/BL2007121800862.html?hpid=opinionsbox1&sub=AR
Funes, M.J. 1998. 'Social responses to political violence in the Basque Country: peace movements and their audience', *Journal of Conflict Resolution*, 42, 493–510.
Furedi, F. 2002. *Culture of Fear. Risk taking and the morality of low expectation*. (Continuum: London).
Gardham, D. and R. Bedi. 2007. 'Car bomb suspect had visited al-Qa'eda's heartland', *Daily Telegraph*, 9 July.
Gardner, F. 2006. *Blood and Sand: Love, death and survival in an age of global terror*. (Bantam Press: London).
Garland, D. 2000. *The Culture of Control*. (Oxford University Press: Oxford).
Garland, D. and R. Sparks. 2000. 'Criminology, social theory and the challenge of our times', *British Journal of Criminology*, 40, 189–204.
Gattrell, V. 2006. *The Hanging Tree*. (Oxford University Press: Oxford).
Gearty, C.A. 2005. 'Terrorism and human rights', *European Human Rights Law Review*, 1–6.
Gearty, C.A. 2005a. 'Legitimising torture – with a little help', *Index on Censorship*: http://www.indexonline.org/en/news/articles/2005/1/international-legitimising-torture-with-a-li.shtml
Gearty, C.A. 2007. 'Rethinking civil liberties in a counter-terrorism world', *European Human Rights Law Review*, 2, 111–19.
Geddis, A. 2004. 'Free speech martyrs or unreasonable threats to social peace? – "Insulting Expression and Section 5 of the Public Order Act"', *Public Law*, Winter, 853–74.
van Gemert, F. 1998. *Ieder voor zich. Kansen, cultuur en criminaliteit van Marokkaanse jongens*. (Het Spinhuis: Amsterdam).
Gibson, R. 2004. 'Bin Laden very nice: Roche', *The West Australian* (Perth), 21 May.

Gil-Robles, A. 2005. *Report by Mr Alvaro Gil-Robles Commissioner for Human Rights on his visit to the United Kingdom* CommDH (2005) 6. (Council of Europe: Strasbourg).

Gill, P. 1994. *Policing Politics: Security intelligence and the liberal democratic state.* (Frank Cass: London).

Gill, P. 2000. *Rounding Up the Usual Suspects? Developments in Contemporary Law Enforcement Intelligence.* (Ashgate: Dartmouth).

Gill, P. 2004. 'Securing the globe: Intelligence and the post 9/11 shift from "Liddism" to "Drainism"', *Intelligence and National Security,* 19 (3), 467–89.

Gill, P. 2006. 'Not just joining the dots but crossing borders and bridging the voids: Constructing security networks after 11 September', *Policing and Society,* 16, (1), 27–49.

Glover, J. 2005. 'Two-thirds believe London bombings are linked to Iraq war', *The Guardian,* 19 July.

Glover, J. and D. Milmo. 2006. 'Travellers keep flying despite terror alerts', *The Guardian,* 22 August.

Goldsmith, J. 2007. *The Terror Presidency: Law and judgment inside the Bush Administration.* (W.W.Norton: New York).

Goldsmith, J. 2007. *Lord Goldsmith, QC,* Centre for Public Law, University of Cambridge, 21 April.

Gotterson, B. 2004. *Letter to the Hon Philip Ruddock, Attorney-General.* 3 March. http://www.lawcouncil.asn.au/get/submissions/2392370367

de Graaf, B. 2007. 'Wanneer stoppen terroristen? Het historisch referentiekader als aanknopingspunt', in Duyvesteyn and De Graaf (eds.), *Terroristen en hun bestrijders.* (Uitgeverij Boom: Amsterdam), pp. 105–19.

Greenberg, K.J. 2005. *The Torture Debate in America.* (Cambridge University Press: Cambridge).

Greenberg, K.J. and J.L Dratel. 2005. *The Torture Papers: The road to Abu Ghraib* (Cambridge University Press: Cambridge).

Grey, S. 2006. *Ghost Plane: The inside story of the CIA's secret rendition programme.* (C. Hurst & Co.:).

Grice, A. 2005. 'We failed to foresee the level of sheer anarchic violence in Iraq', *The Independent,* 25 July.

Gross, O. 2003. 'Chaos and rules', *Yale Law Journal,* 112 (5), 1011–34.

The Guardian. 2003. 'A mosque is no sanctuary', 21 January.

Hamilton, N. 1998. *Zealotry and Academic Freedom.* (Transaction: NewBrunswick).

Hansard. 2006. Ivan Lewis in reply to Vincent Cable. 27 February. http://www.publications.parliament.uk/pa/cm200506/cmhansrd/vo060227/text/60227w84.htm#60227w84.html_spnew0

Hansard. 2006. Ed Balls in reply to George Osborne. 19 October. http://www.publications.parliament.uk/pa/cm200506/cmhansrd/cm061019/text/61019w0019.htm#0610209001327

Hansard. 2007. Ed Balls in reply to Mr. Greg Hands. 31 January. http://www.publications.parliament.uk/pa/cm200607/cmhansrd/cm070131/halltext/70131h0010.htm#070131100000624

Hansard. 2007. Kitty Ussher. Written ministerial statement on the UK asset freezing regime. 11 October. http://www.publications.parliament.uk/pa/cm200607/cmhansrd/cm071011/wmstext/71011m0001.htm#07101121000085

Harnden, T. and M. Ansari. 2005. 'Pakistan: The incubator for al-Qaeda's attacks on London', *Sunday Telegraph*, 24 July.

Harvey, J. 2005. 'An evaluation of money laundering policies', *Journal of Money Laundering Control*, 8 (4), 339–45.

de Hart, B. 2005. 'Het probleem van dubbele nationaliteit: Politieke en mediadebatten na de moord op Theo van Gogh', *Migrantenstudies*, 21 (4), pp. 224–238.

Haubrich, D. 2006. 'Anti-terrorism laws and slippery slopes: A reply to Waddington', *Policing and Society*, 16 (4), 405–14.

Hegland, C. 2006. 'Empty evidence,' *National Journal*, 3 February.

Hencke, D. and H. Muir. 2006. 'Kelly: Imams failing to deter extremism', *The Guardian*, 14 August.

Her Majesty's Government. 2006. *Report of the Official Account of the Bombings in London on 7th July 2005*, HC 1087 (May 2006).

Herbert, I. and K. Sengupta. 2005. 'Revealed: How Aldgate bomber became a single-minded jihadist killer', *The Independent*, 10 September.

Heymann, P.B. 2003. *Terrorism, Freedom and Security. Winning without War*. (MIT: Cambridge, MA/London).

Hitchens, P. 2004. *The Abolition of Liberty. The decline of order and justice in England*. (Atlantic: London).

Hillyard, P. 1987. 'The normalization of special powers: From Northern Ireland to Britain', in Scraton, P. (ed.), *Law, Order and the Authoritarian State*. (Open University Press: Milton Keynes). pp. 270–312.

HM Inspectorate of Constabulary. 1997. *Policing with Intelligence*. (HMIC: London).

HM Inspectorate of Constabulary. 2003. *A Need to Know*. (HMIC: London).

HM Treasury. 2002. *Combating the Financing of Terrorism: A report on UK action*. (HMSO: London).

HM Treasury, Home Office, Serious and Organized Crime Agency, and Foreign and Commonwealth Office. 2007. *The Financial Challenge to Crime and Terrorism*. (HMSO: London).

Hocking, J. 2003. 'Counter-terrorism and the criminalisation of politics: Australia's new security powers of detention, proscription and control', *Australian Journal of Politics and History*, 49 (3), 355–71.

Hoekstra, F. 2004. *In dienst van de BVD. Spionage en contraspionage in Nederland*, (Tree: Amsterdam), pp. 67–76.

Hoffman, B. 2001. 'Change and continuity in terrorism', in *Studies in Conflict & Terrorism*, 24, 417–28.

Holland, J. and S. Phoenix. 1997. *Phoenix. Policing the shadows*. (Hodder and Stoughton: London).

Home Affairs Select Committee. 2005a. 'Uncorrected minutes of evidence,' 1 March, HC 156-v.

Home Affairs Select Committee. 2005b. 'Counter-terrorism and community relations in the aftermath of the London bombings, evidence of Rt Hon. Charles Clarke, MP', 13 September.

Home Affairs Select Committee. 2006. 'Terrorism detention powers', in *Fourth Report of Session 2005–06*, Volume 1. (The Stationery Office: London).

Home Office. 2002. *Police and Criminal Evidence Act 1984 Code A: Exercise by Police Officers of Statutory Powers of Stop and Search*, http://police.homeoffice.gov.uk/

news-and-publications/publication/operational-policing/PACE_Chapter_A. pdf?view=Binary

Home Office. 2004a. *Bichard Inquiry Recommendations: Progress report.* (Home Office: London).

Home Office. 2004b. *Counter Terrorism Powers.* Cm. 6147. (Home Office: London).

Home Office. 2005a. *Preventing Extremism Together,* London. http://communities. homeoffice.gov.uk/raceandfaith/reports_pubs/publications/race_faith/255560

Home Office. 2005b. *Press Release,* 24 August.

Home Office. 2005c. *Press Release,* 'Tackling extremism together: Working groups report back to Home Secretary', 22 September.

Home Office. 2005d. *Preventing Extremism Together: Places of worship,* 6 October.

Home Office. 2006a. *Countering International Terrorism: The United Kingdom's strategy.* Cm.6888. (Home Office: London).

Home Office. 2006b. *New Powers Against Organised and Financial Crime.* Cm. 6875. (Home Office: London).

Home Office. 2006c. *Statistics on Race and the Criminal Justice System 2005.* (Home Office: London) http://www.homeoffice.gov.uk/rds/pdfs06/s95race05.pdf

Home Office (n.d.), *Counter-Terrorism Strategy* http://security.homeoffice.gov.uk/ counter-terrorism-strategy/about-the-strategy/

Home Office (n.d.), *Facts and Figures* http://www.homeoffice.gov.uk/security/ terrorism-and-the-law/ (statistics as of 31 March 2007).

Honigsbaum, M. and V. Dodd. 2005. 'From Gloucester to Afghanistan: The making of a shoe bomber', *The Guardian,* 5 March.

Hope, D. 2004. 'Torture', *International and Comparative Law Quarterly,* 53 (4), 785–807.

House of Commons Constitutional Affairs Committee. 2005. *The Operation of the Special Immigration Appeals Commission (SIAC) and the Use of Special Advocates.* 2004–05 HC 323-I.

House of Commons. 2004. Debates vol.418 col.303 (25 February 2004) (David Blunkett).

House of Commons. 2005a. Debates vol.431 col.153 (22 February 2005) (Charles Clarke).

House of Commons. 2005b. Debates vol.431 col.1626 (9 March 2005) (Hazel Blears).

House of Commons. 2006. *Report of the Official Account of the Bombings in London on 7th July 2005.* HC 1087.

House of Lords. 2005a. Debates vol.670 col.163 (1 March 2005) (Lord Lloyd).

House of Lords. 2005b. Debates vol.670 col.371 (3 March 2005) (Lord Carlile).

House of Lords. 2005c. Debates vol.670 col.121 (3 March 2005) (Lord Falconer).

House of Lords. 2005d. Debates vol.431 col.339 (23 February 2005) (Charles Clarke).

House of Lords. 2007. Debates vol.688 col.WS33 (16 January 2007) (Baroness Scotland).

Huber, P. 1991. *Galileo's Revenge: Junk science in the courtroom.* (Basic Books: New York).

Human Rights Watch. 2004. *Still at Risk: Diplomatic assurances no safeguard against torture.* Human Rights Watch.

Human Rights Watch. 2005. *Leadership Failure: Firsthand accounts of torture of Iraqi detainees by the US army's 82nd airborne division.* Human Rights Watch.

Human Rights Watch. 2006. *Dangerous Ambivalence: UK policy on torture since 9/11*. Human Rights Watch.

Hurd, D. 2005. 'You cannot divorce Iraq from the terror equation', *The Independent*, 28 July.

Husain, E. 2007. *The Islamist*. (Penguin: London).

Hutton, Lord. 2004. *Report of the Inquiry into the Circumstances Surrounding the Death of Dr David Kelly*. 2003–04 HC 247.

Ingraham, B.L. 1979. *Political Crime in Europe*. (University of California Press: Berkeley).

Intelligence and Security Committee. 2003a. *Annual Report 2002–03*. Cm.5837. (HMSO: London).

Intelligence and Security Committee (ISC). 2003b. *Iraqi Weapon of Mass Destruction – Intelligence and Assessments*. Cm.5972. (HMSO: London), September.

Intelligence and Security Committee. 2004. *Annual Report 2003–2004*. Cm.6240. (HMSO: London).

Intelligence and Security Committee. 2006. *Report into the London Terrorist Attacks of 7 July 2005*. Cm.6785. (HMSO: London), May.

Intelligence and Security Committee (ISC). 2007. *Rendition*. Cm.7171. (HMSO: London), July.

Irujo, J.M. 2005, *El agujero. España invadida por la yihad*. (Aguilar: Madrid).

Jaime, O. 2002, *Policía, Terrorismo y Cambio Político en España, 1976–1996*. (Tirant lo Blanch: Valencia), pp. 167–217.

James, A. 2003. 'The advance of intelligence-led policing strategies: the emperor's new clothes?', *Police Journal*, 76 (1), 45–59.

Jenkins, S. 1996. *Accountable to None. The Tory nationalisation of Britain*. (Penguin: London).

John, T. and M. Maguire. 2004. 'The National Intelligence Model: Key lessons from early research'. *Home Office Outline Report*, 30/04 http://www.homeoffice.gov.uk/rds/pdfs04/rdsolr3004.pdf

Johnson, A., M. Woolf and M. Whitaker. 2007. 'The security industry: Britain's private army in Iraq', *Independent*, 3 June.

Joint Committee on Human Rights. 2004–05. *Fourth Report*, H.L. 26; H.C. 244.

Joint Committee on Human Rights. 2006a. *Counter-Terrorism Policy and Human Rights: Terrorism bill and related matters*. 2005–06, H.C. 561-I, H.L. 75-I.

Joint Committee on Human Rights. 2006b. *Counter-Terrorism Policy, and Human Rights: Prosecution and pre-charge detention*. 2005–06, H.C. 1576, H.L. 240.

Joint Committee on Human Rights. 2006c. *Counter-Terrorism Policy and Human Rights: Draft Prevention of Terrorism Act 2005*. (Continuance in Force of Sections 1 to 9) Order 2006, 2005–06, H.L. 122, H.C. 915.

Joint Committee on Human Rights. 2006d. *The UN Convention Against Torture (UNCAT) Nineteenth Report of Session*, 2005–06, H.L. 185 I/H.C. 701-I, H.L. 185 I/H.C. 701-II.

Joint Committee on Human Rights. 2007. *The Council of Europe Convention on the Prevention of Terrorism*, 2006–07, H.L. 26/H.C. 247.

Joint Committee on Human Rights. 2007. 'Counter-terrorism policy and human rights', *Nineteenth Report, Session 2006–07*. (The Stationery Office: London).

Judd, T. 2007. 'Politics, propaganda and persecution: How Muslims see the raids', *Independent*, 2 February.

JUSTICE. 2006. *Intercept Evidence: Lifting the ban*. London.

Kampfner, J. 2002. 'Why the French call us Londonistan', *New Statesman*, 9 December.

Kampfner, J. 2004, *Blair's Wars*. (Free Press: London).

Kassimeris, G. 2006. 'The warrior's dishonour', in Kassimeris, G. (ed.), *Warrior's Dishonour: Barbarity, morality and torture in modern warfare*. (Ashgate: Aldershot), pp. 1–19.

Katz, I. 2008. 'Top Blair aide: We must talk to al-Qaida', *The Guardian*, 15 March.

Kepel, G. 2004. *The War for Muslim Minds: Islam and the West*. (Belknap/Harvard University Press: Cambridge, MA).

King, A. 2005. 'One in four Muslims sympathises with motives of terrorists', *Daily Telegraph*, 23 July.

Kleijwegt, M. 2005. *Onzichtbare ouders. De buurt van Mohammed B.* (Plataan Zutphen).

Kleinman, S.M. 2006. 'KUBARK counterintelligence interrogation review: Observations of an interrogator – Lessons learned and avenues for further research,' in Swenson, R. *Educing Information: Interrogation: Science and art – foundations for the future*. (National Defense Intelligence College: Washington, D.C.).

Klerks, P. 1989. *Terreurbestrijding in Nederland 1970–1988*. (Ravijn: Amsterdam).

Koh, H.H. 2005. 'A world without torture', *Columbia Journal of Transnational Law*, 43, 641–61.

Lagas, T. and Peter Sierksma, 1993. BVD-Infiltrante als spijtoptant, *Trouw*, 15 September.

Laqueur, W. 2006. 'Postmodern terrorism', in Kegley, C. (ed.), *The New Global Terrorism. Characteristics, Causes, Controls*. (Prentice Hall: New Jersey), pp. 151–9.

Laville, S. 2007. '21/7 bombers: Ringleader slipped through police net', *The Guardian*, 10 July.

Lawrence, B. (ed.). 2005. *Messages to the World: The statements of Osama Bin Laden*. (Verso: London).

Leppard, D. 2006a. 'Iraq terror Backlash in UK "for Years"', *Sunday Times*, 2 April.

Leppard, D. 2006b. 'New MI5 boss is top expert on Al-Qaeda', *Sunday Times*, 17 December.

Lester, A. and K. Beattie. 2005. 'Risking torture', *European Human Rights Law Review*, 6.

Levi, M. 1997. 'Evaluating the "new policing": Attacking the money trail of organised crime', *Australian and New Zealand Journal of Criminology*, 30 (1), 1–25.

Levinson, S. 2004. 'Contemplating torture', in Levinson, S. (ed.), *Torture: A reader*. (Oxford University Press: Oxford).

Liberty. 2004. *The Impact of Anti-Terrorism Legislation on British Muslims*. (Liberty: London).

Liberty. 2006. *Renewing the Prevention of Terrorism Act 2005*. (Liberty: London).

Lord Carlile. 2002. *Report on the Operation in 2001 of the Terrorism Act 2000*. (TSO: London).

Lord Carlile. 2004. *Report on the Operation in 2002 and 2003 of the Terrorism Act 2000*. (TSO: London).

Lord Carlile. 2005. *Report on the Operation in 2004 of the Terrorism Act 2000*. (TSO: London).

Lord Carlile. 2006a. *First Report of the Independent Reviewer Pursuant to Section 14(3) of the Prevention of Terrorism Act 2005*. (Home Office: London).

Lord Carlile. 2006b. *Report on the Operation in 2005 of the Terrorism Act 2000*. (TSO: London).

Lord Carlile. 2007a. *Second Report of the Independent Reviewer Pursuant to Section 14(3) of the Prevention of Terrorism Act 2005*. (Home Office: London).

Lord Carlile. 2007b. *Report on the Operation in 2006 of the Terrorism Act 2000*. (TSO: London).

Lynch, A. 2006. 'Legislating with urgency – The enactment of the Anti-Terrorism Act [No. 1] 2005', *Melbourne University Law Review*, 30(3), 747–81.

Lynch, A. and A. Reilly. 2007. 'The constitutional validity of terrorism orders of control and preventative detention', *Flinders Journal of Law Reform*, 10 (1), 105–42.

Lynch, A. and G. Williams. 2006. *What Price Security?* (UNSW Press: Sydney).

MacDonald Commission of Inquiry. 1981. *Concerning Certain Activities of the RCMP*. (Second Report: Freedom and Security). (Minister of Supply and Services: Ottowa).

MacDonald, H. 2005. 'How to interrogate terrorists', in Karen J. Greenberg (ed.), *The Torture Debate in America*. (Cambridge University Press: Cambridge).

Mackey, C. 2004. *The Interrogator's War: Inside the secret war against al Qaeda*. (Little Brown:New York).

MacMaster, N. 2004. 'Torture: from Algiers to Abu Ghraib', *Race & Class*, 46 (2), 1–21.

Malik, Shiv. 2007. 'My brother the bomber', *Prospect*, June.

Manningham-Buller, E. 2005. 'The international terrorist threat and the dilemmas in countering it', Speech at the Ridderzaal, Binnenhof, The Hague, Netherlands, 1 September. www.mi5.gov.uk/print/Page387.html

Manningham-Buller, E. 2006. 'The international terrorist threat to the UK', Speech at Queen Mary's College, London, 9 November. www.mi5.gov.uk/output/Page374.html

Marighela, C. 1971. *For the Liberation of Brazil*. (Penguin: Harmondsworth).

Martin, G. 2006. *Understanding Terrorism*. 2nd edn. (Sage: California).

Martínez-Torrón, J. 2002. 'Religious liberty in European jurisprudence', in Hill, M. (ed.), *Religious Liberty and Human Rights*. (University of Wales Press: Cardiff).

Mata, J.M. 1993. *El nacionalismo vasco radical. Discurso, organizaciones y expresiones*. (Universidad del País Vasco: Bilbao).

Matthew, R. and G. Shambaugh. 2005. 'The pendulum effect: Explaining shifts in democratic response to terrorism', *Analyses of Social Issues and Public Policy*, 5, 223–33.

McCoy, A.W. 2006. *A Question of Torture: CIA interrogation, from the cold war to the war on terror*. (Metropolitan Books: New York).

McGuffin, J. 1974. *The Guineapigs*. (Penguin: London).

Menand, L. 2001. *The Metaphysical Club: A story of ideas in America*. (Farrar, Strauss and Giroux: New York).

Mental Health Advisory Team (MHAT) IV. 2006. *Operation Iraqi Freedom 05–07, Final Report*.

Mesure, S. 2002. 'Lack of trust bigger threat to firms than terrorism', *Independent*, 13 November.

Metcalf, E. 2004. 'Representative but not responsible: the use of special advocates in English law', *JUSTICE Journal*, 1 (2).

Metropolitan Police (n.d.) http://www.met.police.uk/so/counter_terrorism.htm.

MI5. 2006. 'Countering international terrorism' http://www.mi5.gov.uk/output/Page307.html

Michaelsen, C. 2003. 'International Human Rights on Trial – The United Kingdom's and Australia's legal response to 9/11', *Sydney Law Review*, 25 (3), 283–4.

Michaelsen, C. 2005a. 'Why everybody should hear Habib's story', *Canberra Times*, 3 February.

Michaelsen, C. 2005b. 'Antiterrorism legislation in Australia: A proportionate response to the terrorist threat?', *Studies in Conflict and Terrorism*, 28 (4), 329–34.

Michaelsen, C. 2005c. 'Australia's antiterrorism laws lack adequate oversight mechanisms', *Democratic Audit of Australia*, November. http://democratic. audit.anu.edu.au/papers/200511_michaelsen_anti_terror.pdf

Milmo, C. 2007. 'Failed 21/7 bombers given 40 years jail for mass murder attempt', *The Independent*, 12 July.

Milne, S. 2005. 'It is an insult to the dead to deny the link with Iraq', *The Guardian*, 14 July.

Milne, S. 2007. 'Denial of the link with Iraq is delusional and dangerous', *The Guardian*, 5 July.

Minister of Justice (Netherlands) 2003. Letter, 24 June: TK 27925, Nr. 94.

Ministers of the Interior and Justice (Netherlands). 2006. Letter to the Second Chamber. 24 January 2006. Second Chamber (*Tweede Kamer*, TK), 2004–2005, 29754, Nr. 5: 2–3.

Ministry of Justice (Netherlands). 2005. *Radicalisme en radicalisering*. The Hague.

Ministry of Justice/Directie Algemene Justitiële Strategie (Netherlands). 2005. *Nota radicalisme en radicalisering*. The Hague: 19 August.

Moloney, E. 2002. *A Secret History of the IRA*. (Penguin Allen Lane: London).

Moore, M. 2006. 'Al-Qa'eda a greater threat than Nazis', *Daily Telegraph*, 24 December.

Moran, J. 2008. *Policing the Peace in Northern Ireland. Politics, Crime and Security after the Belfast Agreement*. (Manchester University Press: Manchester).

Moran, J. 2005. 'State power in the war on terror: A comparative analysis of the UK and USA', *Crime, Law and Social Change*, 44 (4–5), 335–59.

Moran, J. 2007a. 'Can the New Home Office beat Al Qaeda?', *Parliamentary Brief*, 11 (5), 29–30.

Moran, J. 2007b. 'Generating more heat that light? Debates on civil liberties in the UK', *Policing*, 1 (1), 80–93.

Moran, M. 2001. 'The rise of the regulatory state in Britain', *Parliamentary Affairs*, 54, 19–34.

Moran, M. 2003. *The British Regulatory State. High modernism and hyper innovation*. (Oxford University Press: Oxford).

Morán, S. 1997. *ETA entre España y Francia*. (Editorial Complutense: Madrid).

Morris, N. 2006. 'Reid says terror threat is worse than Cold War', *Independent*, 1 November.

Morris, N. 2007. 'Government Rejects Call for 21 July Inquiry', *The Independent*, 11 July.

Mouer, R. and Y. Sugimoto. 1986. *Images of Japanese Society*. (Kegan Paul: London).

Muller, E.R. 1994. *Terrorisme en politieke verantwoordelijkheid. Gijzelingen, aanslagen en ontvoeringen, in Nederland* (Gouda Quint: Arnhem), pp. 370–6.

Muslim Youth in Europe: Addressing Alienation and Extremism. Report on Wilton Park Conference, WPS05/3, 7–10 February 2005. http://www.wiltonpark.org.uk/ documents/conferences/WPS05-3/pdfs/WPS05-3.pdf

National Centre for Policing Excellence. 2005a. *Guidance on the National Intelligence Model*, http://www.acpo.police.uk/asp/policies/Data/nim2005.pdf

National Centre for Policing Excellence. 2005b. *Code of Practice on the Management of Police Information*, http://police.homeoffice.gov.uk/ news-and-publications/ publication/operational-policing/CodeofPracticeFinal12073.pdf

National Commission on Terrorist Attacks upon the United States. 2004. *The 9/11 Commission Report.*

Naylor, R.T. 2006. *Satanic Purses: Money, myth and misinformation in the war on terror.* (McGill-Queen's University Press: Canada).

NCTb. 2006. *Jihadisten en het internet.* (The Hague).

NCTb/Directie Beleid en Strategie. 2006. *Vierde voortgangsrapportage terrorismebestrijding.* 7 June. (The Hague).

Newman, C. 2006. 'Allowing free speech and prohibiting persecution – A contemporary Sophie's choice', *Journal of Criminal Law*, 70 (4), 329–50.

Norman, P. 1998. 'The terrorist finance unit and the Joint Action Group on Organised Crime: New organisational models and investigative strategies to counter "organised crime" in the UK', *Howard Journal of Criminal Justice*, 37 (4), 375–92.

Northern Ireland Office. 2006. *Northern Ireland Statistics on the Operation of the Terrorism Act 2000: Annual Statistics 2005.* (NIO: Belfast).

Norton-Taylor, R. 2005a. 'Security services face worst scenario', *The Guardian*, 13 July.

Norton-Taylor, R. 2005b. 'MI5 links Iraq to extremists in UK', *The Guardian*, 29 July.

Norton-Taylor R. 2006. 'Minister admits "rendition" planes used RAF bases,' *The Guardian*, 7 March. http://politics.guardian.co.uk/foreignaffairs/story/ 0,,1725223,00.html

Norton-Taylor, R. 2007. 'More Britons travelling to Bangladesh to train in terror', *The Guardian*, 9 July.

Norton-Taylor, R. and I. Cobain. 2007. 'Threat level lowered as inquiry examines foreign connections', *The Guardian*, 5 July.

Norton-Taylor, R. and V. Dodd. 2006. 'Officials admit doubt over chemical plot', *The Guardian*, 5 June.

Norton-Taylor, R., S. Laville and V. Dodd. 2006. 'Terror plot: Pakistan and al-Qaeda links revealed', *The Guardian*, 12 August.

Nowak, M. 1993. *UN Covenant on Civil and Political Rights: Commentary.* (N.P. Engel: Kehl).

NRC Handelsblad. 2006. 'Hofstadgroep wilde "rechtsorde vernietigen"', *NRC Handelsblad*, 11 March 2006.

OBIV. 1998. *Operatie Homerus. Spioneren voor de BVD.* (Papieren Tijger: Breda), pp. 28–30.

O'Malley, P. 2004. *Risk, Uncertainty and Government.* (Glasshouse: London).

O'Neill, B.E. 2005. *Insurgency and Terrorism: From revolution to apocalypse.* (Potomac: Washington, D.C).

O'Neill, S. 2007. 'Pressure grows on Reid over leaked terrorism operation', *The Times*, 27 April.

O'Neill, S., M. Evans and N. Woolcock. 2007. 'British bombers and the lost links to 7/7', *The Times*, 1 May.

Oborne, P. 2006. *The Use and Abuse of Terror.* (Centre for Policy Studies: London).

Omand, D. 2006. 'Ethical guidelines in using secret intelligence for public security', *Cambridge Review of International Affairs*, 19 (4), 613–28.

Ongering, L. 2007. 'Homegrown terrorism and radicalisation in the Netherlands', Testimony before the U.S. Senate Homeland Security and Governmental Affairs Committee. 27 June. http://hsgac.senate.gov/_files/062707Ongering.pdf

O'Rourke, A., V. Chaudri, and C. Nyland. 2005. 'Torture, slippery slopes, intellectual apologists, and ticking bombs: An Australian response to Bagaric and Clarke', *University of San Francisco Law Review*, 40 (1), 1–17.

Owen, T., A. Bailin, J.B. Knowles, M. Ryder, D. Sayers, and H. Tomlinson. 2006. *Blackstone's Guide to the Serious Organised and Police Act 2005*. (Oxford University Press: Oxford).

Pallister, D. 2007. 'Three men jailed for engaging in "Cyber Jihad" for al-Qaida', *The Guardian*, 6 July.

Palmer, A. 2005. 'Is torture always wrong?', *The Spectator*, 24 September.

Parker Committee. 1972. *Report of the Committee of Privy Counsellors Appointed to Consider Authorised Procedures for the Interrogation of Persons Suspected of Terrorism*. Cmnd.4901. (HMSO: London).

Parker, T. 2005. 'Counterterrorism policies in the United Kingdom', in Heymann, P.B. and J. Kayyem (eds.), *Protecting Liberty in an Age of Terror*. (MIT Press: Cambridge, MA).

Penna, S. 2005. 'The Children Act 2004: Child protection and social surveillance', *Journal of Social Welfare and Family Law*, 27 (2), 143–57.

Peppard, D. 2006. 'Reid fights to end torture shield for terror suspects', *Sunday Times*, 1 October.

Peters, B. 2004. *Tödlicher Irrtum. Die RAF in Deutschland*. (Argon: Berlin).

Phythian, M. 2005. 'Intelligence, policy-making and the 7 July 2005 London bombings', *Crime Law and Social Change*, 44 (4–5), 361–85.

Picco, G. 2005. 'The challenges of strategic terrorism', *Terrorism and Political Violence*, 17 (1–2), 11–16.

Pitchford, I. 2003. 'How terrorism ends', 21 July. http://www.interdisciplines.org/terrorism/papers/1/24/printable/discussions/view/823

Plaxton, M. 2006. 'Justifying absolute prohibitions on torture as if consequences mattered', in Kassimeris, G. (ed.), *Warrior's Dishonour: Barbarity, morality and torture in modern warfare*. (Ashgate: Aldershot).

Plett, B. 2007. 'Pakistani links to terror in UK', BBC News, 2 May. http://news.bbc.co.uk/1/hi/uk/6615235.stm

Poole, S. 2007. *Unspeak*. (Abacus: London).

Prenzler, T. 2000. 'Civilian oversight of police. A test of capture theory', *British Journal of Criminology*, 40, 659–74.

Priest, D. 2005. 'Wrongful imprisonment: Anatomy of a CIA mistake', *Washington Post*, 4 December, A01.

Posner, E.A. and A. Vermeule. 2005. 'Should coercive interrogation be legal?', *University of Chicago Public Law and Legal Theory Working Paper*, 84.

Posner, E.A. and A. Vermeule. 2006. 'Should coercive interrogation be legal?', *Michigan Law Review*, 104, 671–708.

Posner, E.A. and A. Vermeule. 2007. *Terror in the Balance: Security, liberty and the courts*. (Oxford University Press: Oxford).

Posner, R.A. 2004. 'Torture, terrorism, and interrogation', in Levinson, S. (ed.), *Torture: A collection*. (Oxford University Press: Oxford).

Posner, R.A. 2006. *Not a Suicide Pact: The Constitution in a Time of National Emergency.* (Oxford University Press: New York).

Raban, J. 2005. 'The truth about terror', *New York Review of Books,* 13 January 2005.

Rapoport, D. 2004, 'The four waves of modern terrorism', in Cronin, A.K. and Ludes, J.M., *Attacking Terrorism: Elements of a Grand Strategy.* (Georgetown University Press: Washington, D.C.), pp. 46–73.

Rapoport, D. 2006, 'Then and now: the significance or insignificance of historical parallels?', paper presented at the II International Conference on Terrorism organised by Fundación Manuel Giménez Abad, Zaragoza (Spain), Palacio de la Aljafería, 30 November 2006.

Rasiah, N. 2006. 'A v Secretary of State for the Home Department (No.2): Occupying the Moral High Ground?', *Modern Law Review,* 69 (6), 995–1005.

Ratcliffe, J. 2002. 'Intelligence led policing and the problems of turning rhetoric into practice', *Policing and Society,* 12 (1), 53–66.

Rawnsley, A. 2001. *Servants of the People.* (Penguin: London).

Razavy, M. 2006. 'Hawala', *Crime, Law and Social Change,* 44 (3), 277–99.

Rees, D. 2003. *Get Your War On.* (Serpent's Tail: London).

Reeve, S. 1999. *The New Jackals: Ramzi Yousef, Osama Bin Laden and the future of terrorism.* (André Deutsch: London).

Reid, J. 2006a. 'Speech to the Labour Party conference', http://bbc.co.uk/1/hi/uk-politics/5389542.stm

Reid, J. 2006b. 'Speech to Muslim groups in East London', (20 September), http://press.homeoffice.gov.uk/Speeches/sp-muslim-group-20-09-06

Reinares, F. 2003. 'Democratization and state responses to protracted terrorism in Spain', in van Leeuwen, M. (ed.), *Confronting Terrorism. European experiences, threat perceptions and policies.* (Kluwer International: The Hague), pp. 57–70.

Reinares, F. 2006. 'Coinciden el Gobierno y los ciudadanos en qué medidas adoptar contra el terrorismo internacional?', *Análisis del Real Instituto Elcano,* ARI No. 35/2006.

Reinares, F. 2006. 'Hacia una caracterización social del terrorismo yihadista en España: implicaciones en seguridad interior y acción exterior', *Análisis del Real Instituto Elcano,* ARI No. 34/2006.

Reinares F. and Alonso, R. 2007. 'Confronting ethnonationalist terrorism in Spain. Political and coercive measures against ETA', in Art, Robert J. and Richardson, L. (eds.), *Democracy and Counterterrorism: Lessons from the past,* (United States Institute of Peace Press; Washington, D.C.), pp. 105–32.

Reiner, R. 2000. *The Politics of the Police.* 3rd edn. (Oxford University Press: Oxford).

Rejali, D. 2007. *Torture and Democracy.* (Princeton University Press: Princeton).

Resolución de Lucha contra el Terrorismo (Fight Against Terrorism), Resolution number 32 approved by the Spanish Congress in plenary session; *Boletín Oficial de las Cortes Generales, número 206, Congreso de los Diputados, VIII Legislatura,* 20 May 2005.

Review of the Northern Ireland (Emergency Provisions) Act 1991. 1995. Cm.2706, London.

Risen, J. 2006. *State of War: The secret history of the CIA and the Bush Administration.* (Free Press: London).

250   *Bibliography*

Robbins, J. 2007. 'Right to protest: Protesting too much?', *Law Gazette*, 18 January.

Robertson, K.G. 1987. 'Intelligence, terrorism and civil liberties', *Conflict Quarterly*, 7 (2), 43–62.

Robinson, J. 2006. 'Brown's war just doesn't add up: You can't kill terrorists with a calculator', *The Times*, 14 February. http://www.timesonline.co.uk/tol/comment/columnists/guest_contributors/article730508.ece

Rodríguez, J. 2006. 'Batería de medidas', *El País*, 8 January.

Roebuck, J.B. 1978. *Political Crime in the United States*. (Praeger: New York).

de Roos, T. 2006. 'Terrorisme en strafrecht in Nederland', in Harchaoui, S. (ed.), *Hedendaags radicalisme*. (Het Spinhuis: Amsterdam), pp. 81–113.

Roper, L. 2006. *Witch Craze: Terror and fantasy in Baroque Germany*. (Yale University Press: Yale).

Rose, D. 2005. 'Revealed: Britain's role in Guantánamo abduction,' *The Observer*, 6 February, http://observer.guardian.co.uk/uk_news/story/0,6903,1407040,00.html

Rose, N. 2006. 'Goldsmith calls for US to close down Guantanamo and back the rule of law', *Law Gazette* (21 September).

Ross, D. 2004. *Violent Democracy*. (Cambridge University Press: Cambridge).

Ross, J.I. 2002. *The Dynamics of Political Crime*. (SAGE: Thousand Oaks, CA).

Rotella, S. 2005. '6 Convicted in Paris in US Embassy plot; the Islamic Militants conspired to bomb the building, a court finds. The investigation traced the rise of a European terrorist network', *Los Angeles Times*, 16 March.

Rubin, A.J. 2007. '3 suspects talk after Iraqi soldiers do dirty work', *New York Times*, 22 April.

Rumney, P. 2005. 'The effectiveness of coercive interrogation: Scholarly and judicial responses', *Crime, Law and Social Change*, 44 (4–5), 465–89.

Rumney, P. 2006. 'Is coercive interrogation of terrorist suspects effective? A response to Bagaric and Clarke', *University of San Francisco Law Review*, 40 (2), 479–513.

Rumney, P. and M. O'Boyle. 2007. 'The torture debate', *New Law Journal*, (9 November), 1566–8.

Rumney, P. and M. O'Boyle. 2008. 'A tortured debate', *New Law Journal*, (25 January), 121–2.

Russell, B. 2005. 'Straw backed memo saying war would anger Muslims', *The Independent*, 31 August.

Saar, E. and V. Novac. 2005. *Inside the Wire: A military intelligence soldier's eyewitness of life at Guantanamo*. (Penguin: London).

Scheffer, P. 2000. 'Het multiculturele drama', *NRC Handelsblad*, 27 January.

Schmid, A.P. 1989, 'Terrorism and the media: The ethics of publicity', *Terrorism and Political Violence*, 1 (4), 539–65.

Schmid, A.P. 1993, 'Terrorism and democracy', in Schmid, A.P. and Crelinsten, R.D., *Western Responses to Terrorism*. (Frank Cass: London), pp. 14–25.

Schmid, A.P. 2000, 'Towards joint political strategies for de-legitimising the use of terrorism', in *Countering Terrorism through International Cooperation*, ISPAC, International Scientific and Professional Advisory Council of the United Nations Crime Prevention and Criminal Justice Programme, Proceedings of the International Conference on 'Countering Terrorism Through Enhanced

International Cooperation', Courmayeur, Mont Blanc, Italy, 22–24 September 2000, pp. 260–5.

Schmitt, E. and C. Marshall. 2006. 'Before and after Abu Ghraib, a US unit abused detainees', *New York Times*, 19 March.

Schmidt, M. 1998. ' "Tektsanalyse" leest in BVD-raportage wat er niet staat', *Het Parool*, 9 December.

Schulte, A. 2004. 'Cliteur is een ijdeltuit, die stopt niet', *Het Parool*, 24 March.

Shamsi, H. 2006. *Command's Responsibility: Detainee deaths in US custody in Iraq and Afghanistan.* (Human Rights First: New York).

Shane, S. and M. Mazzetti. 2007. 'Advisers fault harsh methods in interrogation', *New York Times*, 30 May.

Simon, J. 2007. *Governing Through Crime.* (Oxford University Press: Oxford).

Simpson, A.W.B. 1992. *In the Highest Degree Odious.* (Clarendon Press: Oxford).

Smith, A.T.H. 1986. *Offences against Public Order.* (Sweet and Maxwell: London).

Sproat, P.A. 2007.'An evaluation of the UK's anti-money laundering and asset recovery regime', *Crime Law and Social Change*, 47 (3), 169–84.

Stafford-Smith, C. 2007. *Bad Men: Guantánamo Bay and the secret prisons.* (Weidenfeld & Nicolson: London).

Strawson, J. (ed.) 2002. *Law after Ground Zero.* (Glasshouse Press: London).

Sunier, T. 2006. 'Radicalisme als politieke stijl', in Harchaoui, S. (ed.), *Hedendaags radicalisme. Verklaringen en aanpak.* (Apeldoorn: Antwerpen), pp. 61–80.

Suskind, R. 2006. *One Percent Doctrine: Deep inside America's pursuit of its enemies since 9/11.* (Simon and Schuster: New York).

Sydney Morning Herald. 2005. 'Jack Roche's nine-year sentence upheld', 14 June.

Taylor, I. 1999. *Crime in Context: A critical criminology of market societies.* (Polity: Cambridge).

Taylor, P. 1980. *Beating the Terrorists? Interrogation in Omagh, Gough and Castlereagh.* (Penguin: London).

Taylor, P. 2002. *Brits. The War against the IRA.* (Bloomsbury: London).

Taylor, P. 2005. 'Just waiting to happen', *The Guardian*, 8 July.

Temko, N. 2006. 'Beckett in policy row with Muslim MPs, *The Observer*, 13 August.

Thachuk, K.L. 2006. 'Countering terrorism across the Atlantic', *Defense Horizons*, 53, 1–8.

Tilly, C. 2004. 'Terror, terrorism, terrorists', *Sociological Theory*, 22 (1), 5–13.

Townsend, M. 2006. 'Official: Iraq war led to July bombings', *The Observer*, 2 April.

Travis, A. 2008a. 'Terror bill could put off Muslim informers, consultation finds', *The Guardian*, 25 January.

Travis, A. 2008b. 'Whitehall draws up new rules on language of terror', *The Guardian*, 4 February.

Tremewan, C. 1994. *The Political Economy of Social Control in Singapore.* (Macmillan: London).

Trouw. 1997. 'BVD-rapport is demagogie', *Trouw*, 17 July.

Trouw. 2000. 'Meer racistisch geweld in Nederland', *Trouw*, 6 September.

Tucker, D. 2001. 'What is new about the new terrorism and how dangerous is it?', *Terrorism and Political Violence*, 13 (3), 1–14.

Twemlow, S.W. and F.C. Sacco. 2002. 'Reflections on the making of a terrorist', in Covington, C. et al. (eds.), *Terrorism and War: Unconscious dynamics of political violence* (Karnac: London), pp. 97–123.

Tyrie, A. 2006. Note from Andrew Tyrie to the Intelligence and Security Committee, 30 October. http://www.extraordinaryrendition.org/

UK Government. 2006a. *Report of the Official Account of the Bombings in London on 7th July 2005*. (The Stationery Office: London).

UK Government. 2006b. *Response to the Intelligence and Security Committee's Report into the London Terrorist Attacks on 7 July 2005*. (The Stationery Office: London). Cm.6786, May.

Unzueta, P. and Barbería, J.L. 2003. *Cómo hemos llegado a esto. La crisis vasca.* (Taurus: Madrid).

Uriarte, U. 2003. *Cobardes y Rebeldes. Por Qué Pervive el Terrorismo.* (Temas de Hoy: Madrid).

US Department of Defense. 2005. *Guantánamo Provides Valuable Intelligence Information.*

US Department of Defense. 2005a. *JTF-GTMO Information on Detainees*, 4 March.

Useem, M. 1986. *The Inner Circle. Large Corporations and the Rise of Business Political Activity in the US and UK.* (Oxford University Press: USA).

Valenzuela, J. 2002. *España en el punto de mira. La amenaza del integrismo islámico.* (Temas de Hoy: Madrid).

Schans, Wil van der, E. Timmerman and W. Wagenaar, 2003. *De snuffelstaat: Nederland en de BVD.* (Buro Jansen & Janssen: Amsterdam).

Van Duyne, P.C. 1998. 'Money-laundering: Pavlov's dog and beyond', *The Howard Journal of Criminal Justice*, 37 (4), 359–74.

Van Boxtel, R. 2000. 'BVD terecht alert', *NRC Handelsblad*, 7 October.

Verbij, A. 2005. *Tien rode jaren: Links radicalisme in Nederland 1970–1980.* (Ambo: Amsterdam).

Verkaik, R. 2007. 'Human Rights in Iraq: A case to answer', *The Independent*, 29 May.

Vidal-Naquet, P. 1963. *Torture: Cancer of democracy.* (Penguin: London).

Waddington, P.A.J. 2005. 'Slippery slopes and civil libertarian pessimism', *Policing and Society*, 15 (3), 353–75.

Waddington, P.A.J. 2006. 'Terrorism and civil libertarian pessimism continuing the debate', *Policing and Society*, 16 (4), 415–21.

Walker, C. 1984. 'Irish Republican prisoners – political detainees, prisoners of war or common criminals?', *Irish Jurist*, 19, 189–225.

Walker, C. 2002. *Blackstone's Guide to the Anti Terrorism Legislation.* (Oxford University Press: Oxford).

Walker, C. 2004. 'Terrorism and criminal justice: Past present and future', *Criminal Law Review*, May, 311–27.

Walker, C. 2005. 'Intelligence and anti-terrorism legislation', *Crime, Law and Social Change*, 44 (4–5), 387–422.

Walker, C. 2006a. 'Police powers – whether authorisation given under terrorism legislation lawful, case comment', *Criminal Law Review*, August, 751–7.

Walker, C. 2006b. 'Clamping down on terrorism in the United Kingdom', *International Journal of Criminal Justice*, 4 (5), 1137–51.

Walker, C. 2007a. 'Keeping control of terrorists without losing control of constitutionalism', *Stanford Law Review*, 59 (5), 1395–464.

Walker, C. 2007b. 'The legal definition of "terrorism" in United Kingdom law and beyond', *Public Law*, 331–52.

Walker, C. 2007c. 'The treatment of foreign terror suspects', *Modern Law Review*, 70 (3), 427–57.

Wall, I. M. 2001. *France, the United States and the Algerian War*. (University of California Press: Berkeley).

Walsh, K. 2003. 'Be calm, but here's your "terrorist kit"', *Sydney Morning Herald*, (2 February).

Ward, J. 2007. 'Spain's peace process in tatters after Basque separatist bombing', *The Washington Post*, 18 February.

Watt, N. 2008. 'Revealed: Blair's offer to meet masked IRA leaders', *The Guardian*, 17 March.

Werdmölder, H. 2005. *Marokkaanse lieverdjes. Crimineel en hinderlijk gedrag onder Marokkaanse jongeren*. (Balans: Amsterdam).

White, A.J. 1977. *Special Branch Security Records, Initial Report to the Hon. Donald Allan Dunstan, Premier of South Australia*. (Government Printer: Adelaide).

White, G.E. 1992. 'Justice Holmes and the modernization of free speech jurisprudence: The human dimension', *California Law Review*, 80 (2), 391–467.

Whitaker, R., P. Lashmar and A. Buncombe. 2007. 'Al-Qa'ida's voice threatens once more – But what control does he have over atrocities in Britain?', *Independent on Sunday*, 15 July.

Wilkinson, P. 2000. *Terrorism versus Democracy*. (Frank Cass: London).

Williams, G. 2002. 'Why the ASIO Bill is rotten to the core', *The Age* (Melbourne), 27 August.

Williams, G. 2003. 'Australian values and the war against terrorism', *University of New South Wales Law Journal*, 26 (1), 191–9.

Williams, G. 2004. *The Case for an Australian Bill of Rights: Freedom in the war on terror*. (UNSW Press: Sydney).

Williams, G. and E. MacDonald. 2006. 'This plodding monster faces its own day of judgement', *Sydney Morning Herald*, 30 August.

Williams, J. 2001. 'Hunger-strikes: A prisoner's right or a "wicked folly"?', *Howard Journal of Criminal Justice*, 40 (3), 28596.

Willink, T. 2007. *Speech Delivered at the International Symposium on Accountability of Intelligence and Security Agencies and Human Rights*, The Hague, 7 June.

Wintour, P. 2007. 'Ministers step up Muslim hearts and minds campaign', *The Guardian*, 3 July.

Woodward, W. 2006. 'Reid: Christmas terror attempt highly likely', *The Guardian*, 11 December.

Woodward, B. 2006. *State of Denial: Bush at war, Part III*. (Simon and Schuster: New York).

Woodward, W. and S. Bates. 2006. 'Muslim leaders say foreign policy makes UK target', *The Guardian*, 12 August.

Woodworth, P. 2001. *Dirty Wars, Clean Hands: ETA, the GAL and Spanish Democracy*. (Cork University Press: Cork).

Woolf, M. 2005. 'Conflict motivates extremists, says report', *The Independent*, 16 September.

Wroe, D. 2003. 'Ruddock restarts push for tougher law', *The Age* (Melbourne), 4 November.

Wright Mills, C. 1956. *The Power Elite*. (Oxford University Press: USA).

Yoo, J. 2006. *War by Other Means: An insider's account of the war on terror*. (Atlantic Monthly Press: New York).

Younge, G. 2005. 'Newspapers warn of threat to America from "Londonistan"', *Guardian*, 12 July. http://www.guardian.co.uk/uk_news/story/ 0,3604,1526379,00.html

Zedner, L. 2005. 'Securing liberty in the face of terror', *Journal of Law & Society*, 32 (4), 507–33.

Žižek, S. 2002. *Welcome to the Desert of the Real*. (Verso: London).

Index

9/11 attacks, 46–7, 75, 99, 100, 140, 150, 190

A and others v. Secretary of State for the Home Department (2004), 99

A v. Secretary of State for the Home Department (No.2) (2005), 61, 66

Abu Ghraib, 146

Account Monitoring Orders, 83, 95

Ackerman, Bruce, 150

Afghanistan, 11, 15, 30, 32, 38, 40, 43–4, 46–7, 52, 53n, 70, 90–1, 133, 142, 159, 168, 171, 189, 224, 227–8

AIVD (Alegemene Inlichtingen- en Veiligheidsdienst), 191–6, 198, 200

al-Jazeera, 44, 219

al Kahtani, Mohamed, 151

al-Muhajiroun, 123

al-Qaeda, 22, 24–5, 39, 40–2, 44–5, 50, 84, 87, 89–90, 94–5, 123–4, 142, 145, 151, 153–4, 203–4, 216, 220–1, 229

al-Rawi, Bisher, 224–5

al-Zawahiri, Ayman, 40, 44

Albert v. Levin (1982), 112

Alexander, Douglas, 43

Algeria, 15, 123, 143–4, 152, 214

All-Party Parliamentary Group on Extraordinary Rendition, 224

Amnesty International, 170

Amoore, Louise, 89

Anti-Terrorism Act 2004 (Cth), 173

Anti-Terrorism Act 2005 (Cth), 175–9

Anti-Terrorism, Crime and Security Act 2001 (ATCSA), 20, 55, 58, 82–5, 89, 121, 133, 178

Assets Recovery Agency (ARA), 23

Association of Chief Police Officers, 54

Auld, Lord Justice Robin, 108

Australian Federal Police (AFP), 175–8

Australian Security Intelligence Organisation (ASIO), 160, 169, 171–3, 177, 179

Australian Security Intelligence Organisation Legislation Amendment (Terrorism) Act 2003 (Cth) (ASIO Act), 160, 164–8

Automatic Number Plate Recognition, 14

Aznar, José María, 52

Badat, Saajid, 49, 129

Bagaric, Mirko and Julie Clarke, 140–1, 146, 149, 151–4

Bali bombing, 2002, 159

Balls, Ed, 88–9

Bangladesh, 50, 123

Banksy, 27

Barot, Dhiren, 31n

Batasuna, 206–9

BBC World Service, 137

Beattie, Kate, 136

Begg, Moazzam, 225

Begum, Shabina, 118

Bichard inquiry, 57, 74, 76

bin Laden, Osama, 40–1, 44, 84, 94, 171, 189, 219, *see also* al-Qaeda

Bingham, Lord Thomas, 66, 77n, 112

Blair, Tony, 17, 32, 36, 42–3, 45–6, 116–17, 123, 229

Blair governments, 15, 17, 28, 52, 226, 228

Blears, Hazel, 121

Blum, Stephen, 105

Blum v. Director of Public Prosecutions and other appeals (2006), 105–6, 114

Bosnia, 47

Bourgass, Kamel, 129

Bouyeri, Mohammed, 183, 195, 201

Brigitte, Willie, 168–72, 179, 181n

British National Party, 108

Brown, Gordon, 15, 18, 25, 79–80, 90–2, 221
Brown, Lord Simon, 70, 122
Brown, Melanie, 169
Brown government, 29, 219, 221, 226
Burke, Jason, 16–17, 22
Bush, George W., 99–100, 149
Bush, George W. Administration, 15–16, 32, 150, 152–4
Butler inquiry, 50–1, 57–8
BVD (Binnenlandse Veiligheidsdienst), 183, 185–90, 202n

Canada, 130–1, 164–5, 180
capital punishment, 13
Carlile, Lord Alex, 27, 59, 66–7, 86, 179
Carrasco, Isaias, 221
Casablanca bombing, 2003, 211
CCTV, 13–14, 26
Central Intelligence Agency (CIA), 137, 149, 152–4
Centre for the Protection of the National Infrastructure, 54
Charities Act 1993, 130
Chechnya, 47, 116, 191
Cheney, Dick, 149
Child Support Agency, 14
China, 13
Clarke, Peter, 24, 49
CNI (Centro Nacional de Inteligencia) (Spain), 212–15
CONTEST strategy (Prevent, Pursue, Protect, Prepare), 20, 54, 56, 80, 85, 94–5, 227–8
Control Order Review Group, 67
Conway v. Rimmer (1968), 72
Cook, Robin, 45
Cottee, Simon, 140
Crime and Disorder Act 1998, 108
Criminal Assets Bureau (CAB), 23
Criminal Code Amendment (Terrorist Organisations) Act 2004 (Cth), 163
Criminal Damage Act 1971, 110
Criminal Justice Act 2003, 73
Criminal Justice and Public Order Act 1994, 101, 110–12, 121
Criminal Law Act 1967, 110
Customer Information Orders, 82

Data Protection Act 1998, 74
de Menezes, Jean Charles, 31n
Dear, Lord Geoffrey, 223
Denmark, 127
Dershowitz, Alan, 141, 145
DIB (Directie Inlichtingen Buitenland), 192
DNA databases, 13–14, 26
Donahue, Laura K., 86–90
Dratel, Joshua, 141, 150–1
Drug Trafficking Act 1994, 83

Egypt, 123
el-Banna, Jamil, 224–5
Ertzaintza, 206
ETA (Euskadi Ta Askatasuna), 25, 187, 203–10, 211–13, 216, 220–2
European Convention on Human Rights (ECHR), 58–60, 67, 69, 100, 102–3, 106–9, 112–13, 117, 119, 121, 124, 127, 130, 135–8, 179
European Court of Human Rights (ECtHR), 26, 67–8, 73, 106, 108, 119–20, 124, 126–7, 131, 167, 170
European Union (EU), 84–5, 89–90, 193, 212, 215
Evans, Maya, 106

Farrakhan, Louis, 128
Fenwick, Helen, 136–7
Ferrari, Silvio, 119, 132–3
Financial Investigation Orders, 82
Financial Investigation Unit (FIU), 82, 91
Finsbury Park mosque, 129–30
Fish, Stanley, 139
Foreign Affairs Committee, 137
Forest Gate raid, 51
Fortuyn, Pim, 190–1
France, 139, 143–4, 168–9, 170, 206, 208, 215

GAL (Grupos Antiterroristas de Liberación), 207–8
Gambia, 224
Gardner, Frank, 42–3

GCHQ (Government
Communications Headquarters),
19
Germany, 180, 187, 189, 215
Gillan, Kevin, 103
Glasgow airport attack, 2007, 18, 24,
38, 50
globalisation, 12–13
Goldsmith, Lord Peter, 24
Gotterson, Bob, 163
GRAPO (Grupo de Resistencia
Antifascista Primero de Octubre),
203
Guantánamo, 78n, 116, 137, 142, 145,
150–1, 173, 182n, 224–5
Guardia Civil, 206, 211–13,
215, 217
Guerin, Veronica, 23
Guevara, Ché, 223

Hamza, Abu, 125, 129–30
Hanif, Asif, 49
Harkat ul-Mujahedin, 39
Haw, Brian, 104–5
Hayman, Andy, 24
Hegland, Corine, 142
Hewitt, Patricia, 45
Hizb ut Tahrir, 123
Hocking, Jenny, 162
Hoffmann, Lord Leonard, 60, 66,
110–11, 114
Hofstad group, 195–6, 199
Home Affairs Select Committee, 24,
27, 121, 128
Hoon, Geoff, 46
Howard, John, 159
Howard government, 173, 180
Human Rights Act 1998, 26, 58, 60,
69, 100, 102, 106–9, 119, 130, 179
Human Rights Watch, 136
Hurd, Lord Douglas, 43
Hussein, Hasib, 33
Hutton inquiry, 58

Ibrahim, Muktar Said, 36–7, 39
ID cards, 13
Independent Police Complaints
Commission (IPCC), 27
Indonesia, 41, 159, 171, 186, 214

Intelligence and Security Committee
(ISC), 27, 33–6, 39, 42, 45, 51–2,
57, 224–5
Intelligence Services Act 1994, 58
Intelligence Services Commissioner,
27, 66
Inter-Services Intelligence (ISI)
(Pakistan), 38–9
Interception of Communications
Commissioner (ICC), 27
Iraq, 11, 13–15, 17, 22, 30, 39, 42–7,
52, 53n, 68, 99–100, 104, 106,
109–11, 133, 142, 147, 159, 221–2,
227–9
Israel, 43, 46, 48–9, 139, 142
Istanbul bombing, 2003, 16
Italy, 215
Izzadeen, Abu, 131–2

Japanese Red Army, 185
Jay, Sir Michael, 45
Jemaah Islamiah, 171
Joint Committee on Human Rights,
24, 27, 64, 127–8, 179
Joint Intelligence Committee (JIC),
45–6, 49
Joint Terrorism Analysis Centre
(JTAC), 19, 33, 41, 45, 54
Jones, Margaret, 109, 111–12
Jordan, 214

Kashmir, 47, 191
Kassimeris, George, 139, 143–4, 146
Kepel, Gilles, 40–1, 48
Khan, Mohammad Siddique, 33–4,
36–9, 40, 44, 48, 57, 134n
Khan, Parviz, 37
Khan, Sadiq, 43–4
Khyam, Omar, 35–6, 39
kidnap and behead British Muslim
soldier, plot to, 37, 87
Kleinman, Steven, 154–5
Koh, Harold, 146
Kok, Wim, 190
Kosovo, 15

Lashkar-e-Taiba, 168–9
Laws, Lord Justice John, 61
Lebanon, 43, 123, 128

Lester, Anthony, 136
Liberty, 27
Libya, 123, 214
Lindsay, Jermaine, 33
London bomb plot, 21 July 2005
    (21/7), 36–7, 88, 92–3, 115
London bombings, 7 July 2005 (7/7),
    11, 33–6, 42, 46–7, 49–52, 63, 88,
    92–3, 99, 115, 131–2, 174, 179, 216
'Londonistan', 16
Lynch, Andrew, 177–8

Macdonald, Sir Ken, 226
MacMaster, Neil, 140
Madrid train bombings, 11 March
    2004, 41–2, 44, 49, 52, 193–4,
    204, 210–11, 213–14, 216
Malaysia, 159
Malik, Shahid, 43
Mance, Lord Jonathan, 112–13
Manningham-Buller, Dame Eliza, 33,
    36, 41, 47–8, 50–2
Marcuse, Herbert, 223
Marighela, Carlos, 223
Marr, Andrew, 42–3
McCoy, Alfred, 143, 150
McGuffin, John, 148
Menzies, Robert, 164
Metropolitan Police, 82, 101, 102–4,
    115
MI5 (Security Service), 19, 25, 33–8,
    41–3, 47, 49, 54–5, 56–7, 66, 68,
    87–8, 94, 131, 225
MI6 (Secret Intelligence Service), 19
Milling, Paul, 109, 111–12
Milne, Seamus, 47
Ministry of Sound, 35
Mohammed, Khaled Sheik, 152–3,
    171
Mohammed, Omar Bakri, 123, 128
Moussaoui, Zacarias, 129
Mubanga, Martin, 225

National Coordinator for Counter
    Terrorism (NCTb) (Netherlands),
    184, 194–5, 199
National Counter Terrorism Security
    Office, 54
National Criminal Intelligence
    Service (NCIS), 82

National Intelligence Model (NIM),
    56–7
National Security Strategy, 19, 226–9
National Terrorist Finance
    Investigation Unit (NTFIU), 82,
    88, 92–3
Nicholls, Lord Donald, 66, 120
Northern Ireland, 18, 21, 23, 28–30,
    55, 81, 86, 90, 124, 136, 142,
    144–9, 155, 223, 229, *see also*
    Provisional IRA
*Norwood v. Director of Public
    Prosecutions* (2003), 108

Operation Crevice, 34–6, 39, 52, 57

Pakistan, 12, 15, 25, 37–40, 50, 116,
    123, 142, 154, 168–9, 214
Palestine, 44, 116, 123
Palestine Liberation Organisation
    (PLO), 185
Pearl, Daniel, 39
Percy v. Director of Public Prosecutions
    (2001), 108
Philippines, 159, 214
Plaxton, Michael, 146
Poland, 215
Police Act 1997, 74
Police and Criminal Evidence Act
    1984 (PACE), 27, 83, 101
Police International Counter Terror
    Unit, 55
Policía Nacional, 205–6, 211–13, 215
Portugal, 208
Posner, Eric, 138, 141–5, 149
Posner, Richard, 135, 146
Powell, Jonathan, 229
Prepare, *see* CONTEST strategy
Prevent, *see* CONTEST strategy
Prevention of Terrorism (Temporary
    Provisions) Act 1974, 124
Prevention of Terrorism (Temporary
    Provisions) Act 1989, 101
Prevention of Terrorism Act 2005, 20,
    55, 58–63, 64–8, 68–73 passim,
    174, 179
Proceeds of Crime Act 2002 (Cth),
    173
Proceeds of Crime Act 2002 (PoCA),
    14, 20, 82–4, 88–9, 95

Protect, *see* CONTEST strategy
Provisional IRA, 30, 93, 143, 147–9,
      187, 202n, 221, 229; *see also*
      Northern Ireland
Public Order Act 1986, 105, 107, 111,
      113, 125–6
Pursue, *see* CONTEST strategy

Qatada, Abu, 129, 134n, 138

R v. Jones and others (2006),
      110, 114
*R (on the application of Laporte) v. Chief
      Constable of Gloucestershire* (2004),
      112–13
*R (on the application of Gillan) v.
      Commissioner of Police for the
      Metropolis* (2006), 102–4, 113–14,
      122–3
*R v. Secretary of State for the Home
      Department ex parte Hosenball*
      (1977), 100
*R (on the application of Brian Haw) v.
      Secretary of State for the Home
      Department* (2005), 105–6, 114
Raban, Jonathan, 40
Racial and Religious Hatred Act 2006,
      126
RAF Fairford, 109–15
Rai, Milan, 106
Rapoport, David, 203
Rauf, Rashid, 39
Red Army Faction, 186
*Redmond-Bate v. Director of Public
      Prosecutions* (2000), 108
Rees, David, 11
Regulation of Investigatory Powers
      Act 2000, 27, 64
Reid, John, 17–18, 73, 138, 221
Reid, Richard, 16, 49, 129
Reiner, Robert, 100
rendition, 137, 142–3, 150, 224–6
Roche, Jack, 168, 171–3, 179
Ruddock, Philip, 170, 172–4
Russia, 13

Saudi Arabia, 150, 214
Scheffer, Paul, 190
Secret Intelligence Service (SIS), *see*
      MI6

*Secretary of State for the Home
      Department v. E and another*
      (2007), 70–2
*Secretary of State for the Home
      Department v. JJ and others* (2007),
      70–1
*Secretary of State for the Home
      Department v. M* (2004), 61
*Secretary of State for the Home
      Department v. MB* (2006), 68–70
*Secretary of State for the Home
      Department v. Rehman* (2001),
      60–1
Security Legislation Amendment
      (Terrorism) Act 2002 (Cth),
      160–4
Security Service, *see* MI5
Security Service Act 1989, 58
Sedley, Lord Justice Stephen, 108–9
Serious and Organised Crime Agency
      (SOCA), 23, 82, 91–2
Serious Crime Act 2007, 75
Serious Crime Prevention Orders, 75
Serious Organised Crime and Police
      Act 2005 (SOCPA), 20, 100,
      104–6, 111
Shaer, Aqil, 105
Sharif, Omar, 49
Sierra Leone, 15
Somalia, 123
South Africa, 50
South Moluccan radicals, 184–6
Special Immigration Appeals
      Commission (SIAC), 58, 61, 64,
      66, 134n, 138, 165
Spicer, Robert, 139
Statewatch, 85
Straw, Jack, 46, 133, 134n
Sudan, 189
Suskind, Ron, 150, 153–4
Suspicious Activity Reporting regime
      (SARs), 80, 82, 89, 91–6
Syria, 68, 214

Taliban, *see* Afghanistan
Tanweer, Shazad, 33–4, 36–40, 44, 57
Taylor, Peter, 42, 148–9
Terrorism Act 2000, 20, 26, 55, 80–2,
      86, 88–9, 94–5, 101–3, 109,
      113–14, 121–3, 130, 160

Terrorism Act 2006, 20, 55, 67, 81,
   117, 123–4, 131–2, 221
Terrorism (United Nations Measures)
   Order 2001, 89
Terrorist Finance Action Group, 85
Thailand, 159
Thomas, Mark, 27
'ticking bomb' scenario, 145, 147
Tunisian Fighting Group, 70
Turkey, 124
Turnbull, Sir Andrew, 45
Tyrie, Andrew, 225

Ukraine, 191
United Nations, 84–5, 87, 89, 130, 163,
   166
   UN Convention for the Suppression
      of the Financing of Terrorism,
      193
   UN Convention on the Rights of
      the Child, 167–8
   UN International Covenant on
      Civil Political Rights (ICCPR),
      166, 178–9
United States, 19, 22, 25, 27, 29, 32,
   39–40, 45–6, 93, 139, 140,
   149–51, 164–5, 200, 213, 224–5,
   228, *see also* Bush, George W.;
   Bush, George W. Administration;
   Central Intelligence Agency;
   Cheney, Dick; rendition

Universal Declaration of Human
   Rights, 167
Uzair, Abu, 131
Uzbekistan, 12, 15, 123

van Duyne, Petrus C., 92
van Gogh, Theo, 183, 195–6, 201
Vermeule, Adrian, 138, 141–5, 149

Walker, Lord Robert, 120–1
Wallinger, Mark, 27
Wannsee conference, 141
West, Sir Alan, 15
Westminster CC v. Haw (2002),
   104–5
White Overall Movement Building
   Libertarian Effective Struggles
   (WOMBLES), 112
Williams, Daryl, 164
Williams, George, 177–8
Woodward, Bob, 150
Woolf, Lord Harry, 61
World Trade Centre bombing,
   1993, 47

Yemen, 68, 123

Zambia, 225
Zapatero, José Luis Rodríguez, 210
Žižek, Slavoj, 141
Zubaydah, Abu, 153–4